Planning for the
Internal Audit Function

by J. Efrim Boritz, Ph.D.

The Institute of Internal Auditors Research Foundation
249 Maitland Avenue, P.O. Box 1119
Altamonte Springs, Florida 32701, U.S.A.

ISBN 0-89413-107-9
83163 JUL83
87016 JAN87

Foreword

Planning is one of the more critical aspects of internal auditing. This is a vital element which can consume up to two-thirds of an internal audit manager's time and resources. It is important enough to be contained in the *Standards for the Professional Practice of Internal Auditing* as explicit directives of sections 400 and 500.

The Research Foundation of The Institute, responding to the continued challenges of our profession, commissioned this work to provide pioneering research for a comprehensive audit planning mechanism as well as a determination of the state of the art on this topic. The intent is to elevate the audit planning process to a level of sophistication above that which is achievable by intuitive or judgmental means. These tools and techniques recommended by Professor Boritz in this study have paved the way for further research and development of a computer-assisted system which is now underway.

On behalf of The Institute and the Board of Trustees of the Research Foundation, I express much appreciation to J. Efrim Boritz for his enthusiasm and perseverance with this project. His contribution will surely lead the profession to a greater appreciation and understanding of a strategic audit planning process.

William C. Anderson, CIA, CBA
IIA Research Foundation
President
1983-1984

Preface

This book deals with planning and coordinating internal audit activities. Its appeal may range outside the internal auditing profession. Management, external auditors, academicians, and students may be interested in the issues and concepts discussed here. This publication attempts to provide materials of interest to these diverse audiences; consequently, there are portions of this study that may fall outside the areas of interest of any given group. The information herein is sufficiently comprehensive and rich so that the different parties may delve into preferred topics.

There are three major components to this research study:

• A broad review of relevant literature with the goal of summarizing the underlying principles and concepts applicable to a study of planning and coordinating internal audit activities.

• Case studies of a number of planning and coordinating approaches in use with the goal of identifying the state of the art in this area.

• A detailed, systematic study of planning and coordinating activities, including analyses of processing activities, information flows, and information structures involved in the important aspects of planning in internal audit departments.

These three components will vary in terms of their relevance to specific readers. Some readers may wish to concentrate on the case studies. Others may emphasize the broad planning concepts. And others may wish to delve into the detailed analyses provided in the latter chapters. All of these are legitimate approaches to a selective reading of what turned out to be a fairly lengthy publication. Throughout the book, adequate cross-referencing is provided to permit readers to pursue their particular interests.

Some readers may wonder whether planning merits the amount of attention given to it in this publication. It does. And this publication merely scratches the surface of what might be said about planning. I hope, of course, that the scratch is deep enough to provide new insight and information. I have no illusions, however, about this being the last word. Indeed, I hope to continue exploring many more of the important facets of the theory and practice of planning which, I believe, are crucial to professional practice in any field of endeavor.

J. Efrim Boritz

Altamonte Springs, Florida
July 1, 1983

Acknowledgements

This project owes much to many. Most will not be mentioned by name, but several must. First, I must thank The Institute of Internal Auditors, particularly Paul Nelson and Ken Meuwissen of IIA's Twin Cities Chapter, who involved me in this project that provided me with a valuable research opportunity. Also, IIA staff members John Dattola, Rob Muirhead, and Richard Holman administered and conducted this project in a professional and supportive way.

Two research assistants, Wan Ling Kung and Theresa Tiu, made important contributions to the project.

A number of reviewers provided valuable feedback that helped improve various aspects of this report. In particular, Ron Lynch, Larry Noxon, and Brad Schweiger provided in-depth reviews and comments. Although our views differed in some cases, their comments pointed out important areas requiring clarification.

Gordon Duke, Charles Brown, and Betty Kercher submitted comments on an earlier draft. Many others contributed with their valuable suggestions and time, but it would be impossible to list them all here.

I would be remiss were I to omit mentioning the members of the internal audit departments that served in the case studies. Although unable to enter their names here, I certainly appreciate their contributions to this project, expecially their professionalism and helpfulness.

About the Author

J. Efrim Boritz is assistant professor in the accounting group at the University of Waterloo, Canada. He holds a Ph.D. from the University of Minnesota in accounting and management-information systems. In addition, he is a chartered accountant and certified information-systems auditor. Professor Boritz has extensive practical experience in many auditing fields and has written books, articles, and research papers on various aspects of auditing.

Contents

List of Figures

4 Developing Comprehensive Plans

5 A Structured Analysis for a Comprehensive Audit-Planning System

1

Overview of the Study

. . . because the one thing that makes man superior to the rest of the animals is his ability to think ahead – to plan. Planning means laying out a course of action that we can follow that will take us to our desired goals. (Churchman, 1968, p. 146, see bibliography)

No one would disagree with the statement that effective planning and coordinating are key factors in the proper management of an internal audit department. Surprisingly, little research has been done to examine the critical issues and decisions involved in the effective planning and coordinating of internal audit departments' activities. It is fair to say that the general principles of planning are relatively well known and are applicable to the activities of a variety of organizational subunits, including internal auditing. However, implementing such principles, the "how to's" of effective planning and coordinating, is not as well understood. This is true of auditing and of other functional areas as well.

Formal Versus Intuitive Planning

Although the value of formal planning is generally well accepted, it is carried out far less often than might be expected, given the high regard everyone seems to have for it. Even though much has been written about planning from a conceptual perspective, when it comes right down to actually doing it, it seems that the implementation burden is often so overwhelming that it actually prevents formal planning activities from being adequately instituted, despite everyone's wishes to the contrary. This is not to say that no one does any planning. It is probably impossible to survive in the corporate world without making some effort at planning (i.e., anticipating events and providing for them.)[1] The important distinction that must be made and emphasized is one between minimal, informal planning efforts and formal, well-institutionalized planning activities. The former is a product of necessity and represents the bare essentials for survival. The latter is a product of optimizing behavior and represents a well-thought-out approach to managing.

In his exposition on comprehensive managerial planning, George Steiner emphasized that – in contrast with intuitive-anticipatory planning based on past experience, "gut" feeling, judgment, and intuition – formal planning systems are organized and based on a given set of procedures. They are explicit, based on evidence, and result in explicit written plans.

During the case studies reported in Chapter 3, several internal audit managers expressed doubts about formal planning systems. They seemed to feel that formalities in planning were somehow at odds with initiative or judgment-based planning activities. It should be recognized that a good planning system does not eliminate judgment; rather, it organizes it so that its exercise is balanced. An important premise of this study is that the failures in blending intuition and formality are failures of implementation, not evidence of fundamental incompatibilities between them. The prevailing view of researchers in the behavioral sciences, particularly in the area of judgment and decision making (e.g., see Ashton and Libby for an introduction), suggests the necessity of tightening rather than relaxing the formalities involved in identifying, evaluating, and selecting (in short, planning) courses of action.

Steiner emphasized that, although in practice these approaches to planning (i.e., intuitive versus formal) often clash, there should be no conflict between them; rather, they should complement one another. The formal system should draw judgment and intuition into it and should help managers hone their intuitive evaluations. The comprehensive planning system described in chapters 4 and 5 incorporates judgments into all its phases yet does so in an explicit and controlled way.

Planning as a Managerial Activity

Six activities are widely accepted as key functions of internal audit management (Chambers, 1981): planning, organizing, staffing, directing and leading, controlling, and coordinating.

Planning includes selecting objectives, identifying alternatives, decision making, and adopting implementation plans and procedures to achieve specified goals. It is a process of deciding what to do and how to do it before some action is required (Moskow, 1978).

Organizing involves implementation of appropriate organizational structures and roles to suit the goals of the organization, the department, and its individual members as well as appropriate assignments of activities, delegation of responsibility, and providing for communication vertically and horizontally and formally and informally.

Staffing involves the determination of personnel requirements, keeping records of available personnel time by skill level, and personnel recruitment training and development to ensure that specified goals can be attained.

Directing and leading involve provision for appropriate guidance to subordinates to ensure that assignments can be viewed with clarity.

Controlling involves monitoring and evaluating departmental and staff activities and taking appropriate corrective action when necessary. It is not possible to control without an appropriate plan against which performance may be compared.

Coordinating involves synchronizing and harmonizing both within a department and between the department and the organization which it is designed to serve.

These six activities create a network of managerial responsibility tied to planning. They describe what should be expected of management at all levels within an organization, including internal audit management. Ansoff and Brandenburg identified three important and time-consuming activities performed by managers:

● Responding to problems which are brought up by others in the organization; for example, in the context of internal auditing, requests made by management for special studies, investigations, and so on.

● Continuously searching for opportunities which permit improvements in a firm's or a department's performance; for example, in the context of internal auditing, this would be illustrated by an active search for audit opportunities and adding these to the inventory of auditable units, including changing the definition of what constitutes an auditable unit whenever such a change becomes appropriate.

● Periodically reviewing past performance; for example, in the context of internal auditing, this would be illustrated by an annual review and summary of work done by the department and periodic reviews of departmental activities in general through

3

the mechanism of peer reviews, internal task forces, or by external consultants.

Ansoff and Brandenburg described the second phase as being virtually ignored relative to the others. Although this has possibly improved somewhat since they made their comments, it seems that this activity still suffers. For example, a recent survey[2] of long-range planning and audit-universe control concluded that planning procedures by the internal audit function should be given more serious consideration and that an adequate level of audit-universe identification and definition may be lacking in many audit departments. A 1982 study by Urton Anderson involving peer reviews of internal audit departments found a wide variation in the sophistication of planning that varied from a formal, systematic, and computerized approach to "seat-of-the-pants" procedures. None of the departments systematically assessed risk (although all showed some evidence of considering it in their choice of specific audits to be scheduled and their frequency).

Certainly, audit management is not to be singled out for criticism; it shares many of the issues and problems associated with establishing and implementing effective planning and coordinating mechanisms faced by many other functional areas such as production, marketing, and information systems. There are also specific considerations in managing activites of audit departments requiring approaches tailored to audit functions.

Professional Standards

Managing the internal audit function, the director of internal audit[3] is responsible for ensuring that:
- Audit work accomplishes the purposes of the function and its responsibilities as set out in its charter.
- Resources of the function are efficiently and effectively employed.
- Audit work conforms to generally accepted standards for the professional practice of internal auditing.

According to Section 500 of the *Standards for the Professional Practice of Internal Auditing* (published by The Institute of Internal Auditors in 1978 and hereafter referred to as the *Standards*), effective discharge of management responsibilities requires the director of internal audit to:
- Ensure the existence of an appropriate statement of corporate policy dealing with the purpose, authority, and responsibility of

the internal audit function.

• Develop plans for carrying out the audit work. These plans should be consistent with the goals of the corporation and with its statement dealing with internal audit. For example, as part of their planning and coordinating activities, audit managers must:

1. Establish appropriate long-range goals that can be measured and evaluated.

2. Identify all auditable areas within the organization and set priorities for selecting areas to audit.

3. Establish varying degrees of scope and intensity of audit effort to be applied, commensurate with the exposures faced by the organization.

4. Balance the mix of skills to be utilized within and across audits.

5. Prepare and maintain written work schedules indicating timing and estimated time requirements of each audit.

6. Prepare staffing plans, operating budgets, and mechanisms for status reporting.

• Establish written policies and procedural guidelines appropriate in form and context so as to suit the size and the structure of the department and the nature of its activities.

• Manage and develop the human resources of the function through a program which provides for:

1. Developing written job descriptions for each level of the internal audit staff.

2. Selecting qualified and competent personnel.

3. Training and providing continuing education opportunities for each staff member.

4. Appraising each member's performance at least annually.

• Coordinate internal and external audit efforts to ensure that adequate audit coverage is provided with a minimum of duplication.

• Establish and maintain a quality assurance program to assure that the audit work conforms with corporate goals and policies, the policies and procedures of the internal audit function, and generally accepted standards and rules of conduct for internal auditing. (See Figure 1.1 for the full text of Section 520 (Planning) of the *Standards* and Appendix A for the full text of Section 500 (Management of the Internal Auditing Department).)

Figure 1.1
Professional Standards: Planning*

520 Planning
The director of internal auditing should establish plans to carry out the responsibilities of the internal auditing department.

.01 These plans should be consistent with the internal auditing department's charter and with the goals of the organization.

.02 The planning process involves establishing:
.1 Goals
.2 Audit work schedules
.3 Staffing plans and financial budgets
.4 Activity reports

.03 The *goals* of the internal auditing department should be capable of being accomplished within the specified operating plans and budgets and, to the extent possible, should be measurable. They should be accompanied by measurement criteria and targeted dates of accomplishment.

.04 *Audit work schedules* should include (a) what activities are to be audited; (b) when they will be audited; and (c) the estimated time required taking into account the scope of the audit work planned and the nature and extent of audit work performed by others. Matters to be considered in establishing audit work schedule priorities should include (a) the date and results of the last audit; (b) financial exposure; (c) potential loss and risk; (d) request by management; (e) major changes in operations, programs, systems, and controls; (f) opportunities to achieve operating benefits; and (g) changes to and capabilities of the audit staff. The work schedules should be sufficiently flexible to cover unanticipated demands on the internal auditing department.

.05 *Staffing plans and financial budgets,* including the number of auditors and the knowledge, skills, and disciplines required to perform their work, should be determined from audit work schedules, administrative activities, education and training requirements, and audit research and development efforts.

.06 *Activity reports* should be submitted periodically to management and to the board. These reports should compare (a) performance with the department's goals and audit work schedules and (b) expenditures with financial budgets. They should explain the reasons for major variances and indicate any action taken or needed.

*Excerpted from the *Standards for the Professional Practice of Internal Auditing,* published by The Institute of Internal Auditors in 1978, pp. 500-1 and 500-2.

As discussed in this study, planning and coordinating audit activities involves a comprehensive network of tasks encompassing virtually all the managerial tasks entrusted to the director of the internal auditing function. At best, these are difficult tasks to accomplish. Today's pressures upon internal audit departments make these tasks even more difficult.

Research Issues

Fifteen years ago, Ansoff and Brandenburg posed a number of questions about planning:
- How much planning is enough?
- What are the cost-benefit relationships in planning?
- How should uncertainty be handled?
- What kinds of planning approaches and practices are appropriate to different industries, different firms and departments within them, and different business conditions?
- How is planning related to control?
- How should departments organize for planning?
- What is the role of computers in planning?
- How can we tell whether a proposed plan is good?

Fifteen years later, a number of additional, equally relevant questions have been added by Herbert Simon:
- How can we represent the problems to solve with the aid of plans in such a way as to compensate for human problem-solving limitations?
- How do we cope with imperfect or unavailable information upon which to base plans?
- For whom is the planner planning?
- How do we measure progress toward a planned goal, how do we maintain a proper perspective, and how do we focus attention on key issues?
- How do we deal with ambiguity and conflicting goals?

Dealing with these questions is a tall order for any research study, and it is not possible to study planning and coordinating in any depth and not touch on many of the issues raised in the questions above at least briefly and some of them in-depth. Some tentative answers are offered to these questions on the basis of the research conducted herein and the literature cited.

How Much Planning Is Enough? Planning should encompass the major areas of concern to an organization. These areas might be highlighted by management, or they may be established by outside authorities. In internal auditing, management has traditionally provided little planning guidance. However, this can and should be amended. The Institute of Internal Auditors (IIA) has provided a set of standards which outlines the minimum planning requirements which should guide the planning activities of internal auditors. It appears from the surveys cited previously that current planning practices can stand improvement. A comprehensive planning system is described in chapters 4 and 5 which is consistent with professional standards and which incorporates a role for management to provide specific guidance to enhance the general guidelines provided by the professional standards.

What Are the Cost-Benefit Relationships in Planning? Planning might pay for itself, but little can be gained by expending resources to prove this within each and every organization. Planning facilitates good management. The consensus in the planning literature seems to be that it is the planning *process,* rather than specific plans, which makes the greatest impact. To the extent that it is deemed necessary or desirable to improve the quality of departmental activities, personnel utilization, audit emphasis, and relations between the department and outside parties, planning can offer important benefits. The costs pertain primarily to the time and the effort required to institute a comprehensive planning system.

How Should Uncertainty Be Handled? Planning serves to reduce some of the uncertainties in decision making. Systematic procedures and guidelines eliminate some alternatives from consideration, reducing other uncertainties. Finally, appropriate analyses of risk and probabilistic models such as conditional investigation models, network models, and simulation can help manage uncertainty related to audit selection, work scheduling, and plan preparation and keep uncertainty within tolerable bounds. Chapters 4 and 6 describe these techniques.

What Kinds of Planning Approaches and Practices Are Appropriate? The approach described herein is a comprehensive, top-down, systems-oriented, modular approach. It permits the explicit identification of the major processes, information flows, data stores, and parties involved in planning and coordinating internal audit activities. It also draws upon practices observed in a number of organizations whose planning activities were studied (reported in Chapter 3) as well as practices recommended in the relevant literature.

As described here, internal audit planning approaches should encompass six main sets of activities:

● Planning the role, responsibility, and audit orientation of the internal audit department.

● Planning the facilities and procedures to use.

● Planning the portfolio of auditable units and activities.

● Planning personnel-skill availability and utilization commensurate with the inventory of audit tasks.

● Planning work activities and resource requirements of the department and its staff over appropriate time horizons and coordinating them with outside parties.

● Scheduling, monitoring, and evaluating departmental work activities.

Figure 1.2 illustrates the relationships among these six sets of activities. Chapters 4 and 5 provide a detailed analysis of these activities.

How Is Planning Related to Control? Planning permits the exercise of control by:

● Constraining the activities of a department to a subset of the universe of all possible activities.

● Providing guidelines and rationale for selecting the activities to be emphasized or de-emphasized.

● Setting specific goals and targets to permit measurement and evaluation of a department's and its personnel's accomplishments.

What Is the Role of Computers in Planning? Some aspects of planning can be substantially enhanced through the use of computer-assisted planning tools and techniques. Most of our case companies used such techniques; however, in the profession as a whole, the use of computers in planning is at a relatively primitive stage. It is doubtful whether substantial improvements in planning can be achieved without equal improvements in tools.

How Can We Tell Whether a Proposed Plan Is Good? A good plan is complete, unbiased, implementable, and verifiable and leads to good results. Sometimes it is possible to evaluate the individual aspects of plans, but it is rarely possible to evaluate a plan without actually implementing it and seeing whether it works. It is a wise strategy to test plans (for example, through simulation) prior to their full implementation to determine their

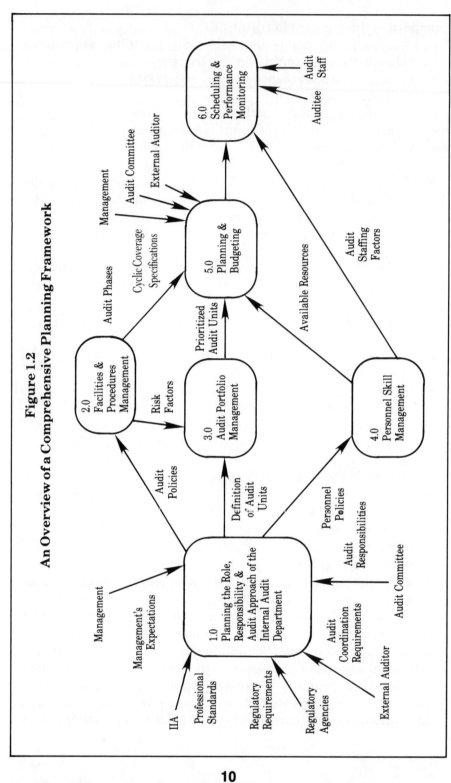

Figure 1.2
An Overview of a Comprehensive Planning Framework

resiliency. Ultimately, the measure of the quality of a plan must be based upon the results achieved by using it; but this cannot be a foolproof measure of goodness. Even the best plans may not lead to good outcomes, as discussed in Chapter 2.

How Can We Represent Problems to Solve with the Aid of Plans in Such a Way as to Compensate for Human Problem-Solving Limitations? By using "hierarchical decomposition" which serves to simplify and modularize decisions, it is possible to reduce the complexity and the cognitive stress associated with planning. Also, the use of computer-assisted planning tools and techniques, as aids for enhancing planning, can reduce the sometimes overwhelming burden of information processing associated with effective planning.

How Do We Cope with Imperfect or Unavailable Information upon Which to Base Plans? By making plans flexible and building in monitoring and feedback facilities into the planning system, it is possible to permit ongoing revision of the information base. Thus, plans which are prepared on the basis of the information can be revised in a timely fashion. Also, by seeking information from a number of possibly conflicting sources, it is possible to reduce the chance of being misled.

For Whom Is the Planner Planning? Although this may seem to be out of keeping with some normative writings in this area, the planner is essentially planning for himself. It is desirable to have the planner plan for the sake of the larger goals of the organization. This, however, is difficult to achieve. Systematic procedures might be implemented to encourage the plans to be congruent with the overall objectives of the organization. In chapters 2, 4, and 6, we suggest methods for ensuring that key planning decisions are made in accordance with organization-wide priorities.

How Do We Measure Progress Toward a Planned Goal, How Do We Maintain a Proper Perspective, and How Do We Focus Attention on Key Issues? We focus attention on key issues by setting audit goals congruent with them. If goals are stated carefully and with due consideration of the need for subsequent measurement of progress and if measures are defined in advance, the problem is reduced. An appropriately designed planning system permits follow-up and continuous monitoring of progress relative to goals.

How Do We Deal with Ambiguity and Conflicting Goals? By bringing parties with different goals into the planning process, it is possible to coordinate or at least make provision for different goals and different interpretations. In chapters 2, 4, and 6, we identify relevant parties and outline methods for including their perspectives.

An Overview of This Study

This research study deals with difficult planning and coordinating issues confronting directors of internal audit departments. The basis for the information contained in this study is (1) the researcher's review of planning and coordinating activities in a number of internal audit departments, (2) his previous experience in this area, and (3) a review of relevant literature.

This study is based upon the premise that planning is important and that effective planning involves a set of activities that, although simple when considered one at a time, creates a complex and integrated network of activities which is difficult to understand, design, implement, and manage. Finally, it is the researcher's belief that we have the capability to substantially improve the state of the art of planning and coordinating audit activities.

The contribution of this study for improving planning is threefold:

● It contributes to our understanding of planning theory and practice.

● It breaks down the complex network of related activities which falls under the umbrella of planning into its component tasks and deals with each task in some detail so as to guide directors of internal audit departments seeking to enhance their overall planning activity or to improve specific aspects of their planning practices.

● It provides a structured analysis of the information and processing requirements for developing a computer-based set of planning aids and suggests techniques for enhancing aspects of planning.

This study consists of six chapters and is quite comprehensive in its coverage but may offer more detail than some readers might wish to delve into. This is particularly true of chapters 4 and 5 which, of necessity, are fairly detailed since they deal with specific information-processing requirements of a comprehensive planning system. It is unlikely that the system described in this study will be applicable in all aspects to any single reader or organization. It is impossible to predict which aspects of planning are most important to a given reader. During the case studies, we found that different companies emphasized different aspects of planning, although there were many similarities as well. It is up to the reader, then, to choose which parts to concentrate on and which to skip over. Sufficient information is provided to fill the needs of a variety of planning philosophies and practices.

Most internal auditors and directors will probably want to read only the first four chapters. However, if enhancements to an existing planning system are contemplated, they will find chapters 5 and 6 to be extremely useful for additional and detailed information.

Chapter 1 is an overview and introduction to the study.

In Chapter 2, general planning and coordinating concepts are discussed as a basis for understanding the substantive issues underlying the administrative tasks entrusted to the director of internal audit.

In Chapter 3, we discuss a number of case studies so as to inform the reader about the various planning methods, tools, and techniques used by internal audit departments which have attempted to formalize their planning and coordinating activities. The case studies cover companies in a range of sizes, industries, attitudes, and sophistication; thus, they provide an informative and interesting background for the rest of the study.

Chapter 4 provides an outline of how to prepare a comprehensive plan for coordinating activities of internal audit departments and delves into important issues involved in each major planning phase.

Chapter 5 provides a blueprint for a comprehensive planning system. It draws upon the case studies, the literature review, and the researcher's personal experience, eclectically combining what appear to be the best techniques into a unified approach. Included is an analysis of information requirements and a definition of processing steps necessary to automate substantial portions of the planning and coordinating activities described in Chapter 4. It is the researcher's belief that, in both large and small internal audit departments, an important obstacle to improvements in planning activities can often be attributed to the absence of appropriate tools.

Chapter 6 covers tools and techniques which may be useful for planning and coordinating departmental activities. The previously cited survey of long-range planning and audit-universe control found that, for key aspects of planning and coordinating activities to be discussed herein, computers were used little, if at all.[4] Computer-assisted techniques can effectively reduce the overwhelming clerical and administrative efforts that a comprehensive planning and coordinating system may impose upon internal audit departments. In addition, other techniques not necessarily involving computers are suggested for enhancing aspects of planning.

There are numerous reasons why such technical innovations may not be acceptable – hence, not widely adopted – including political reasons (Benveniste, 1972; Kling, 1981), economic reasons (Sutton, 1980), sociological reasons (Bostrum and Heinen, 1977), and psychological reasons (Keen and Morton, 1978; Brehm, 1966). These reasons may be the more important considerations in the move toward technical innovation in the managing and planning functions overriding technical efficiency-effectiveness arguments. These very important considerations are, regrettably, outside the scope of this study.

This study deals with fundamental planning and coordinating issues involved in managing the activities of internal auditing functions. In large measure, these activities depend upon the skills, experience, and wisdom of directors of internal audit. However, a properly implemented set of procedures can help institutionalize a sound management approach within internal audit functions.

Footnotes:

[1]For an interesting discussion of economic aspects of planning refer to Sutton's work.

[2]This 1981-82 survey was conducted by the Tulsa Chapter of The Institute of Internal Auditors (by Mark Randle and Deborah Kelly) and covered a sample of the Fortune 500 industrial companies. The Tulsa Chapter's survey selected a random sample of 200 of these industrial companies and received 136 responses, a response rate of 68 percent. In addition, 25 of 42 locally mailed responses were collected. Unlike other surveys (described in footnotes 16, 17, and 18), this survey was specifically aimed at exploring planning issues.

[3]The title director of internal audit is according to the *Survey of Internal Auditing: 1979* the most commonly used title referring to the person with overall responsibility for the day-to-day operations

of internal auditing activity. Consequently, it will be used throughout this study.

[4]The Tulsa Chapter's survey found that 56 percent of its sample companies did not use or made only nominal use of computers in audit-universe control and risk analysis. Only 14 percent made heavy use of EDP in planning and coordinating.

2

Planning Concepts

This chapter outlines and discusses general planning concepts, the need for and importance of planning, the usefulness of plans, and some important aspects of planning approaches and plans. The purpose of this discussion is to provide the reader with insight into the theory of planning and a basis for evaluating planning systems used by many internal audit departments.

Planning is a process which is part of a larger process – the process of managerial decision making. Planning is used to select a course of action to follow on the basis of predefined policy statements. Although the planning process should not lead to excessive rigidity in the plans adopted, one of the important features of planning is that it does limit what is to be done and constrains and guides the activities of a department. Deviations from plans require a rationale, and this may explain the reluctance of some managers for implementing a comprehensive planning system.

The lengthening time span of managerial decisions, volatility and change in organizational and business environments, complexity of business and information-processing activities, and changing locus of managerial decision making emphasize the need for comprehensive approaches to planning and coordinating departmental activities. The usefulness of the planning *process* may exceed the usefulness of the specific plans that are generated, but the benefits achieved may not be easily measurable. In particular, the planning process may contribute to improvements in the efficiency and the effectiveness of departmental operations through improved communication with management and auditees, improved allocation of departmental resources, better emphasis of departmental efforts in areas warranting more attention with a corresponding de-emphasis in areas which are not corporate priorities.

Planning is a process involving many interrelated tasks and activities and is considered from a broad systems perspective. This perspective is slightly broader than that outlined in Section

17

520 of the *Standards,* but it is consistent with the planning and coordinating issues which pervade the broader discussion in Section 500 of the *Standards.* As viewed in this study, planning and coordinating departmental activities involves an integrated set of activities which may be conceptualized in a hierarchic fashion. It starts with defining the objectives and the character of the internal audit function and proceeds to defining and selecting schemes for identifying and measuring the importance of audit projects with the judicious assignments of professional audit personnel (the major resource of the department) to specific audit tasks and monitoring and evaluating the department's activities. These activities involve direct or indirect coordination internally as well as with external parties such as audit committees and regulatory (occasionally) bodies. These groups have different interests. Coordination can be enhanced through formally documented and defensible plans of departmental activities.

A comprehensive planning system involves a hierarchy of plans which take into account:

- Different planning horizons over which departmental resources are committed.
- Different planning concerns encountered at different levels of management.
- Systematically related phases of managerial decision making of which planning is a part.
- Characteristic risks to be managed as part of the planning process.
- Performance evaluation and feedback mechanisms used for monitoring and controlling the quality of plans.
- Knowledge requirements involved in planning and coordinating professional activities.

General Planning Concepts

The essential ingredients of a plan are described by C. West Churchman (considered by many as one of the founders of systems analysis):

> A goal is set, a group of alternatives is created, each alternative is scanned as to whether it will or will not effectively lead to the goal, one of the alternatives is selected, the plan is implemented, and the decision maker checks to see how well the plan worked. The last piece of information will be used to control the operation of the plan as well as to plan better in the future. (Churchman, 1968, p. 147)

According to Anderson, plans serve two functions. They help prevent costly mistakes and simplify problems. Planning may help reduce some of the uncertainties involved in problem solving and decision making and may be used to defend decisions that have already been made. It may also be used to control the activities of subordinates or, conversely, to limit the basis upon which policies are made at higher levels (Benveniste, 1972).

Comprehensive Planning

Steiner emphasized the following four aspects of planning:

- Planning involves tracing the pattern of cause-effect relationships leading to future consequences of an intended decision today. This is termed the "futurity of current decisions." Thus, he argues, a systematic identification of opportunities and threats is the essence of planning. Presumably, in an audit context, there should be a set of benefits associated with an audit plan. An auditor should be able to estimate the risks and benefits associated with auditing a given auditee with a given frequency and a given degree of intensity.
- Comprehensive planning is a multiphase process which involves developing objectives, defining strategies and policies for achieving them, and developing detailed plans for implementing the policies. It is a process of defining in advance:
  1. What is to be done?
  2. When it is to be done?
  3. How it is to be done?
  4. Who is going to do it?
  5. How long will it take?

(In an audit context, these decisions involve establishing the audit purpose and direction for the internal audit function and its personnel, including an audit framework, and a set of plans to determine what is to be audited, timing of audits during the planning period, procedures to follow, staff members to assign to projects, and estimated duration of audits.)
- It is a philosophy or way of life – not a haphazard project to be adopted, discarded, and adopted once again.
- Comprehensive planning is a hierarchic structure of plans which, when integrated, affect all functions of an organization/department from the top levels to the lower levels of activity. (In an audit context, certain planning considerations will affect audit personnel; others will involve supervisory staff, affect man-

agerial staff, and have implications for outside parties with an interest in the activities of the internal auditing function.)

These four points summarize a number of key aspects of planning as discussed by writers during the last 25 years and will be discussed further. Although planning is sometimes treated as less of an art than a science, this overlooks its relative "youth" as a field of study and research. It is easy to discuss planning, but doing it is somehow never quite as easy. There are good reasons for this. Planning is usually not taught formally, yet it takes great skill and experience to create good plans. Planning requires discipline and formal procedures which are often neither instituted nor maintained. It involves a complex network of interrelated activities which are difficult to manage and control.

Since its infancy, planning has been treated conceptually. Writings in the area are typically quite general and aimed at laying out the conceptual frameworks and building professional management skills. Little empirical evidence has been gathered about planning.

More than 20 years ago, Peter Drucker described what planning is and what it is not. For example, he emphasized that planning is not forecasting but that it is necessary because we cannot forecast future events accurately. Also, planning does not deal with future decisions but with the future consequences of present decisions. Moreover, planning is not an attempt to eliminate risk; instead, it is a process that leads to taking the "right risks." Drucker adds:

> To do this, however, we must know and understand the risks we take. We must be able to rationally choose among risk-taking courses of action rather than plunge into uncertainty. (Drucker, 1959, p. 111)

It is not up to the decision makers to choose whether they want to make planning decisions. They can be made by default, responsibly or irresponsibly, rationally or irrationally, as a blind gamble. However, they are always made.

According to Herbert Simon, planning is a technique by which the skills of a variety of specialists can be brought to bear on a problem before the formal stage of decision making is reached. In addition, planning, as a process of setting formal guidelines, constrains behavior by choosing certain avenues to pursue and others to eliminate. Simon states:

> It should be made clear that actual events are determined by choice among on-the-spot alternatives for immediate behavior. In a strict sense, a decision can influence the future in only two ways: (1)

present behavior, determined by this decision, may limit future possibilities and (2) future decisions may be guided to a greater or lesser degree by the present decision. It is from this possibility of influencing future choice by present decisions that the idea of an interconnected plexus of decision derives. (Simon, 1976, p. 97)

Simon adds that, when a problem of a particular kind has recurred several times, it may lead to a generalized set of actions being adopted for guiding all further decisions by selecting particular:

- Values for later decisions.
- Items of knowledge to use in a later decision.
- Alternatives to consider (and others to not consider) for a later choice.

Ansoff and Brandenburg follow a similar line of reasoning. They place planning within the management-decision process since it "seeks to change and guide organizations through the specific means of strategies, policies, standing rules, plans, and budgets." Their view of the management process seems to be particularly appropriate and encompasses both Simon's and Drucker's conceptions of planning. Thus, long-range planning is the continuous process of making present risk-taking decisions systematically and with the best possible knowledge of the future consequences, systematically organizing the efforts needed to carry out these decisions, and measuring the results of these decisions against expectations through organized and systematic feedback. As will become apparent in the latter parts of this section, this view of planning as a multiphase process involving decision analysis, programming, implementation, and feedback has become the basis for virtually all major writings on planning.

Substantive Versus Procedural Planning

Herbert Simon distinguishes between substantive planning and procedural planning. Substantive planning involves making broad decisions about:

- Goals to which activities will be directed.
- General methods to use to achieve these goals.
- Knowledge, skill, and information required to make and to implement particular decisions within the limits of the policies laid down.

Procedural planning involves designing and implementing mechanisms that will direct attention and channel information

21

and knowledge in such a way as to cause specific day-to-day decisions to conform with the substantive plan. In this research study, both types of planning will be considered, although attention is focused primarily upon substantive planning.

Procedural planning involves the prescription of procedures to be used by audit personnel. These are often compiled within technical manuals, guidelines, preprinted audit checklists, computer programs, and so on. This type of professional work planning is as important as the broader administrative type of planning contemplated by substantive planning; however, a detailed examination of procedural planning is outside the scope of this study. Thus, although the facilities-and-procedures-planning phase is included in the comprehensive planning system, the primary focus here will be on broader planning considerations.

The Need for and Importance of Planning

As the complexity of organizational business activities increases, as information systems grow in sophistication, and as regulatory factors become more prominent, audit departments are asked to participate in a variety of evaluative capacities beyond their traditional financial audit role; for example, operational audits, reviews of systems under development, reviews of data processing security, and so on.

As the scope of audit activities increases, the complexity and the difficulty of planning and coordinating do too. The sheer volume and the increasing competition among demands for audit attention create a large and complex set of decisions involved in a proper allocation of audit efforts. This presents a difficult environment for many audit directors.

Drucker identified four characteristics of the decision-making environment which serve to emphasize the importance of formal planning: lengthening time span of managerial decisions, volatility of the environment, growing organizational and environmental complexity, and changing locus of decision-making authority and responsibility.

Lengthening Time Span of Managerial Decisions. Audit directors must often commit themselves to departmental work plans with three-to-five-year horizons. For example, in cyclical audit-coverage plans, a complete cycle may require three to five years to complete. In the audit-personnel recruitment, promotion, and training areas, similar long-range perspectives are often taken by directors and staff members as well. Comprehensive training programs may span two to five years in departments with a moderate level of sophistication and size.

Volatility and Change. The environment is increasingly volatile and fast paced. This underlines the need for planning as a means of providing stability in an ever-changing corporate environment.

Complexity. Another factor contributing to the need for planning is the growing complexity of business organizations and also the economy and the society in which they function. It is increasingly less viable to carry out audits without adequate preparation. It is difficult, if not impossible, to effectively manage a moderately large audit department without adequate planning.

Locus of Decision Making. The continuous shift in locus of decision making from top management to professional managers at various levels in the organizational hierarchy, having both specialized knowledge and the authority to exercise relatively autonomous judgment, emphasizes procedures aimed at achieving an adequate understanding of various operating units of the organization and eliciting the cooperation of managers throughout the organization in planning audits. Top-management directives are less and less effective means for ensuring adequate auditor involvement in various areas of organizations and for having audit services appreciated.

In addition to these four factors which lend emphasis to planning and coordinating audit activities, the number of parties with an interest in the work of an internal audit department requires the capability on the part of internal audit management to describe, coordinate, and defend its work on a regular and frequent basis (see Figure 2.1). Among the most interested parties with the ability to influence the work of an internal audit department are the audit committee, top management, the external auditor, the auditee, and regulatory agencies.

Each of these groups has its own special interests in the nature, scope, and conduct of the activities of an internal auditing department. For example, the audit committee is typically concerned that the company's financial statements present fairly the financial position and results of operations and that the auditors (both external and internal) have no reservations about them.[5] Top management, on the other hand, may be primarily interested in cost savings associated with the internal auditors' activities

Figure 2.1
Influence Relationships

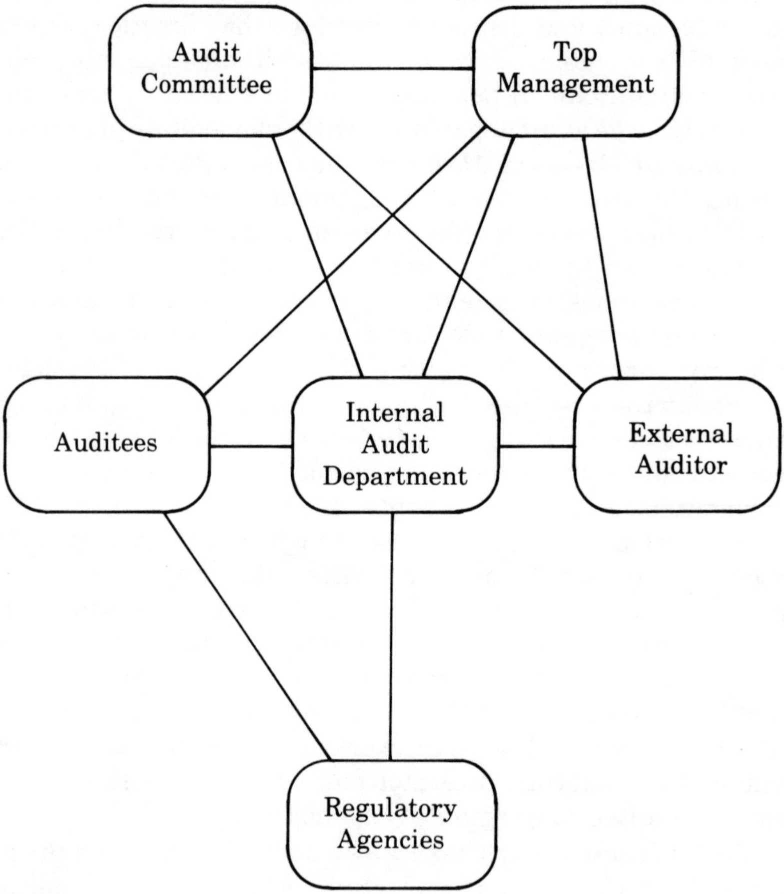

and enforcement of corporate control systems (Macchiaverna, 1978). External auditors may be primarily interested in controlling audit fees and audit risks through reliance upon the work of internal auditors.[6] Regulatory agencies, such as those sponsoring state bank and insurance examiners, may have interests similar to those of external auditors, although they may have different audit mandates. Auditees have a variety of interests but, in many cases, look to the audit function for help in controlling the functions under their administration and for suggestions about potential improvements in procedures and operations.

The Usefulness of Plans

Rappaport suggested that the goodness of a plan might be determined by assessing its relevancy, verifiability, freedom from bias, and quantifiability. More recently, Freedman and Weinberg compiled a comprehensive list of criteria by which to evaluate a set of plans:[7]

- Completeness.
- Correctness.
- Precision (i.e., clarity, nonambiguity).
- Consistency and defensibility.
- Relevance.
- Testability/verifiability.
- Traceability (i.e., from generalities to specifics and vice versa).
- Feasibility (i.e., implementability).
- Appropriate level of detail.
- Manageability.

Although it would be difficult to dispute the merit of these criteria as a basis for assessing the quality of any information, more specific investigation into what constitutes a good set of plans is required to provide useful planning guidelines.

It is important to distinguish between the "goodness" of a plan and the "usefulness" of the results achieved by using it. The two may not be related owing to a number of factors. Good plans may be poorly implemented and lead to poor results. Bad luck often interferes too, causing the best of plans to simply not produce the desired outcomes. However, Steiner (1972, p. 57) recalls a military saying: "Plans sometimes may be useless, but the planning process is always indispensable." Plans bring with them no guarantees. However, participation in the planning process may

25

improve the quality of management.

A 1974 conference on planning [8] emphasized the need for more formal planning for these reasons and suggested a number of additional potential benefits:
- Improved communication with auditees.
- Improved communication with top management.
- Enhanced support of audit activity by top management.
- Improved forecasts of resource requirements and, consequently, improved resource allocation.
- Identification of important audit areas to be emphasized and also less important areas to be de-emphasized.

Although the goodness of plans is independent of the actual outcomes achieved at a point in time, over a long run, there must be a demonstrated "payoff" from the planning process. This payoff might be viewed in relatively broad terms as indicated above rather than in terms of the outcomes from a particular decision based upon a plan.

There are limitations to planning. For example, planning does not actually get departmental work done. This is why it may often be sacrificed or given insufficient attention. Also, planning is costly. It consumes resources and may not contribute benefits sufficiently quantifiable to justify the costs associated with planning. Furthermore, planning deals with future events, whereas we all live in the present. Consequently, current "fires" always take precedence and should often do so. However, there is a danger of remaining perpetually in the day-to-day "fire-fighting" mode and managing from crisis to crisis rather than anticipating and preparing for a variety of possible challenges.

In the long run, success of an audit department hinges on a number of important factors – among them the credibility of its activities – which in turn depends upon the appropriateness of its planning approach and the quality of specific planning and coordinating activities. Simon highlights a number of obstacles to designing appropriate planning mechanisms which must be considered:
- The means used for representing the problems to be solved by plans to cope with the limited problem-solving capabilities of humans.
- The unavailability of information and the inadequacies of available data for effective planning.
- Identification of the "client" for whom the planning is being

26

carried out (e.g., the corporation, the department, the director of internal audit) and whose goals must dominate the analysis.

- The limitations of time and the ability to pay attention to the right problems and to measure progress toward goals.
- Ambiguity and conflicts of goals (e.g., as hinted in item three above).

Top-down Versus Bottom-up Planning Approaches

Formal planning approaches fall along a continuum from "controlled-reaction" tactics for evaluating and ranking known audit projects, to the strategic analysis of the organization's operating and information-processing activities, and to identifying auditable units with a high potential payoff. The former approach represents the state of the art today. The latter approach is rarely found, but several organizations are considering such an approach.

In a top-down approach, the director of internal audit identifies the important aspects of current corporate strategy with an impact upon internal audit then uses these in conjunction with the departmental charter to define specific departmental policies and a long-range plan for departmental activities, including what should be audited and to what extent. This plan is subsequently used to schedule audits and make staffing decisions and other audit-planning decisions.

In a bottom-up approach, managers or senior auditors plan audit activities relatively freely without much concern about departmental strategies or charters. In particular, they have a relatively free hand in deciding how much auditing to do in any given assignment, which audits to do, and when to do them. Their plans are then passed to the directors of internal audit who put them together into departmental plans and, if necessary, rationalize their relationship to departmental charters. When major disruptions to a plan owing to strategic shifts at the corporate level occur, a flurry of "activity" occurs at the department level in response, as audits are rescheduled, dropped, or "scoped down."

Strategic top-down analysis requires that an organization be viewed by an auditor from a corporate perspective. A systems approach is used to define and then hierarchially subdivide all of the organization's operations into successively smaller subsystems. The way in which the subdivision is carried out will depend upon the specific characteristics of the organization being analyzed. For example, a functionally organized, centralized business might require one type of definition for auditable unit, whereas a product-centered, decentralized business might require another type of definition of what constitutes an auditable unit. Typically, several definitions will be required in very large organizations. The important point to note, however, is that, regardless of the definition used, a formal hierarchical subdivision is used.

The subdivision process may be viewed as the imposition by an auditor of a template or a series of templates upon the business as a whole (see Figure 2.2). The example, drawn from a banking organization, may serve to clarify this formal subdivision process. The organization is a holding company with about 90 locations. Each location has been conceptualized as consisting of 20 auditable "modules." The same 20 modules apply across all 90 locations, although they vary in importance from location to location. Each audit module has been further subdivided into ten audit units of more or less importance depending upon the location.

As a result of this hierarchical subdivision, audits may be viewed in two ways. First, they may be viewed as consisting of a series of organized components defining the audit of a given location. Or for the company as a whole, one may "turn the hierarchy upside down" and view the corporate-wide audit as a specific audit step executed across 90 locations. Both views are useful at different times and for various specific purposes. The result is an identification of auditable units possibly quite different from those typically identified by many organizations today.

In contrast to the approach above, the controlled reaction or bottom-up approach simply inventories project names as they come up. An auditable unit may be anything that has been audited in the past or that has been requested for audit in the future. The lunchroom, a financial system, an operating division, and so on may all find themselves on the list of auditable units, creating a hodgepodge of audits often not linked to any specific corporate view of the business and generally displaying little homogeneity. This lack of homogeneity often hinders, and may even preclude, any formal quantitative approach to ranking audits according to priorities.[9]

It must be emphasized that these approaches are not mutually exclusive. They can coexist and may be emphasized to different degrees by the judicious exercise of choice on the part of the

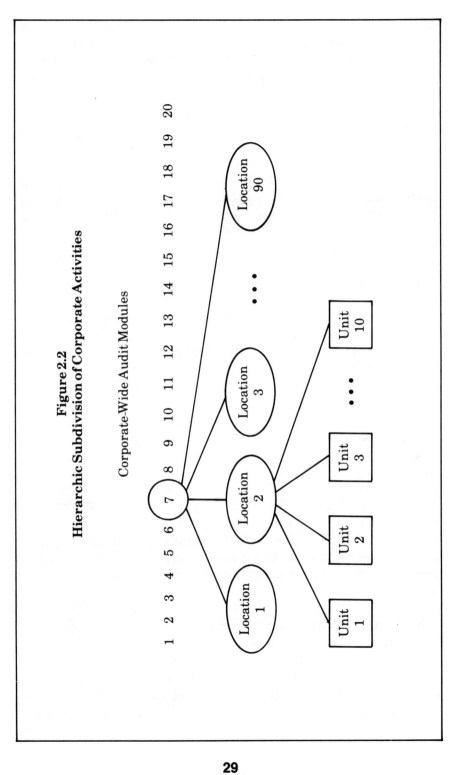

Figure 2.2
Hierarchic Subdivision of Corporate Activities

director of internal audit. However, where the controlled-reaction approach is solidly embedded within existing audit procedures and patterns of activity, the resistance to change may be so overwhelming as to prevent any systematic top-down approach to planning.

It should be recognized that the definition of what is an auditable unit powerfully dominates the nature of audit procedures and the nature of benefits to be derived from audit activity. An example of this is most evident in the public accounting realm where the cycle approach to defining internal control systems has dramatically changed the way in which audits are viewed. The cycle approach, for example, emphasizes relationships among certain accounting activities and forces explicit consideration of these to become part of standard audit procedures. As a result, weaknesses and errors in one subsystem are traced and evaluated as to their effects on other subsystems rather than being treated in isolation.

In an internal auditing context, the definition of an audit unit as a location may lead to location-centered audit procedures. However, if the locations have common features, then feature-centered audit procedures may be more appropriate. This is especially true where centralized information systems exist with applications uniformly applied across locations.

Selecting a particular approach requires careful balancing of such factors as the role of the audit department within the organization, its degree of maturity, the sophistication of the organization, its management, and the audit staff. Implementing the top-down approach in an organization which is not ready for it may prove to be disastrous and should be approached with caution. Moreover, a wholesale change in approach is not only undesirable but also unnecessary. Gradual implementation of the top-down approach could be considered as part of an evolutionary process by many organizations that have hitherto hesitated to use it.

A Systems Approach to Planning

Churchman discusses a most appealing approach to planning which views planning from a broad systems perspective. As such it identifies four main components of the activity to be served by a planning system. A planning system serves (1) decision makers, who select from among (2) alternative courses of action, in order to reach (3) specific goals which, if reached, contribute to the (4) overall objectives set for the activity for which planning is carried out.

Churchman goes on to provide a program description of a planning system consisting of three programs and a number of subprograms (see Figure 2.3). The three programs involve:

- Social interaction between the planning activity and the activity for which planning is being performed.
- Measurement and analysis.
- Verification.

A number of subsystems and components are identified for each of the three main programs as follows (Churchman, 1968, pp. 151,152):

Program 1 – Social Interaction
Subprograms:

(a) Justifying the planning system and its proper role.

(b) Organizing the subsystem by staffing the planning system and establishing its responsibility and authority (i.e., where it "belongs" in the organization).

(c) Explaining the subsystem:

(1) Persuasion (selling the plan).

(2) Mutual education (teaching the planning system about the requirements of the work system it is to serve and teaching the work system about the plans for it by the planning system).

(3) Politics (identifying and changing the power structure of the organization).

(d) Implementing the subsystem (installing the plan).

Program 2 – Measurement and Analysis
Subprograms:

(a) Identifying the decision makers and "customers" to be served by the planning system.

(b) Discovering and inventing the alternatives.

(c) Identifying first-stage goals.

(d) Identifying ultimate objectives.

(e) Measuring the effectiveness of each alternative for each first-stage goal (i.e., describing links between alternatives and goals).

(f) Measuring the effectiveness of each first-stage goal for the ultimate objectives (links between goals and objectives).

(g) Estimating the optimal alternative.

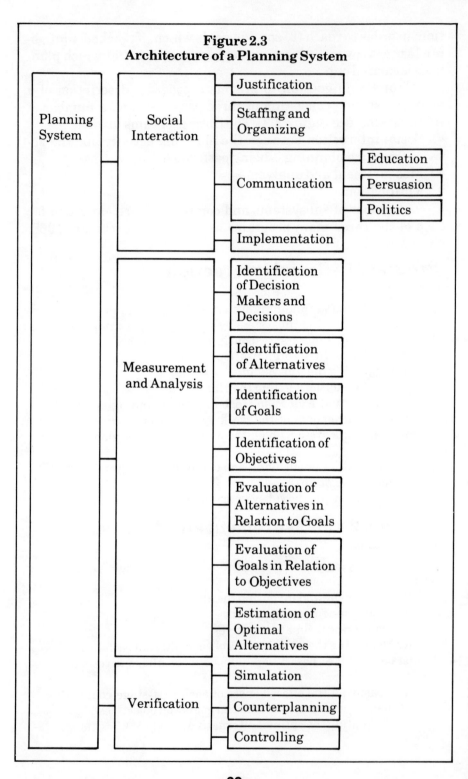

Figure 2.3
Architecture of a Planning System

Planning System
- Social Interaction
  - Justification
  - Staffing and Organizing
  - Communication
    - Education
    - Persuasion
    - Politics
  - Implementation
- Measurement and Analysis
  - Identification of Decision Makers and Decisions
  - Identification of Alternatives
  - Identification of Goals
  - Identification of Objectives
  - Evaluation of Alternatives in Relation to Goals
  - Evaluation of Goals in Relation to Objectives
  - Estimation of Optimal Alternatives
- Verification
  - Simulation
  - Counterplanning
  - Controlling

Program 3 – Verifying, Testing, and Evaluating the Plan

Subprograms:

    (a) Simulation and parallel testing.

    (b) Counterplanning (opposing the plan by its "deadly enemy").

    (c) Controlling the implemented plan.

Churchman discusses these activities and assesses the time, cost, and potential role for technological aids associated with each of these aspects of planning. Although much of Churchman's discussion focuses on corporate planning, many of the principles enunciated by him have immediate implications for planning within a function such as internal auditing. A brief summary of the main points made by him and their application in an internal audit context follow.

Social Interaction. Although much attention has been given to the justification of planning, Churchman believes that a manager considering a planning system should not bother to justify it. Such justification, he believes, is a waste of time with doubtful results.

Planners should be responsible for their plans. They should have the authority to act on their plans and bear responsibility for the outcomes. The planning effort should be visible, and it should be subjected to periodic measurements and evaluation.

Plans must be *used.* Consequently, an effort must be made to have them understood, accepted, and acted upon. In some internal audit departments, management by objectives is used as a technique to help ensure that plans are not devoid of meaning. This technique functions by enumerating explicit goals which both managers and subordinates agree upon and which are then used as a measure of performance. Of course, this technique may not contribute to accepting a plan outside the department; for example, by senior management, auditees, and external auditors. Persuasion, education, and politics may be required to achieve such acceptance.

Internal auditors often mention politics as an important part of their interactions with parties outside their departments. At this time, however, it is not clear what their considerations ought to be regarding the power relationships within their organizations. Churchman suggests that the amount of time devoted to politics, as opposed to persuasion and education, depends upon the relationship between an audit department and the parties external to it. This implies that, if politics are viewed as an unnecessary burden upon the department, they can be reduced by strategic action with regard to the "proper" organizational placement of the department, the development of "good" relationships between the department and the auditees, and the development of a "good" relationship between the department and external auditors.

A plan should explicitly state who is to do what and when. Sometimes, it must also specify "how." In auditing, procedural guidelines and technical manuals play a prominent role in specifying many of the "how's."

Measurement and Analysis. A critical issue in departmental planning involves: Who is the department to please? Whose goals are to be met? It is trite to say that a department's goals must be congruent with the overall goals of the corporation. How can they be made congruent? Many theorists believe that individuals are first and foremost driven by their own self-interests, although what comprises individuals' preferences may be difficult to determine and may vary. Thus, in keeping with such a view, we would presume that directors of internal audit departments will tend to make decisions which serve their self-interests. When there is congruency between the goals of corporations and those of the individuals, all is well. But how can this be guaranteed?

Let us consider a central problem which epitomizes this potential dichotomy in interests. Internal auditors typically determine what is to be audited. Some departments perform a formal evaluation of risk-exposure concerns associated with specific audit units. However, the evaluations are made by internal auditors and may not reflect the concerns of senior management. Thus, the audit plan may not be consistent with what senior management's evaluations would lead to in terms of audit priorities. Internal auditors cannot escape outside their skins and make objective evaluations as if they were automatons. Their subjective evaluations may be perceptive and made in the best of faith; however, they will reflect their preferences, which may not be the same as those of senior management.

Is this a problem area? We cannot know unless we systematically and concurrently collect the evaluations of senior management and internal auditors and resolve the differences, if there are any. Some organizations now require that directors of internal audit prepare evaluations of the risk-exposure concerns associated with various audit units and present to their audit committees and senior management the resulting priorities assigned to audit units. Such communication can enhance the prioritization process.

The proper identification of alternatives upon which plans are based must be considered a critical issue in planning. The nature and the completeness of the population of alternatives determine the nature of the eventual plan and results achieved when the plan is acted upon. Restricting the scope of alternatives will restrict the scope of internal audit's contribution to an organization.

Long-range objectives serve to provide a perspective for short-range goals and provide guidelines and restrictions which help direct activities toward some overriding purpose. For example, in some organizations, operational audits are strongly emphasized in mandates or charters of internal audit departments. This emphasis serves to highlight what types of audit activities should be planned each year.

Objectives may be stated so vaguely as to provide little guidance to a department. Although this may permit the maximum freedom for the department to plan its activities any way it chooses, it may also fail to adequately channel departmental efforts toward corporate goals. It appears that many companies have not given serious consideration to the role of internal audit in the corporate scheme of things. IIA's *Standards* provides general objectives around which departments can plan their activities, but they are not designed to provide explicit guidance about which units to audit and to what extent.

With respect to evaluating alternative plans and making decisions in the light of goals and objectives set for departments, Churchman suggests that technology can be most helpful in providing tools for enhancing the evaluation process and contributing to sound choices of specific plans.

Verifying, Testing, and Evaluating the Plans. Technology will enhance plan testing; for example, by simulation, sensitivity analysis, and so on. Simulation involves changing the premises upon which plans are based (e.g., available man-hours) to determine their repercussions on plans.

Churchman also highlights a technique he calls "counterplanning." The purpose of counterplanning is to help identify the hidden assumptions which might not have been adequately considered by managers in arriving at the original set of plans. Counterplanning involves challenging basic concepts such as the definition of the audit unit or the audit approach taken.

Although some readers may wonder whether internal audit planning is worth this much work, it should be noted that moderate-to-large departments have budgets running into the millions of dollars. This warrants a good deal of careful planning of their activities. Smaller departments might not need to engage in quite as comprehensive a planning effort.

Auditors generally do not engage in testing plans before implementing them except by means of discussion within their departments or with outside parties. In many cases, this is perfectly justifiable and sufficient. In other instances, it may be worthwhile to subject plans to more rigorous tests as by means of simulation.

Eventually, plans must be put into operation: their ultimate test. If a plan is not monitored or not monitored on a timely basis, corrections cannot be made midway; and the activities of the department could wind up being unproductive or out of phase with the goals previously set. Consequently, actual performance must be periodically and timely compared and assessed as to its impact upon the plan.

Key Factors Governing the Nature of Plans

The previous discussion identified a number of key factors which all planning approaches must take into account:
- Time dimensions of plans.
- Level of the organizational unit or subunit carrying out the planning.
- Structure of the specific decisions which the planning activity seeks to enhance.
- Characteristics (categories) of risks faced by both the organization and the department.
- Measurements to use for performance evaluation of the department and its staff and for providing feedback.
- Nature and extent of managerial knowledge about the specific subunits for which plans are made, including the nature of their operations and their strengths and limitations.

Figure 2.4 summarizes the main concepts to be discussed

later in detail. Each of the six factors governing the nature of plans is listed, and a brief explanatory summary of the essential attributes of the factors is provided. Later, these six factors will be used as categories for planning activities of internal audit departments and summarizing their key features.

Time Dimensions

Planning may take place along several time dimensions from the very long run covering several years to day-to-day planning horizons. Since different time horizons are used, a number of different plans must be prepared, each focusing upon a specific time dimension. Typically, planners deal in four time dimensions:

- Very long run (more than five years).
- Medium range (two to five years).
- Short range (one year).
- Immediate time horizon (weeks).

Each time horizon represents planning activities which require the requisite degree of preparedness for action but which also represent a varying degree of volatility of decision variables. In the very short run, day-to-day planning dominates the activities of the department. These typically involve specific audit projects and procedures that are either responses to unplanned requests or preplanned behavior in accordance with the departmental work plan.

It is rare to have sufficient resources to audit every important auditable activity within a corporation each year.[10] Consequently, a two-to-five-year horizon is often used for planning a relatively complete cycle of audit coverage. Of course, a long-range plan cannot be fixed, since the corporation and the audit department are continuously undergoing change: growth in some areas, decline in others, changes in methods and practices employed in different areas (e.g., automation/computerization of various activities), changing emphasis by management in response to environmental pressures (e.g., the Foreign Corrupt Practices Act), and so on.

To provide long-term stability to a department in the midst of these types of changes, a long-term-defining "character" must be established for it. This serves to provide its members with a perspective upon their role in the organization and the value of their specific audit activities.

Figure 2.4
Summary of Key Factors Governing the Nature of Plans

Key Factors	Explanation
Time Dimensions	The time dimension constrains what aspects of the department can be manipulated over a specific time horizon; for example, during the short run, personnel are fixed and must be utilized as given. Over the long run, personnel skills may be increased, staff may be increased, and so on.
Level of Planning	The organizational level of the planner determines which variables will be emphasized in the planning process.
Structure of Decisions and the Planning Process	Planning at all levels must include the four key phases: analysis, programming, implementation, and performance and feedback.
Characteristic Risks	The failure of a plan has consequences attached to it. Each plan has different characteristic risks to be considered depending upon the party most concerned.
Performance Measures	Each plan should have associated with it some type of measure reflecting its quality.
Knowledge Requirements	Different plans have different knowledge requirements. If these knowledge requirements are not met, the plan's quality will suffer.

Level of Planning

Anthony suggested a multilevel model of managerial activity and identified three classes of activity:

- Strategic planning.
- Management planning and control.
- Operational planning and control.

We can view some of a department's activities as a hierarchy of planning activities associated with departmental operations. This is illustrated in Figure 2.5, which shows a five-tier hierarchy of planning activities which can be easily mapped onto Anthony's three-level approach:

- The strategic planning level includes the corporate plan for the internal audit department's role and scope of activities to pursue and the department's long-range plan for best serving the organization.

- The management planning and control level includes planning audit activities aimed at complying with the mandate or charter, specifically managing the portfolio of auditable units and the resources (personnel, facilities, and procedures) to permit cost-effective audits to be carried out.

- The operational planning and control level includes specific audit project plans and activities.

Strategic Planning. According to Anthony, strategic planning is a process having to do with formulating long-range plans and policies that determine or change the character or direction of an organization. Such plans in the context of internal audit departments define how and why they operate. Included under this heading is the plan of the internal audit organization, personnel policies, and specific policies as to audit activities to emphasize; for example, the emphasis on operational, as opposed to financial, audits; the degree of independence of the internal audit department; the extent to which the standards of the internal auditing profession govern the conduct of the audit department; and the relationship between internal and external auditors. Typically, these are codified and incorporated within the mandate or charter of a department and further explained in its manual for the professional staff.

Strategic decisions such as the above would typically be made jointly by corporate top management and the chief internal auditor. The audit committee might also be involved.

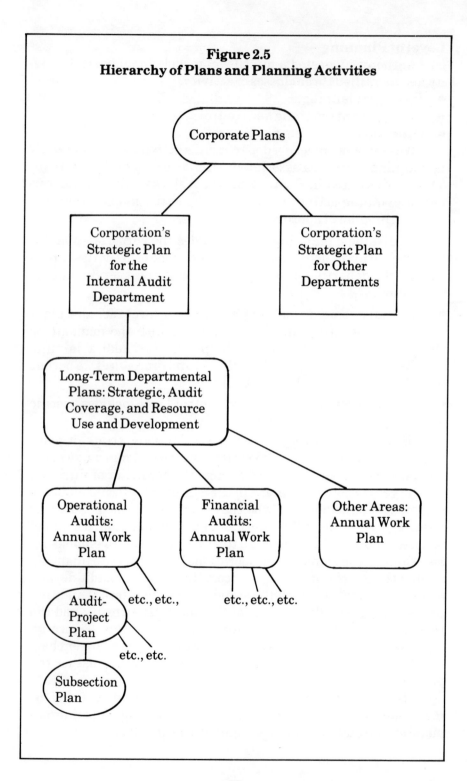

Figure 2.5
Hierarchy of Plans and Planning Activities

Corporate Plans

Corporation's Strategic Plan for the Internal Audit Department

Corporation's Strategic Plan for Other Departments

Long-Term Departmental Plans: Strategic, Audit Coverage, and Resource Use and Development

Operational Audits: Annual Work Plan

Financial Audits: Annual Work Plan

Other Areas: Annual Work Plan

Audit-Project Plan

etc., etc.,

etc., etc., etc.

etc., etc.

Subsection Plan

At the departmental level, it is possible to subdivide departmental planning into two main types of plans. The first type of plan deals with setting the character of the audit organization. The second type deals with the audit organization's planned response to strategic plans at the corporate level. Each type of plan has its own difficulties.

Character-defining plans are supposed to restrict and direct the audit focus of a department. They should define the goals of a department and the type of professional conduct to be expected. For example, some internal audit departments are defined to be a training ground for managers,[11] whereas others are defined to be professional specialties within the organization. In some organizations, these definitions are taken very seriously; in others, they are disregarded. In yet others, they are not made at all.

The response-to-corporate-strategy types of plans are a difficult problem for most departments. Typically, top management does not share its strategic plans with lower management levels. Of course, this makes it exceedingly difficult for directors of departments to plan for departmental activities which are congruent with the strategic plans of top management. The MIS function, for example, has been burdened with the problem of inaccessibility to top-management strategies yet, at the same time, is at the mercy of strategic changes which have important and pervasive effects upon MIS. To overcome some of the problems, King suggests a guessing-game approach called "strategy-set transformation." The idea is that, if strategic plans of top management are important but if top management fails to adequately communicate them, it is incumbent upon MIS managers to take active steps to determine what the strategies are and ensure that they are prepared for the important contingencies. King provides some guidelines that MIS managers might use in transforming perceived corporate strategies into department-level-strategy sets. A formal document is prepared and then presented to management for feedback. Once the initiative is taken by the department, it is hypothesized that top management will respond by providing further guidelines and other informative comments.

In auditing, management's strategies may have less severe impacts than might be the case in other areas; yet there are some important problems to consider. For example, suppose a new line of business is acquired without adequate warning being given to the audit department. In such circumstances, the audit department might be literally incapable of carrying out adequate audits if the newly acquired business is very different from the old lines. Well-defined auditing procedures may not exist and may not be easily and "instantly" created. Accounting-systems technologies – such as data-base-management systems, on-line systems, and distributed-processing systems – used by the new business may require skills which the audit department's personnel may simply not possess or in which it may lack adequate proficiency. Another possible consequence might be stretching the existing audit resources so thin as to detract from the overall quality of departmental audit work.

The Foreign Corrupt Practices Act created difficulties for some departments which did not possess sufficient expertise and/ or resources to meet managements' directive to evaluate their organizations' compliance with its provisions.

More recently, the pressure exerted by the Securities and Exchange Commission (SEC) for inclusion in the financial statements of a statement by management regarding the system of internal accounting control bears potential consequences for the long-term character of many internal audit departments (see for example, Wesberry, 1980).

In some instances, by having direct contact with the chief executive officer as part of the formal authority structure or as an informal communication link, the director of internal audit may be well informed and be able to plan for important contingencies. In other instances, the internal audit department may be an active participant; for example, it may carry out a purchase investigation as a special assignment on behalf of top management. Barring such active participation in strategic activities or in the absence of accessible channels of communication with top management, it may be incumbent upon the director of internal audit to adopt King's suggested approach.

Management Planning and Control. Management planning and control involves arranging and ensuring that resources are obtained and used effectively in achieving departmental objectives. This includes planning staff levels and personnel practices, developing procedural guidelines governing the execution of audits, providing audit tools such as audit software, and budgeting for departmental financial resources. In addition, this level of activity involves measuring, appraising, and improving performance of members of the department.

The key management-planning concerns for internal audit departments revolve around the identification of auditable units, ranking them according to their importance, allocating the appropriate resources to them in terms of intensity and frequency of audit coverage, and matching the appropriate resources in terms of personnel skills to each audit project.

In most audit departments, the identification of auditable units or activities is an ongoing process. Often it is carried out haphazardly . . . sometimes not at all. Sometimes it is carried out formally by using a systematic approach as previously described.[12]

The ranking of auditable units according to their importance depends heavily upon the criteria set for assessing importance. In many cases, the criteria reflect the department's view of importance rather than the organization's view. In addition, internal audit management often overrides the formally computed measures of importance; thus, criteria not explicitly incorporated into the formal scheme are sometimes used, even when much effort has gone into developing a formal evaluation approach.

In internal audit departments which lack the resources to audit all significant auditable units each year, audits are planned over cyclic periods of two to five years. The frequency with which a given auditable unit is audited during a cyclic period depends upon its assessed importance.

In some organizations – for example, in banking institutions – all locations are typically audited each year. However, depending upon the audit importance of a given unit, the audit scope and intensity might be adjusted in order to fit all the audits into the year.

Audits require various degrees of skill and expertise; therefore, an important aspect of planning involves matching the requisite skills to the planned audit activities. This type of planning is so obvious that it is often not formally considered. Often a team of auditors with a range of experience and skill is assigned to carry out an audit, and this indirectly obviates the necessity for formal matching of skills to audits.

Another reason that formal planning consideration in this area may be rare is due to the way audit projects are defined. All audits are usually considered as being essentially similar. A typical audit profile might consist of six major phases: (1) preaudit planning; (2) documenting the auditable activity; (3) reviewing and evaluating the activity being audited; (4) testing controls and procedures for adherence to prescribed policies; (5) checking transactions and balances for errors, misstatements, and irregularities; and (6) reporting the results of the audit to appropriate personnel.

Although the emphasis given to these activities varies from audit to audit, most audits adhere to this six-phase scheme. Many audit departments use a less refined three-phase scheme: preliminary work, fieldwork, and reporting. Each phase has its own objectives. The phases differ in their skill requirements and may be carried out independently at different points in time. For example, review and evaluation may require a greater level of skill than checking transactions. These may be carried out at different times by personnel with different skills. If an audit project is defined in terms of a subset of the six phases rather than in terms of all of the phases, matching the requisite skills to audits and using available manpower within the audit department efficiently become more difficult and require formal planning to make it work.

Some important premises and features of the approach outlined above which must be emphasized include the assumptions that:

• Audits can be subdivided into phases (but they do not have to be so subdivided).

• Some phases require different types of audit skills and training.

• All man-hours are not equal. It is more cost-effective to formally assign the appropriate level of skill to the audit phase.

• In order to successfully plan for the acquisition of appropriate resources (e.g., recruiting competent staff), it is essential that the shortfall between skill-level hours required to carry out departmental activities and the skill-level hours currently available be identified.

Operational Planning and Control. Operational planning and control involve implementing the policies established at higher levels, scheduling audit activities, monitoring their execution, and measuring and appraising the work of subordinates.

Once a long-range audit plan is created, each period's "allotment" of audit projects is allocated. Within the period, individual projects and personnel must be matched up and scheduled. Arrangements must be made with auditees unless a surprise audit is planned.[13] Also, preaudit procedural preparations must be undertaken, including revisions to audit approach if necessary, design of techniques (e.g., computer-assisted audit techniques) requiring lead time, and advance planning for important audit-related events (e.g., a stocktaking, a system conversion, a cash count, etc.).

Structure of Decisions and the Planning Process

Regardless of the time horizon or level of planning activity, all decisions, including planning decisions, may be viewed as consisting of certain generic phases and components:

- Decision analysis.

1. A set of alternatives presented to or searched out by the decision maker.

2. A set of anticipated consequences attached to each alternative including risks of failure.

3. A set of information items which assist in selecting a set of alternatives.

4. A set of preferences by those involved in making the choice.

5. An algorithm for weighing and combining the considerations in (1) through (4) above and for arriving at a choice from among the alternatives considered.

- Programming.

1. A set of action plans to support the decision.

- Implementation.

1. A set of actions aimed at achieving the goals by adhering to the planned program of action.

2. A set of consequences which may or may not correspond to those anticipated when contemplating a course of action.

- Performance evaluation and feedback.

1. A measurement scheme for evaluating the search, decision, programming, or implementation phases.

2. A feedback mechanism which presents the outcome to the decision maker and permits him/her to revise planning activities in the future.

Figure 2.6 illustrates these four phases and their interrelationships discussed below.

Decision Analysis. The decision-analysis phase is concerned with the consequences of given alternatives under

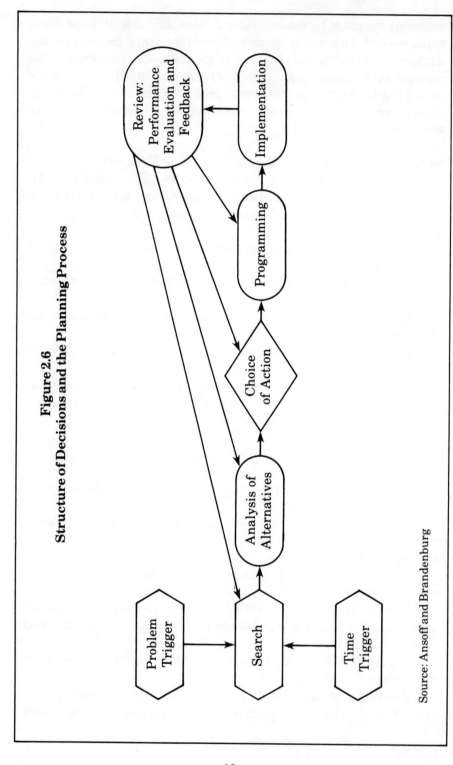

Figure 2.6
Structure of Decisions and the Planning Process

Problem Trigger → Search

Time Trigger → Search

Search → Analysis of Alternatives → Choice of Action → Programming → Implementation → Review: Performance Evaluation and Feedback

Source: Ansoff and Brandenburg

specified conditions. In contrast, the decision-making phase is concerned with choosing one set of consequences over another set. Although recent audit literature shows some progress being made in this area, many flaws in planning are evident today. For example, although planning checklists are sometimes used, little attention is given to formally structured analyses of alternatives, consequences, and rationale for making a particular choice. In some organizations, criteria for making audit-planning decisions have been adopted only to be ignored because they do not reflect the decision environment of the organization. Often "miscellaneous" categories are used to twist decisions into the direction desired, holding sway over the formal models which suggest some other course of action. It is not clear whether such formal models are incapable of reflecting the decision environment of the department or whether insufficient effort has been paid to developing them.

Programming. Selecting a preferred alternative does not end the planning process. Managers must translate their decisions into specific plans for implementation. The main tasks involved in this programming phase include:
- Scheduling activities in support of decisions.
- Assigning and scheduling resources in support of decisions.
- Establishing patterns of work flows in the department.
- Establishing patterns of authority and responsibility.
- Establishing communication flows.

This area of activity seems to have captured the lion's share of attention by planners and authors with less attention being paid to the search and decision-analysis aspects of planning.

Implementation. This consists of the following main tasks:
- Disseminating information about plans and programs.
- Securing their acceptance by responsible participants.
- Triggering organizational action.
- Providing coordination among related activities.
- Providing leadership and motivating the participants.

The program of action must be accepted by the organization within the internal audit department as well as outside it. Management by objectives, for example, is a means of securing an adequate commitment to the plan within the department by using participative techniques. A number of internal audit departments have adopted such an approach for programming and implementing activities. In contrast with traditional programming concerned with resource scheduling, this approach emphasizes activity scheduling by specifying activities to become objectives of participants.

For disseminating a department's plans to the parties outside it such as audit committees, top management, external auditors, and auditees, coordinating and informational meetings are held periodically.[14]

Performance Evaluation and Feedback. Performance evaluation depends upon the programming and implementing philosophies adopted as well as the actual results flowing from the actions of staff members. Herbert Simon identifies four functions served by the review process:

• It is the means by which the administrative hierarchy learns whether decisions (including planning decisions) are being made correctly or incorrectly and whether work is being done well or badly at the lower levels of the hierarchy. It is a fundamental source of information upon which higher levels of the hierarchy must rely heavily for their decisions.

• It is a means by which subsequent decisions may be influenced: by specific directives, policies, and training.

• It is a means by which important decisions may be reconsidered (sometimes by better skilled personnel).

• It is a means by which the exercise of authority may be supported.

The review process may focus on outcomes, processes, or both. However, as was pointed out previously, outcomes alone may not provide adequate insight into the quality of decisions made, since they may be strongly affected by random factors.

The performance-evaluation-and-feedback phase involves four feedback loops with the following action consequences:

• Redirection of implementation activities to promote attainment of planned objectives.

• Reprogramming activities while maintaining the same basic goals.

• Reformulating the decision-analysis process because it has led to selection of a suboptimal decision from an adequate set of alternatives.

• Seeking out different alternatives to replace those being implemented (i.e., the problem lies in the decision chosen rather than in programming or implementing phases).

In some cases, the cause of a plan failure will not be structural (i.e., it will not lie in any of the phases above). Instead, it will sometimes be largely the decision maker who is the source of the problem and not the process.

There is similarity in the structure of planning activities at all five of the levels in the hierarchy of plans. Figure 2.7 summarizes the hierarchic structure of the key planning decisions and is briefly discussed below. Horizontally across the top are the four generic planning phases: decision analysis, programming, implementation, and feedback. Vertically, the five levels of planning (which can also be categorized into three levels) are presented.

At the strategic level, decision analysis involves determining the role, responsibilities, and audit approach of the internal audit department. Once these have been selected, the programming phase must provide a plan for the organizational placement of the department and relations with outside parties such as top management, the audit committee, external auditors, and auditees. The implementation considerations involve a set of explicit policies and guidelines governing the internal audit department, its professional staff, and its work. Feedback is provided through periodic review and evaluation of departmental activities, practices, and procedures in force.

At the managerial level, planning involves management of the audit portfolio and personnel-skill-hour availability. Audit-portfolio management involves identification, evaluation, and definitions of auditable units, risk-exposure factors in setting priorities, the audit framework to use for planning purposes, and the skill requirements associated with various audits.

Once the definitions are made, it is necessary to program methods for evaluating the importance of specific auditable units, prioritize them according to their importance, and estimate the skill-hour requirements of all audits. Once the methods are defined, the program can be executed. A prioritized long-range and "ideal" audit-coverage plan results. This plan will undoubtedly undergo a series of revisions to appropriately adjust it for resource limitations, disagreements about priorities, and other similar implementation reconsiderations. Reviews of audit coverage planned and provided by the internal audit department as well as resources consumed permit an evaluation of the plans constructed in this manner.

Figure 2.7
Hierarchy Structure of Key Planning Decisions

Level of Planning	Generic Planning Phase			
	Analysis	Programming	Implementation	Performance Evaluation and Feedback
Strategic	Analyze: • Role, responsibility, and approach of internal audit department	Define: • Organizational position • Relation with outsiders	Set policies and guidelines governing conduct of: • Audit department • Professional staff • Audit work	Periodic review of: • Department activities and procedures
Managerial	Define and identify: • Auditable units • Risk factors • Audit framework • Skill requirements	Define methods for: • Risk evaluation • Priority ranking • Time requirements estimated	Prepare: • Ideal audit-coverage plan • Work plan adjusted for resource limitations	Review of: • Priorities and planned coverage by audit committees and external auditor • Resource requirements

Managerial	Identification of: • Audit skill requirements and shortfalls	Define plan for eliminating shortfall by: • Training • New tools • Work adjustments	Implement: • Training • Recruitment procedures • Work-Plan adjustment	Review and Evaluation of: • Audit coverage • Findings • Staff skill
Operational	Analyze audit requirement: • Goals, methods, extent, and timing • Personnel requirements Analyze: • Procedures	Define methods for: • Staff to audit assignment • Audit to time-period scheduling Provide procedural guidelines by: • Manuals • Procedural guidelines	• Prepare work schedule • Coordinate with auditees and external auditors • Coordinate Staff • Implement procedures in audit	• Monitor audit work in progress • Review performance • Review of audit-work quality

A long-range plan is a guide. During a given period, only the available staff will be involved in carrying it out. The staff availability may be considered to be a pool of skill hours. Thus, in the short run – say one quarter – work plans must match skill hours available. Over a longer horizon, skill-hour shortages can be corrected to permit annual work plans to be achieved. Programs for adjusting staff shortages (or excesses) will include staff training and planned recruitment, which will affect the pool of available skill hours. Other plans might involve changes in work methods and tools (e.g., statistical sampling, analytical review, software) or in workload adjustments. Periodic evaluations of staff-resource availability, audit coverage provided, and audit findings will permit an evaluation of personnel-skill management.

At the operational level, specific work requirements govern the assignment of specific staff members to audits. In addition, personnel training and developing aspects must be considered. Scheduling audits depends simultaneously upon the availability of specific members, auditees' considerations, and external audit requirements.

Through appropriate monitoring, actual performance can be measured relative to a plan. This entails comparing audits started and completed against planned dates, actual time taken to complete audits against budgeted time, and other aspects.

The final operational planning level is strictly procedural. Certain audit procedures are planned and executed in accordance with professional standards, guidelines, manuals, etc. Reviews of work quality will provide insight into the quality of these *procedural* plans.

Characteristic Risks

In planning, there are a number of risks to consider and weigh. At different levels in the hierarchy of plans hitherto outlined, different risks are important.

Patton *et alii* provide an insight into the relative importance of factors as a basis for determining the audit importance of a given audit unit. They call these "risk factors," but their discussion makes it clear that these are "concern factors" useful in assigning a measure of concern to specific audit units according to a multidimensional scheme which incorporates a variety of criteria for arriving at such a measure. As such, they cover only risks which are useful for constructing cyclical audit plans. On the basis of their riskiness or concern index, individual audit units might be assigned to various categories of frequency or intensity of auditing.

It is important to recognize, however, that these risks are only criteria for determining whether, and the extent to which, specific audit units might be audited and form only one set of criteria useful for one set of planning decisions. At other levels of the planning hierarchy, other concerns might come into play. Even if some of the same concerns exist at different levels, their relative magnitudes may change as one moves from planning level to planning level. It is also important to recognize that concern factors related to an individual audit unit are different from the risk factors which govern broader planning decisions.

In examining the hierarchy of planning activities, the risks to consider and control must be intimately related to the objectives of the planning activity. Thus, the important risks must be related to the consequences flowing from inadequately formulated plans at each level of planning.

Figure 2.8 summarizes the characteristic risks associated with aspects of planning. These risks outline the consequences attached to inadequate plans or planning procedures at each level of the planning hierarchy. Unless these risks are properly considered, it is doubtful that formal audit-planning procedures will be effectively implemented. Instead, they will likely be overridden or fall into disuse.

Performance Measures

Each level of planning activity requires its own set of performance measures to assess the quality of planning. Since quality of planning may not be related in any given period to quality of outcomes, performance measures are not necessarily straightforward to construct. Outcomes must be a part of the performance-measurement scheme since the planning activity, if poorly executed, may have an important effect upon the quality of the outcomes themselves. However, the methods used in planning must also receive a full measure of attention.

A variety of outcome measures are used by internal auditors. For example, often observed measures include:
• Variances between budgeted and actual time or budgeted and actual number of audits (i.e., good planning should lead to low variances).

Figure 2.8
Risks Associated with Failures of Plans

Planning Activity	Characteristic Risks
Strategic corporate	• Poor leadership of department • Wrong emphasis by department • Insufficient "power" to audit
Strategic departmental	• Wrong emphasis by department • Inadequate quality of departmental activities
Cyclic coverage plan	• Omissions of important areas • Isolated rather than integrated audits • Inappropriate audit extents
Resource plan	• Shortage of personnel and other resources • Mismatch between skills required and skills available
Annual work plan	• Mismatch of person and audit • Bad timing • Poor work quality
Audit-project plan	• Inappropriate scope or extent of work • Budget exceeded
Subsection plan	• Inappropriate procedures, timing, and extent of work

- Percentage of available personnel time spent on audit projects (where charge-out systems exist, this may be extended to a measure of financial "recovery" per employee).
- Corporate cost savings owing to findings and recommendations made by auditors (the argument supporting this measure is that proper planning should emphasize high payback audits and de-emphasize low-payoff audits).

Measures of planning performance based on the planning process rather than outcomes may include:
- Feedback from auditees to the extent that they are involved in the planning process (or left out when they should not be).
- Feedback from external auditors.
- Peer reviews or reviews by external consultants, task forces, etc.

Knowledge Requirements

Each type of plan draws on different kinds of expertise, skill, and judgment. Some plans require a broad understanding of the organization and of the department's role within it. Other plans require an intimate knowledge of a particular activity. This aspect of planning is not widely recognized.

Planning knowledge is a particular kind of knowledge typically possessed by experts in a given field; that is, to be able to plan an activity requires a good deal of expertise in that activity. Different activities require different kinds of expertise.

The implications of these observations are that the variety of planning activities performed by internal audit departments will require many participants, depending upon the nature of the plan, which can be partially defined by the other five key factors outlined above. Strategic planning will require a specific set of management skills and knowledge of corporate behaviors, tendencies, and plans. Audit-project planning, on- the other hand, will require an in-depth knowledge of the specific auditee and of professional audit skills.

It is not necessary nor desirable to have all plans carried out by the same individual and at the same management level. Instead, planning activities and outcomes can be enhanced by matching personnel skills and knowledge to those required by the planning activity. Where the skills do not exist, they must be cultivated, acquired, or contracted.

Figure 2.9
Summary of Key Attributes of Internal Audit Plans and Planning Activities

Plan Type	Time Dimensions	Level of Planning	Key Considerations and Related Decisions Flowing from Plan	Key Factors		
				Characteristic Risks	Performance Measures	Knowledge Requirements
Strategic Corporate	5-7 years	Corporate management	• Appoint director • Organizational status of internal audit department • Relations with audit committee	• Poor leadership • Wrong emphasis • No power	• Peer review • Internal task force	• Mettle of director • Alternatives available • Role of internal audit
Strategic Departmental	2-7 years	Corporate management and director of internal auditing	• Role of internal audit • Degree of independence • Relations between internal and external auditors	• Wrong emphasis • Inadequate professionalism	• Peer review • Internal task force • External audit feedback	• Corporate goals for internal audit department • Professional standards of IIA
Cyclic audit-coverage plan	2-5 years	Director and managers	• What is eligible for audit? • What are priorities? • What will be audited, when, how much, by whom, and how often?	• Omissions • Isolated, not integrated audits • Too much/too little auditing	• Independent review • Management review • Audit-committee review • Auditee feedback	• What is auditable? • How to prioritize? • How much skill time required? • How much skill available?

Plan	Time	Responsibility	Activities	Risks	Controls	Considerations
Resource plan	2-5 years	Director and managers	• Skill-hour shortfall • Hiring, training, and subcontracting	• Mismatching of skill/time required and available • Resource mismanagement	• Independent review • Staff feedback	• Long-run-cyclic plan • Skill requirements • Personnel potentials
Annual work plan	1 year	Director and managers	• Staffing: in-charge assistants • Scheduling: personnel, auditee, external auditor	• Mismatch of person to audit • Bad timing, work quality	• Plan versus variance • Findings in audits • Auditee feedback	• Capabilities of staff • Auditee circumstances • Goals of audit
Audit-project plan	Weeks	Manager and in-charge auditors	• Audit issues • Staff assignments • Staff scheduling, supervision	• Too much/too little work • Wrong emphasis • Over budget	• Quality of findings • Budget variance • Quality of work	• Auditee strengths and weaknesses • Staff strengths and weaknesses • Technical skills
Subsection plan	Days	In-charge and auditors	• Specific procedures to perform • Timing • Extent	• Wrong procedures • Bad timing • Too much/too little work	• Work-paper quality • Budget variances	• Audit skills: matching tasks assigned

Planning activity at every level is a demonstration of professional or managerial skill in a particular domain. Where the skill or expertise is missing, effective planning cannot be expected.

Summary

In this part of the study, the general concepts and issues pertaining to planning were discussed. We considered some background information about planning and a conceptual framework for understanding planning approaches as a basis for the following chapters. Our discussion covered general planning concepts, the need and importance of planning, the usefulness of plans for a variety of purposes, top-down versus bottom-up planning approaches, a systems approach to planning, and six key factors governing the nature of plans.

The six factors discussed are important in defining the nature of plans and the characteristics of each type of planning activity. Figure 2.9 summarizes our discussion to this point and is a cross-classification with levels of planning activity down the left-hand side and the six key planning factors across the top. The purpose of this analysis is to help distinguish among the planning activities typically performed within internal audit departments as well as to emphasize the similarities in the planning phases involved at each level.

In contrast with the planning framework summarized here, current audit practices tend to be quite less comprehensive. For example, a Conference Board report on internal auditing (Macchiaverna, 1978) indicates that detailed departmental plans typically include the following components:
- A departmental work-force-allocation schedule by location and activity.
- Budgetary-spending figures.
- A comparison of prior year's activities against plans.
- A narrative description of planned audit objectives.

This observation is significant for what it omits as much as for what it includes. As described in this chapter, planning may require a greater investment of resources than currently is expended or a redirection of resources to different aspects of planning than those currently emphasized. It should be noted, however, that the intent of our discussion is not to raise the importance of planning above the importance of auditing activities themselves.

Many authors in this field believe that there is an important relationship between the quality and comprehensiveness of planning and the quality of work performed. Better insight into the planning process may lead to improvements in planning activities which may then transfer over to improvements in quality of work (including efficiency as well as effectiveness).

Footnotes:

[5]See, for example, Neumann, Mautz and Neary, Shornack, Palmer, and Williams. Commonly, meetings are held with the audit committee and external auditors, the latter at the behest of the audit committee which is apparently interested in ensuring that:
- Audit activities are directed at operations with the highest exposures.
- Audit activities are properly coordinated between the two sets of auditors so that all material corporate activities are covered and that audit costs (i.e., external and internal) are minimized.

According to the *Survey of Internal Auditing: 1979,* most (70 to 90 percent) departments hold periodic meetings with audit committee if they exist.

The Conference Board's survey (Macchiaverna, 1978) reports the frequency of meetings between audit committees and internal audit directors as follows:

Frequency of Meetings with Audit Committee	Percentage of Respondents
0	28
1	17
2	21
3	12
4	16
5 +	6
	100

Typically, the scope of audits, audit findings, and the internal audit organization are discussed at these meetings. Only 38 percent of the respondents indicated that audit committees regularly receive formally written reports of audit findings (other than at such meetings).

[6]See for example, Ward and Robertson, Williams, Rittenberg and Davis, and AICPA's SAS No. 9. The *Survey of Internal Auditing: 1979* indicated that:
- 50 percent of internal auditors complete some work on behalf of external auditors.
- 50 percent of internal audit departments' work papers are used by external auditors.

- More than 80 percent work jointly with external auditors to some extent, and the incidence of no joint programs is low (19 percent).

Further, the survey indicated that 73 percent of internal audit departments cooperatively schedule audit activities.

The Conference Board's survey also adds that most (87 percent) departments furnish reports of their audit findings to external auditors and meet periodically with them to discuss the scope of their audits and their findings:

Frequency of Meetings with External Auditors	Proportion of Responses	
0		13%
1	6	
2	18	
3	7	
4	12	44%
5-12	17	17%
13 +	26	26%
		100%

[7]Although this list is provided in a computer-systems context, it is generally applicable.

[8]As reported by E.R. McLean and J.V. Soden in *Strategic Planning for MIS,* New York: John Wiley & Sons, 1977.

[9]The figures may be computed, but they will not be justifiable. One of the seldom discussed aspects of priority-rating schemes is this issue of comparing dissimilar items. They may simply not be measurable by the same scale.

[10]Surprisingly, the Tulsa Chapter's survey found that only 21 percent of the respondents excluded audit units from their audit coverage because of limited resources as the primary reason.

[11]When a department serves as a training ground, the turnover of personnel precludes a certain degree of audit professionalism from developing, although it certainly does not preclude the development of managerial professionalism. If this character-defining strategy is set, departmental activities must correspond to it; and performance evaluation must also be defined appropriately. In many instances, it is difficult to see a relationship between character-defining plans and departmental activities.

In the *Survey of Internal Auditing: 1979,* 60 percent of the responses indicated that internal auditing departments were used as a training ground for managerial/supervisory positions within their organizations. However, although most view themselves as an important source of future managerial talent, some departments are formally considered by management as part of a managerial training program with an "internship" in the department being an entry-level position to a career with the corporation.

[12]The Tulsa Chapter's survey concluded that (1) a substantial number of internal audit departments had not systematically identified their audit universe and that (2) many internal audit departments did not formally document the results of their audit-universe-risk analysis.

[13]As reported in the *Survey of Internal Auditing: 1979,* only one-quarter of the respondents never perform surprise audits. However, suggestions as to audit coverage are quite commonly solicited from auditees, particularly from top and middle-level executives, and often incorporated into audit plans.

[14]According to the *Survey of Internal Auditing: 1979,* regularly scheduled departmental meetings are relatively atypical and tend toward being informal and without an agenda.

3

Case Studies in Internal Audit Departments' Planning Systems

This chapter describes actual planning activities in a number of organizations and provides insight into specific practices and approaches in use by internal audit departments. The case studies are included for illustrative purposes, and no criticism is made or intended of any of the specific practices described. Although the companies are not identified for reasons of confidentiality, the information provided attempts to be as accurate a representation of the activities reviewed by the researcher as possible.

The companies and the departments range in size. The smallest company has assets of $200 million, and the largest has $15 billion. Several different industries and several different management styles are represented. Industries include manufacturing, banking, agriculture, oil and gas, investment, retailing, and transportation.

Internal audit departments range in size from five to 100 members with budgets ranging from $250 thousand to $7.5 million.[15] Several different audit orientations and organizational roles are represented. Planning systems vary from simple manual systems to complex computer-based systems and from conventional planning to management by objectives and zero-base budgeting.

The case studies provide a rich tapestry of planning practices currently in use and may serve as reference materials, as aids for planning, and also as evidence of the growing sophistication of internal audit managements seeking out and implementing tools and techniques for enhancing the capabilities and the endeavors of internal audit departments.

Each case-study description follows a three-section format. Section 1 provides the company's background and the contextual information for better understanding the planning activities of the internal audit department. Section 2 discusses the role and the responsibilities of the internal audit department and provides a basis for readers to compare their departments to the one described. Section 3 describes the planning activities of the department.

All sections in the case studies are also uniformly subdivided into subsections for ease of comparing the companies. The structure of the case-study descriptions is as follows:

1.0 Company's Background
1.1 Financial Highlights
1.2 Management Style
1.3 Control Atmosphere
2.0 Role and Responsibilities of the Internal Audit Department
2.1 Organizational Position, Department Structure, Size, and Personnel
2.2 Cost Structure and Charge-out Policy
2.3 Mandate or Charter and Audit Orientation
2.4 Relations with External Auditors
2.5 Audit Techniques
3.0 Planning and Coordinating Activities
3.1 Planning Overview
3.2 Audit-Portfolio Management
3.3 Personnel Management, Coordination, and Development

The information contained was gathered through personal interviews with members of the internal audit departments conducted by the author. In addition, supporting documentation was reviewed in all cases (to the extent that it was made available), and excerpts from this documentation are included in some of the case-study descriptions. Other sources of information used to compile these descriptions included:

• A 1978 Conference Board report on internal auditing (Macchiaverna, 1978).[16]

• A 1979 survey of internal auditing [17] published by IIA.[18]

• A 1982 survey of planning practices among large (i.e., Fortune 500 companies) internal audit departments which was carried out by IIA's Tulsa Chapter.[19]

As will become evident from the reports that follow and while there are many differences among internal audit departments, they are similar in several key respects:

- Most have implemented a priority rating-scheme for evaluating the relative importance of individual audits.
- Most have automated some portions of their planning activities, although none have comprehensive planning systems.
- Most expressed that they were contemplating improvements, despite the fact that their practices are probably better than average.
- Most have "reinvented the wheel" when creating their planning systems because no materials such as contained in this study were available.

All the case-study materials included here have been reviewed, approved, and edited by the respective managements of the internal audit departments. Although the information provided makes every attempt at fairness of representation, there are obvious limitations to this type of research in the degree to which the practices described can be generalized and in the objectivity and accuracy of the reports. Even with these limitations, the case studies provide interesting insight into the planning practices of internal audit departments. The summary of this chapter, which follows the case studies, includes additional observations.

A Company

1.0 Company's Background

A Company is a high-technology Fortune 1,000 company founded early in this century. It is one of the world's leading manufacturers of its main line of products and sells principally to equipment manufacturers and to users of its equipment.

1.1 Financial Highlights

Consolidated financial statements for 1981 show sales revenues exceeding one third of a billion dollars on assets of $200 million. Research and development activities account for about six percent of each sales dollar. This reflects the technological leadership position cultivated by A Company.

The company's shares are listed on the New York Stock Exchange and its external auditors are M Company, one of the "big eight" public accounting firms.

1.2 Management Style

The management philosophy at A Company is oriented toward strong, autonomous operating divisions and a small corporate staff. Six divisions carry on operations throughout the world through wholly owned subsidiaries, joint ventures, and licensing arrangements.

Although A Company is a multinational enterprise employing several thousand people, the managements of all the divisions, along with corporate staffs, are housed at the same central site. Audit, data processing, finance, and legal functions are central corporation functions.

1.3 Control Atmosphere

The control atmosphere within the company might be described as relaxed yet well managed. Although accounting controls are considered to be quite strong, operational controls are considered candidates for improvement. The company's financial statements do not carry any statement by management regarding its system of internal control, reflecting a policy of disclosing only what is explicitly required.

Management's chief concern is the possibility of bad decisions resulting from flaws or weaknesses in its information systems. Consequently, all new financial systems are reviewed at the information-requirements-definition stage of the system-development life cycle. This is a change from the previous practice of auditors' involvement at the testing phase and differs from the design-stage-involvement philosophy often espoused by internal auditors.

2.0 Role and Responsibilities of the Internal Audit Department

2.1 Organizational Position, Department Structure, Size, and Personnel

The internal audit department is responsible to the audit committee of the board of directors and reports organizationally to a senior corporate vice president. Meetings with the audit committee are held at least three times annually and more often if required.

The internal audit department at A Company is quite small

in comparison with others participating in this study. The department consists of the director, three auditors, and a secretary.

The auditors are considered strong candidates for management positions within the company. Indeed, the department prides itself on being a training ground for future managers for A Company. This is an attitude quite different from that held by some internal audit departments.

Personnel are hired with strong academic qualifications and work experience. Currently, all the auditors have MBAs and have three to 11 years of experience. Managerial talents rather than audit skills are sought by the department.

2.2 Cost Structure and Charge-out Policy

Departmental costs of $250 thousand may be broken down into:

Salaries and benefits	75%
Travel	16%
Training, space, etc.	9%
	100%

No charge-out system for audit department costs is used. Audit costs form part of corporate overhead which is not a part of divisional profit computation.

2.3 Mandate or Charter and Audit Orientation

The following excerpt is from the company's statement of policy for internal auditing:

The overall objective of internal auditing is to assist all members of corporate and division management in the effective discharge of their responsibilities . . . . *The main role of the internal audit function is to provide a management service* concerned with all phases of the business. In fulfilling this mission, the following principal responsibilities are assigned to the internal audit functions:

• Provide all management levels with an *objective review of operations* and recommend where improvements could be made.

• Review compliance with the company's policies and procedures.

• Evaluate the adequacy of the system of internal control and protection of assets.

• Determine the reliability and timeliness of reporting systems used by management for decision making.

- Be alert to possibilities of fraud.
- Report findings to appropriate management and recommend corrective action. (Emphasis added)

Although most audits have elements of both a financial and operational nature, the emphasis of A Company's corporate audit function is mandated to be in the realm of operational audits. The service aspect is emphasized, and participative involvement by auditees is encouraged.

Audits are highly variable in their scope. Although an audit might be called for a given unit, only specific aspects might be subjected to intensive review. Thus, what constitutes the boundaries of a given audit is very flexible.

2.4 Relations with External Auditors

Although relations with external auditors are cordial, the department does little, if any, work on behalf of external auditors. It emphasizes operational audits and does not attempt to duplicate or replace the audit activities of external auditors.

2.5 Audit Techniques

Procedures and guidelines for performing audits are relatively informal and often developed on an ad hoc basis as required by the auditor. Audit software is available (e.g., PMM & Co., 2190, Data Analyzer).

3.0 Planning and Coordinating Activities

3.1 Planning Overview

A Company's director of internal audit prepares/revises a long-range plan each year that highlights the audit areas to emphasize during a three-year period and projects personnel and facility requirements and related costs over a five-year period. It is based upon the internal audit director's personal knowledge of divisional long-range plans and companywide developments.

A list of the company's audit universe, all the identified auditable units by division, is prepared annually. This list is evaluated by using a relatively complex method, and the auditable units are ranked in descending order of priority based upon this evaluation. Both a three-year-cyclic-coverage plan and a one-year-proposed work plan are prepared by using the prioritized list.

All audits are generally scheduled to last four to six weeks if in town or two weeks if out of town. Since the department is so small, no formal scheduling and coordinating mechanism is deemed necessary. Audit reports are issued within five working days of completion of an audit as a matter of course.

3.2 Audit-Portfolio Management

Identification of Auditable Units. A list is prepared of about 150 auditable units based on an analysis of the general ledger and the company's departmental list. A unit is any identifiable entity with sales, assets, personnel, or some other similar basis for being considered.

Evaluation of Audit-Risk-Exposure Concern. Audit significance is measured by a point system assigned on the basis of 12 differentially weighted criteria (see Figure 3.A.1.)

The total risk for a location is the weighted sum of the 12 risk scores with each score weighted by the global importance weight of each factor. The higher the number of risk points assigned to an auditable unit under this scheme, the higher its audit priority. The 12 risk factors are listed in Figure 3.A.1

The scale of one to four for the risk factors indicates that all 12 are to be considered for each unit. Once the risk factors are evaluated globally, a second level of analysis follows. Each auditable unit (i.e., location) is evaluated according to each of the 12 criteria by using a zero-to-three-point scale with the values assigned as indicated in Figure 3.A.1.

The absolute magnitude of the exposure points computed by this scheme is of little interest. Of primary interest are the relative magnitudes of categories and units within categories. For example, the analysis by division, included in Figure 3.A.1, highlights the relative concern generated by Division E.

A list of all potential audits in descending sequence based on the evaluation system above is produced. It represents a prioritized audit portfolio which may be used to prepare the audit-coverage plan.

Preparation of the Audit-Coverage Cycle and the Work Plan. An audit plan is prepared, guided by this quantitative analysis, but mitigated by such factors as:
- Management requests for audits.
- Related audits or multiple-phase audits.

Figure 3.A.1
Company A: Evaluation of Audit Units
Risk-Exposure-Concern Factors

	Factor 1	Factor 2	...	Factor 12	Audit unit's total exposure (summary of global factor x location risk of all 12 factors)
Global importance weight of this factor	1 2 3 4	1 2 3 4	...	1 2 3 4	
	Degree of factor 1 risk at this location	Degree of factor 2 risk at this location	...	Degree of factor 12 risk at this location	
	0 1 2 3	0 1 2 3	...	0 1 2 3	
Division A					
Auditable unit ABC					
Auditable unit ABD					
etc.					
Division A subtotals	15	34	...	192	1143
Division B					
etc.					
. . .					
Company's Total					4196

List of Risk-Exposure-Concern Factors

1. Access to cash
2. Access to checks
3. Authorize expenditures
4. Access to assets (liquid)
5. Integration with corporate system
6. Visits from corporate
7. Visits to corporation
8. Extent of policies and procedures
9. Local versus U.S. customs
10. Turnover length of service
11. Layoffs or demotions
12. Quality and experience of people

Basis for Location-Risk Assignments

0 = Not considered a problem
1 = Presents some risk
2 = Periodic attention required but not urgent
3 = Significant risk which should be considered

Example of Summary Analysis:

Audit-Unit Category	Total-Risk Points	Number of Audit Units Within Audit-Unit-Category	Average
Division A	1143	48	23.8
B	1367	52	26.3
C	544	23	23.7
D	225	11	20.5
E	917	17	53.9
Total	4196	151	27.8

- Manpower availability.
- Other factors.

Quality of the quantitative assessment is assured by several independent assessments and discussions thereafter until a consensus is reached and by review and approval by the vice president, president, and chairman of the board.

3.3 Personnel Management, Coordination, and Development

Due to the size of the department, personnel management, coordination, and development activities are quite informal. Auditors submit weekly time reports which are filed and periodically summarized, but this is only done when necessary and not on an ongoing basis.

For the most part, monitoring and supervising staff activities depend upon the internal audit director's personal contact and involvement with both the audits and the auditors.

No formal training programs exist since personnel hired are expected to have adequate experience and background and to acquire specific training on the job.

B Company

1.0 Company's Background

B Company is a diversified transportation company with more than ten major lines of business and is one of the nation's largest corporations.

1.1 Financial Highlights

Consolidated financial statements for 1981 show sales revenues in excess of $4 billion on assets in excess of $5 billion. The company's shares are listed on several stock exchanges, including the New York Stock Exchange; and its external auditors are N Company, one of the "big eight" public accounting firms.

1.2 Management Style

The management philosophy at B Company is oriented toward maintaining relatively strong profit control over its many subsidiaries. The audit function is centralized at corporate headquarters.

1.3 Control Atmosphere

The control atmosphere within the company is relatively stringent, particularly with regard to costs. The company's financial statements include a statement by management regarding the effectiveness of its system of internal control and the substantial activities of the internal audit department, including a reference to the role of the professional standards of the internal audit profession as a determinant of the company's internal audit program as the following excerpt illustrates:

> In the opinion of management, the financial statements are fairly stated; and to that end, the company maintains a system of internal control which *provides* reasonable assurance that transactions are recorded properly for the preparation of financial statements, safeguards assets against loss or unauthorized use, maintains accountability for assets, and requires proper authorization and accounting for all transactions. Management is responsible for the effectiveness of internal control. This is accomplished through established codes of conduct, accounting and other control systems, policies and procedures, employee selection and training, appropriate delegation of authority, and segregation of responsibilities. To further assure compliance with established standards and related control procedures, *the company maintains a substantial program of internal audit in accordance with recognized professional standards for that activity.* (emphasis added)

2.0 Role and Responsibilities of the Internal Audit Department

2.1 Organizational Position, Department Structure, Size, and Personnel

The internal audit department reports to the corporate controller and is quite far removed from direct access to the chief executive officer and the board of directors, although periodic meetings are held which include management, the vice president of corporate internal audit, the external auditor, and the audit committee of the board of directors (composed solely of outside directors) to coordinate audit activities. The internal auditor has full and free access to the audit committee.

The internal audit department at B Company is quite substantial – about ten times the size of A Company – consisting of about 40 auditors, clerical, and supervisory personnel. The department is subdivided into four audit sections: financial, information systems, disbursements, and remote locations. In contrast with A Company, the department considers itself to be primarily a professional audit service function rather than a management-training facility. Personnel are generally recruited out of college and provided with a comprehensive training program, as the cost structure provided below indicates.

2.2 Cost Structure and Charge-out Policy

Departmental costs may be broken down into:

Salaries and benefits	70%
Travel and related	15%
Training	10%
Software	3%
Other	2%
	100%

Costs are charged out in some cases, but no uniform charge-out policy is currently in existence.

2.3 Mandate or Charter and Audit Orientation

B Company's charter is very much in keeping with IIA's recommended practice and explicitly incorporates the professional standards of the internal audit profession as a governing policy for the department's activities.

The department's audit activities are broken down into the following categories:

Compliance reviews	40%
Financial audits	40%
Operational audits	15%
(primarily information systems related)	
Fraud investigations	5%
	100%

2.4 Relations with the External Auditors

The department closely coordinates its work with the external auditors and carries out specific audits on their behalf (sometimes under their supervision).

2.5 Audit Techniques

Procedural guidelines exist for all established segments of the business, and a variety of sophisticated audit software is available and used (e.g., DYL280, Auditape, Culprit, SAS).

3.0 Planning and Coordinating Activities

3.1 Planning Overview
B Company's internal audit department prepares a cyclical coverage plan, as well as an annual work plan and budget, that is broken down into monthly segments.

Auditors submit weekly time reports which are used to prepare monthly summaries for comparisons with budgets. For scheduling, monitoring, and managing audit activities within the four audit groups, 13-week Gantt charts are used. A simple computerized scheme is used for audit-portfolio management and is discussed below.

3.2 Audit-Portfolio Management
Identification of Auditable Units. The corporation is subdivided by functional units based on the corporate organization chart. Thus, there are 30 groups, each with 100 to 150 auditable units, having a total of about 4,000 audit units. An inventory of these units is maintained with the aid of a computer program.

Evaluation of Audit-Risk-Exposure Concern. Audit significance is measured by a point system assigned on the basis of five equally weighted criteria, each measured on a scale from zero to five (see Figure 3.B.1).

The points assigned are a sum of the points for each of the five factors. Explicit guidelines are set for translating revenue, expense, asset dollars, and transaction volumes into a score from zero to five, thus providing a relatively objective basis for assigning scores for all but the "other" category, which is a subjective evaluation of audit importance owing to a unit's perceived importance, risk, etc. A computer program automatically assigns the points for all the objective and quantitative criteria, leaving only the subjective criteria to be assigned by the auditor.

Preparation of the Audit-Coverage Cycle and the Work Plan. B Company uses a five-year-audit-coverage cycle. A computer program is used to analyze the 4,000 auditable units' risk-exposure-concern stores and assign them to coverage categories on the basis of their scores. For example, all units with a score in excess of 15 would be audited annually, those with a score between 10 and 15 biennially, and so on. Items with a score of less than three are excluded from consideration.

Figure 3.B.1
Company B: Evaluation of Audit Units

Risk-Exposure-Concern Factors

Auditable Unit	Revenue	Expense	Assets	Volume	Other	Total
Global Factor Weights	0 — 5	0 — 5	0 — 5	0 — 5	0 — 5	0 — 25
ABC	3	2	2	3	4	14
ABD	2	2	2	2	2	10
ABE	4	2	3	3	4	16
• • • etc.						• • • etc.

3.3 Personnel Management, Coordination, and Development

Five managers report to the director of the internal audit department. Each manages a specific group of audits and about seven employees out of the department's pool of employees.

Employees fill out weekly time reports as part of a corporate-wide-time-reporting subsystem of the corporate payroll system. Employees' activities are also monitored via 13-week Gantt charts which indicate to which audit projects each individual is assigned during that period.

C Company

1.0 Company's Background

C Company is a large, closely held multinational corporation with six major lines of business which are fairly autonomous.

1.1 Financial Highlights

Since C is a private company, its financial statements were not available for review. C's external auditors are O Company, one of the "big eight" public accounting firms.

1.2 Management Style

Management at C Company tends to be relaxed and relatively informal. Although there is a tendency toward decentralized autonomous units controlled through a profit-center approach, management by objectives is also used throughout the company. Its method of implementation varies from division to division. For example, the internal audit department requires two sets of objectives to be prepared by each member: a set of performance objectives and a set of personal "growth" (i.e., career development) objectives.

1.3 Control Atmosphere

An accounting-policy manual of the company is held by all divisional controllers. It highlights the key areas of financial control and specific internal accounting controls to enforce and audit.

2.0 Role and Responsibilities of Internal Audit Department

2.1 Organizational Position, Department Structure, Size, and Personnel

The internal audit departments at C Company have about 65 auditors located in four regions throughout the world. All report to the assistant secretary of the audit committee. The account below describes the United States-based group consisting of about 45 auditors divided into three groups. Like A Company, C Company emphasizes the managerial training role of the internal audit department. With promotion from within being a "sacred cow" of C Company, the internal audit department is viewed as an entry-level position into a long-run career with the corporation. Personnel are recruited directly from college and must commit themselves to a minimal three-year stint in internal audit,[20] which is part of the corporation's management-training system. As a result, the department is relatively young.

2.2 Cost Structure and Charge-out Policy

Departmental costs in 1981 were about $2.25 million and may be broken down as follows:

Salaries and benefits	53%
Travel	32%
Training	6%
Miscellaneous	9%
	100%

Costs are charged out 100 percent in keeping with the company's policy for all service functions. Cost savings as a result of audit findings are emphasized as a very important goal of the department. The basis for charging out costs is actual time spent on an audit multiplied by the average cost per chargeable hour (i.e., approximately $26 per hour).

2.3 Mandate or Charter and Audit Orientation

C Company's charter emphasizes reviews of controls and operational audits aimed at cost savings referred to as "auditing for profits." The following excerpts from C Company's accounting-policy manual effectively illustrates the audit orientation of the internal audit department:

> The objective of the internal audit function within the C Company organization is to measure and evaluate the effectiveness of the internal controls which have been established by management . . . . An internal audit department's responsibilities include:
>
> 1. Performing periodic audits of C Company's and subsidiaries' activities in an objective and professional manner as prescribed by the *Standards for the Professional Practice of Internal Auditing.*
>
> 2. Scheduling audits to obtain a high return of audit costs.
>
> 3. Appraising the adequacy of corrective action of audit recommendations. When necessary, internal audit will conduct follow-up reviews to evaluate effectiveness of corrective action taken.
>
> 4. Coordinating audit activities with independent auditors.
>
> 5. Providing audit assistance in special projects such as acquisition audits, accounting assistance, liquidations, fraud investigations, and government reports.
>
> 6. Training and developing auditors to assure that the internal audit functions are at a high level of professional competence.
>
> 7. Developing auditors to assume accounting management positions with the C organization.

There are no surprise audits. Although a priority list is used to help schedule audits, all plans are usually discussed with group controllers. An audit cycle of one and one-half to two years is considered desirable by the auditees and the department.

2.4 Relations with External Auditors

Although external auditors rely upon the internal audit department's activities, there is no direct working relationship between the internal and external auditors.

2.5 Audit Techniques

C Company is active in acquiring new companies but rarely warns the internal audit department, which must often prepare procedural guidelines with no experience in a particular area. Systems-related auditing is relatively weak. In other areas, procedural audit guidelines exist for each major division in addition to a general technical manual.

3.0 Planning and Coordinating Activities

3.1 Planning Overview

No long-term planning is carried out by C Company's internal audit department. The director of internal audit meets annually with the audit committee at which time staffing plans and the departmental budget are reviewed. In addition, the audit committee receives monthly operational reports of the department indicating the audits planned, completed, and their duration.

Management by objectives is used to specify monthly and annual activity targets for departmental personnel at all levels. Some examples of goals used include:

- Audit frequency for each unit is at least once in 24 months.
- Audits are completed within ten percent of budgeted time at least 50 percent of the time.
- Final reports to auditee are issued within 21 working days of completion of field audit.
- Chargeable hours are at least 80 percent.
- Cost savings from recommendations are at least equal to the annual budget.

3.2 Audit-Portfolio Management

Identification of Auditable Units. The corporation is divided into six business groups with multiple locations and numbers about 500 locations in total. These locations are considered auditable units for planning purposes but are further classified into 20 categories according to similarity of product-business lines.

Evaluation of Audit-Risk-Exposure Concern. Audit significance is measured by a complex computer-point-assignment system based around seven differentially weighted factors. In fact, there are 20 different sets of weights – one set for each category – although the same seven factors are used (see Figure 3.C.1).

Although the same seven factors are used in all categories, different category weights are preassigned within the computer program. Each auditable unit is evaluated with respect to each factor on a scale of one to ten, and then the program multiplies the points so assigned by the category weight of that factor. The risk-exposure-concern score for an auditable unit is a weighted sum of the scores on each of the seven factors. When units are ranked according to priority, this is carried out within categories; thus, there are, in fact, 20 sets of ranked units. All subsequent analyses are performed within categories. With reference to the evaluations for locations ABC, ABD, and XYZ in Figure 3.C.1, locations ABC and XYZ were assigned the same factor scores; however, their membership in different categories results in different overall evaluations because of different category weights being used in each case. Locations ABC and XYZ are not comparable, whereas locations ABC and ABD are comparable.

Preparation of the Audit Coverage Cycle and the Work Plan. As mentioned previously, C Company uses a two-year-audit-coverage cycle. Each of the 20 categories is summarized by a computer program producing 20 priority-ranked lists. These lists are then used by the audit managers to schedule audits. Gantt-chart schedules are prepared manually by the audit group managers and are subject to adjustment as circumstances warrant.

3.3 Personnel Management, Coordination, and Development

Three group managers report to the director of internal audit. Each one handles two lines of business and about one-third of the employees. One of the goals is to have employees rotate through all the groups during the first two years in the department and then specialize in one of the groups. Staffing to accomplish this is carried out twice a year with quarterly trades among groups if necessary.

Staff audit assignments are made well in advance, and employees are given assignment sheets indicating future jobs. In-charge auditors submit weekly job-status reports indicating progress on current jobs. Semimonthly time and expense reports are also submitted and summarized on a monthly basis. These are maintained on a computer system which produces periodic reports for internal audit managers' use.

Two one-week-long-staff-training sessions are held each year in addition to a month-long orientation upon entry into the company. An administrative assistant maintains records of these in-house training sessions and outside seminars for each employee.

Figure 3.C.1
Company C: Evaluation of Audit Units

Risk-Exposure-Concern Factors

	Factor 1	Factor 2	Factor 3	Factor 4	Factor 5	Factor 6	Factor 7	Wtd. Avg.

Category 1

Preassigned Category 1 Weights for These Factors*

	C1W1	C1W2	C1W3	C1W4	C1W5	C1W6	C1W7	Wtd. Avg.
	1—10	1—10	1—10	1—10	1—10	1—10	1—10	1—10
Location ABC	5	6	5	4	3	5	4	3.2
Location ABD · · · ·	7	4	4	4	8	5	5	3.7
Category 1 subtotals								

Category 2

Preassigned Category 2 Weights for These Factors**

	C2W1	C2W2	C2W3	C2W4	C2W5	C2W6	C2W7	Wtd. Avg.
	1—10	1—10	1—10	1—10	1—10	1—10	1—10	1—10
Location XYZ	5	6	5	4	3	5	4	4.5
•								
•								
•								

List of Risk-Exposure-Concern Factors

The following is a list of seven factors incorporated into the computer program:
1. New acquisition
2. Time since last audit
3. Score on last internal control evaluation
4. Recent management change
5. Number of employees
6. Risk
7. Special

*C1W1 is the category 1 weight of factor 1 built into the computer program.

**C2W1 is the category 2 weight c. factor 1 built into the computer program.

Scores from 1-10 are entered for each location for each factor.

As part of their supervisory and quality control role, managers are strongly encouraged to perform field reviews of audits nearing completion at audit sites by having the requirement built into their objectives. Upon completion of each audit, a formal evaluation of auditor performance is carried out by the manager.

D Company

1.0 Company's Background

D Company is a bank-holding company formally organized in the late 1920s. It is one of the largest commercial banking organizations in the United States with about 90 commercial banks, several trust companies, and several financial services subsidiaries.

1.1 Financial Highlights

D Company has assets of about $15 billion and has in excess of 13,000 employees. The company's stock is listed on the New York Stock Exchange. Its external auditors are O Company, one of the "big eight" public accounting firms.

1.2 Management Style

D Company's management philosophy and banking regulations lead to decentralized day-to-day operations. It is also management's philosophy that the total operations of all the individual operating units are to be coordinated by and accountable to management and the board of directors in a manner which assures that their responsibilities and accountability to the stockholders are fulfilled.

1.3 Control Atmosphere

The awareness and attitude toward internal control throughout D Company is considered good. The primary objective of the department's audits is to review and evaluate each entity's systems of internal control. This is consistent with the Bank Administration Institute's standards.[21]

The rating by internal audit of each entity's system of internal control is part of the criteria used by corporate management in measuring the performance of each affiliate manager/president.

The company's annual report includes a statement by management regarding its reliance on the system of internal control:

> In preparing the financial statements, management makes judgments and estimates of the expected effects of events and transactions that are currently being accounted for and relies on the corporation's system of internal accounting control. In designing these controls, management recognizes that errors and irregularities may nevertheless occur. Also, estimates and judgments are required to assess and balance the relative costs and expected benefits of the controls. This system is augmented by written policies, operating procedures, accounting manuals, plus a *strong program of internal audit carried out with carefully selected and qualified personnel.* (emphasis added)

2.0 The Role and Responsibilities of the Internal Audit Department

2.1 Organizational Position, Department Structure, Size, and Personnel

The company's internal audit department is an incorporated subsidiary whose president (the director of internal audit) reports to the executive vice president of finance and administration.

The department is administered by the board of directors of the subsidiary company of which the executive vice president of corporate finance is a member. It reports periodically to the corporate board of directors of D Company after review and recommendation by the audit and examination committee of the board of the subsidiary.

The department has approximately 100 employees and maintains 13 regional offices. It is the responsibility of the regional offices to audit all affiliate banks within their geographical areas each year. A sufficient staff size is maintained to permit each location to be visited annually, taking into account anticipated turnover of personnel of 25 percent.

The department is subdivided into five groups. The bank audit group is responsible for auditing all the affiliate banks as outlined above.

The professional practices group is responsible for developing and maintaining audit programs, technical audit manuals, educating and training the staff, general research and development, and coordination of special projects. In addition, this group is responsible for conducting formal, in-depth internal reviews of the audit practices within the department.

The EDP audit group is responsible for auditing computer centers and the corporate office in addition to assisting and complementing the efforts of the professional practices group, particularly in developing computerized applications of quantitative methods.

The corporate and nonbank subsidiary auditing group is responsible for auditing trust companies and all financial service subsidiaries.

The administration and finance group is responsible for administrative policies and procedures, payroll, accounting, and employee-benefits functions of the department.

2.2 Cost Structure and Charge-out Policy

The department's annual budget is about $4.5 million, and its cost structure is broken down as follows:

Salaries and benefits	75%
Travel	12%
Facilities and miscellaneous	11%
Training	2%
	100%

All department costs are charged out. At the end of each year, the department notifies affiliates of their estimated annual audit fees for the coming year. Each month, one-twelfth of the estimated billing is charged directly to the affiliates' accounts.

2.3 Mandate or Charter and Audit Orientation

The primary objective of the audit-services function of D Company (defined in its charter and approved by the audit and examination committee of the board of directors) is . . . to serve the corporation's operating management and its various boards of directors by providing them with information . . . which will help them carry out their responsibilities more effectively and profitably.

The basic responsibilities of the audit-services function as defined in its charter are as follows:

- Evaluate the adequacy of the corporation's network of financial, accounting, and operating systems.
- Determine whether the financial controls being used are ade-

quate for preventing and detecting fraud, loss of assets and revenue, and other irregularities.

- Verify the existence of the corporation's assets and liabilities.
- Evaluate the financial condition of the operating units reviewed within the corporation and use, where appropriate, reports of other divisions of the corporation as the primary basis of the evaluation.
- Evaluate the existence and the adequacy of the corporation's system of management controls in carrying out assigned responsibilities within the corporation.
- Determine whether the financial and operating information that is reported to the various levels of operating management in the corporation and the various boards of directors is current, accurate, and complete.
- Determine the extent of compliance with the corporation's established policies, procedures, and plans with accepted accounting principles and sound business practices and with banking laws and regulations.
- Report to all levels of management within the corporation and to the various boards of directors the results of reviews together with recommendations and possible courses of action that will improve the control and the profitability of the corporation's operations.
- Conduct periodic follow-up reviews and inform senior management.
- Conduct investigations, as deemed necessary, of any irregularities detected during periodic audits or brought to the attention of the chief auditor by operating management.

The charter also sets specific limitations on the internal audit department's authority in the corporation. It has no authority to (1) make operating decisions, (2) directly tell anyone in the corporation what to do, or (3) implement any of its recommendations or suggestions.

2.4 Relations with External Auditors

A close working relationship exists between external auditors and the internal audit department. It performs certain year-end tasks on behalf of and, at times, under the direct supervision of the external auditors. The external auditors, in carrying out their responsibilities, place a great deal of reliance on the work performed by the internal audit group. They receive copies of all departmental plans and audit reports and may choose to participate in planned audits. Quarterly meetings are also held to assess progress toward achieving the annual work plans and coordinating joint efforts.

2.5 Audit Techniques

A technical audit manual is used which discusses D Company's overall audit philosophy and includes approved policies, procedures, and guidelines covering audit approaches and processes. In addition, an audit procedures manual includes comprehensive guidelines for performing virtually all recurring audits. Although no comprehensively integrated, automated planning system is used, a number of automated tools are used to help in planning and coordinating audit department activities.

An automated analytical review (i.e., ratio analysis) package is used for determining which areas should be emphasized in an audit. A timesharing system permits evaluations of data files, especially for testing compliance with prescribed policies, statutes, and so on.

3.0 Planning and Coordinating Activities

3.1 Planning Overview

Planning activities occur at several levels. Long-range planning is performed annually at which time the department's rolling four-year plan is revised. An important basis for the department's long-range plan is the annual memorandum of planning objectives issued by the chief executive officer of the corporation. It includes a summary of economic conditions, new corporate policies and programs, and other similar information.

Each year, an ad hoc committee is formed for updating the long-range plan. This includes audit directors, managers, supervisors, and staff members. The committee is briefed by the corporate planning officer regarding corporate plans, problems, and goals. In addition, a calendar of key events in the corporate planning cycle is presented; for example, financial reporting deadlines, program-implementation dates, etc.

On the basis of the revised long-range plan, specific projects are assigned to management-level personnel; and these then fall into the management-by-objectives program as the relevant annual plans come into effect. The thrust of the long-range plan is to maintain a high level of professional competence and an ongoing capability to provide services to the corporation as needed. To this end, the department maintains a continuous research and development effort aimed at improving audit tools and techniques. It also participates actively with The Institute of Internal Auditors. Since the department is required to audit all locations at least annually, audit-work-planning issues are different from the other cases discussed below.

3.2 Audit-Portfolio Management

Identification of Auditable Units. As previously mentioned, there are three auditing groups in the D Company's internal audit department with three different methods for identifying auditable units. The discussion which follows is restricted to the bank audit group's set of audits.

The bank audit group is charged with visiting each location each year. Consequently, this aspect of identification of auditable units is predetermined. However, the department is developing a hierarchical view of these audits. This view was illustrated in Figure 2.2 in Chapter 2. By subdividing locations into modules for audit-planning purposes, the department believes it can better allocate its audit effort to locations in a systematic way. Since this is still being refined, only the traditional approach, based upon locations, is discussed below.

Evaluation of Audit-Risk-Exposure Concern. The 90 banking locations are evaluated by regional managers who are responsible for six to ten locations. Although the basis for the evaluation is relatively flexible and informal, a suggested set of guidelines is provided to help the managers document their rationale for the schedules they set. In particular, six main factors are used as outlined in Figure 3.D.1.

The priority score is a sum of individual factor scores. Since factors are preweighted, the sum is already weighted. Within the confines of preassigned weightings, however, judgments are quite subjective.

Of particular interest is the approach used for assigning the internal control component of the overall evaluation, since it plays such an important role in planning the department's activities. The format used in evaluating internal control is provided in Figure 3.D.2. Since each location is conceptualized to consist of 20 audit modules, the evaluations take place module by

Figure 3.D.1
Company D: Evaluation of Audit Units

Region A	Asset Size	Quality of Internal Control	Recency of Last Audit	Personnel Quality	Planned Conversions, Expansion, etc.	Audit-Staff Considerations	Total
Weight	1 — 10	1 — 30	1 — 20	1 — 20	1 — 10	1 — 10	Max 100
Location ABC							
Location ABD							
. . . etc.							

module within the location. Five features of internal control are evaluated on a scale of one to ten and are supported by written explanations.

Preparation of the Audit Coverage Cycle and the Work Plan. Each location is subdivided into 20 modules, all of which are typically included as part of an audit. However, within modules, discretion is once again available. Each module consists of ten subsections, and the degree of audit effort within each module depends on the in-charge auditor's judgment.

The annual planning effort at the regional level is aimed at determining the appropriate intensity of the audits and scheduling them at appropriate points in the year. Although an audit for each location is required annually, the discretionary scheduling of audits can stretch the between-audit time period to almost two years if, for example, the audit is carried out very early in one year and then again toward the end of the following year.

The annual planning is carried out in four main phases:

● Regional managers prepare a work plan by evaluating the locations within their regions (as further described below).
● On the basis of this evaluation and prior year's time requirements, an estimate is made for each location and combined into a regional manpower-requirement summary.
● With this summary, a regional mix-of-staff plan is prepared that outlines the region's requirements for entry-level, staff-level, and in-charge-level auditors for the coming audit year.
● When the regional plans are submitted to the central office, a consolidated annual manpower plan is prepared for the entire department. Through a comparison of manpower availability in man-months to manpower requirements in man-months, this plan provides information for hiring, training, and promoting.

3.3 Personnel Management, Coordination, and Development

D Company's internal audit department expects a relatively high staff turnover (typical of the banking industry); nevertheless, if this is not anticipated, it can prevent regional plans from being fulfilled. Currently, the strategy for dealing with this problem is to anticipate a 25 percent turnover and build it into staffing plans.

Like C, D Company uses a modified management-by-objec-

Figure 3.D.2
Company D: Evaluation of the
Quality of Internal Control

Location Name: _____

Module	Internal Control Features					
	Plan of Organization	Policies, Procedures, System of Authorization	Sound Management and Business Practices	Personnel Quality and Practices	Attitude	Average Rating
	1—10	1—10	1—10	1—10	1—10	1—10
1.						
2.						
3.						
4.						
•						
•						
•						
20.						
Averages						

91

tives approach as a means for planning work activity and as a basis for evaluating performance for its senior personnel. However, the objectives are quite different in orientation from those of C Company, being aimed at development of professional staff, procedures, and training programs rather than cost savings, audit-performance guidelines, etc. For example, a statement of D Company's internal audit management's objectives for 1981 included such items as:

- Reevaluate the purpose, scope, and frequency of D's quality-assurance program.
- Develop and finalize questionnaires and audit programs for the corporate treasurer's function.
- Define, develop, and implement a methodology for analyzing exposure and risk to be used to allocate audit resources.

For each of these objectives, a target-completion date was set, and formal responsibility was assigned and published in the document outlining the department's long-range plan.

E Company

1.0 Company's Background

E Company is a large banking subsidiary of a banking organization of about 90 banks (not the same as D Company).

1.1 Financial Highlights

E Company has assets of about $3 billion and about 700 employees. Its (and its parent company's) auditors are M Company, one of the "big eight" public accounting firms.

1.2 Management Style

E Company employs zero-base budgeting as a planning and priority-ranking tool, and the internal audit department does too. The zero-base-budgeting approach requires an annual analysis and reevaluation of all activities, functions, and expenses in each area. As a budgetary and planning tool, it forces:

- Detailed and regular justification of each budget line.
- Breakdown of departmental activities into units which are separable and which can be eliminated if necessary; this also can lead to better identification of packages which are not separable.
- Periodic consideration of the effects upon the department and the corporation of eliminating a particular activity.

1.3 Control Atmosphere

The employees know each other. As a result, both informal as well as formal controls are exercised. Financial controls are stringent (typical in most banking institutions). Management controls are exercised by combining management by objectives and zero-base budgeting.

2.0 Role and Responsibilities of Internal Audit Department

2.1 Organizational Position, Department Structure, Size, and Personnel

Owing to the size of E Company, it has its own internal audit department which reports directly to the chairman of the board of directors and chief executive officer. The internal audit director meets twice yearly with the examining committee or the chairman of E's board of directors and four times annually with E's management committee to discuss audit results.

The department has six financial auditors, one EDP auditor, one supervisor, one secretary, and two managers. Most new auditors are hired from local colleges.

2.2 Cost Structure and Charge-out Policy

Departmental costs totalling about $400 thousand in 1981 may be broken down as follows:

Salaries and benefits	82%
Training	4%
Other	14%
	100%

Audit costs are not charged out.

2.3 Mandate or Charter and Audit Orientation

The audit charter excerpted below is a statement of the primary functions and objectives of internal auditing. It was approved by the board of directors.

Function – Auditing is an independent appraisal activity within the bank for review of operations as a service to management. It is a managerial control which functions by measuring and evaluating the effectiveness of other controls. In developing audit programs, the auditor recognizes that the cost of particular auditing programs must be reasonably related to the risks involved. In discharging its function, auditing does not exercise direct authority over other operations in the bank; nor does it relieve other personnel or activities in the organization of the responsibilities assigned to them; however, the auditor and his representatives are authorized full, free, and unrestricted access to all company functions, records, property and personnel.

Organizational Status – Auditing is a staff function, reporting to the audit committee of the bank, directors' examining committee and, for administrative purposes, the office of the chief executive officer.

Responsibilities – The auditor's responsibilities are these:

1. Developing and conducting a continuing test of the accuracy of income statements and the asset and liability accounts on the bank's books and the integrity of established systems of internal control. This is the traditional internal auditing function of inventorying, checking, counting, and verifying of a financial audit.

2. Evaluating and recommending proper internal controls for all new systems before their introduction and determining periodically that controls in existing systems are functioning in a way to protect against inaccuracies, irregularities, and willful manipulations.

3. Coordinating traditional auditing functions with similar activities of the outside certified public accountants, thereby economizing the time the outside certified public accountants elect to spend on our engagement (and its cost to us). The principal interface between outside auditors and the bank is the comptroller.

4. Liaison with the national bank examiners to relieve them of such inventorying, checking, counting, and verifying responsibility as they elect to delegate to the house auditor. The principal interface between the national bank examiner and the bank is the loan-review officer and the comptroller.

5. Encouraging throughout the bank adherence to managerial policies, laws, regulations of supervisory authorities, and sound fiduciary principles.

6. Promoting throughout the bank operational efficiency recognizing that line management (aided by the systems department) has the primary responsibility to insure that operations are efficient and economical.

7. Performing any services requested by the directors' examining committee; it is understood that the bank management urges the directors' examining committee to use the loan-review officer and comptroller for questions in their field of responsibility and expertise.

2.4 Relations with External Auditors

The department provides direct assistance to external auditors and to national bank examiners and coordinates its own audit activities so as to expicitly include their requirements in all major audit programs.

2.5 Audit Techniques

Detailed guidelines exist, and a technical audit manual serves as an audit aid. Indeed, E's manual contained the most detailed discussion of planning and associated procedures of all the companies studied. The use of audit software is limited. Reports and confirmation notices are requested as needed from the bank-holding company's systems subsidiary, a sister company providing data-processing services to all 90 banks.

3.0 Planning and Coordinating Activities

3.1 Planning Overview

The department does not carry out long-range planning per se, although a three-year horizon serves as an informal basis for discussing plans. Zero-base budgeting is used as a basis for preparing annual audit plans.

Audit plans can be broken down into what will be audited and what will not, and the director of internal audit is required to justify this. Zero-base budgeting, if strictly applied, may lead to some areas not receiving any attention. Thus, an understanding exists that each area, no matter what its importance, should be audited at least once every five years, if possible.

3.2 Audit-Portfolio Management

Definition of Auditable Units. E Company's general ledger accounts and related operating functions serve as the basis for identifying all auditable units. About 60 auditable units have been identified so far. In contrast, recall that D Company identified about 20 auditable units, each with ten subsections, at each location.

Evaluation of Audit-Risk-Exposure Concern. E's audit-risk-evaluation procedures are by far the most comprehensive of all the companies studied. Twenty-two factors grouped into five groups of four to five items each provide the basis for evaluating audit concern. Thus, 22 separate assessments are required for each auditable unit. Each assessment is made on a scale from zero to four. Detailed guidelines are provided for each factor indicating precisely what each value on the scale represents for that particular factor. In some cases, these are objective, quantitative criteria. In other cases, they are subjective, qualitative criteria. Also, each factor has a weight predefined for it (see Figure 3.E.1, which is a representative risk-calculation worksheet). Appendix B provides detailed guidelines for completing the evaluation related to Figure 3.E.1.

Preparation of the Audit Coverage Cycle and the Work Plan. An ordered list of 60 audit units is prepared on the basis of the risk-exposure-concern assessments. A cumulative estimate of time requirements for the audits is added to the list. This list is then subdivided into size blocks or funding levels. For example, assuming a minimal department's size of five financial auditors, a five-person block of audits is identified. Next, a six-person block, a seven-person block, and larger blocks are identified until the entire list is taken into account. Figure 3.E.2 illustrates this type of incremental analysis.

Once this incremental analysis is prepared, it is up to management to decide on the minimal, annual level of auditing which it desires and which it must fund. As currently structured, the department functions at the six-employee level (i.e., about 10,500 hours) carrying out about 30 financial audits and a number of EDP audits. This leaves about 30 audit areas without audit coverage based upon management's choice.

3.3 Personnel Management, Coordination, and Development

The small size of the department permits the director of internal audit to pay close attention to the work of the staff. For example, he personally reviews every set of audit working papers, visits auditees, and monitors the progress of ongoing activities with the aid of a time-keeping system which produces weekly reports summarizing departmental activities for that week and for the year to date. These reports include actual time, budgeted time, and starting and completion dates.

All audits scheduled for the year are assigned to specific personnel on the basis of matching audit skills required by a particular audit project to those possessed by an auditor. A modified

Figure 3.E.1
Company E: Risk-Calculation Worksheet

Activity _____ Category	Factor	Weight × Points = Risk
1. Nature of Transactions	1. Value per transaction 2. Total value of transactions (daily) 3. General ledger balance 4. Liquidity/negotiability 5. Income/expense	_____ _____ _____ _____ _____ _____ _____ _____ _____ _____ _____ _____ _____ _____ _____ Subtotal _____
2. Nature of Operations	1. Pressure (meeting deadlines) 2. Volume of transactions 3. Complexity of transactions 4. Compliance with regulations	_____ _____ _____ _____ _____ _____ _____ _____ _____ _____ _____ _____ Subtotal _____
3. Departmental Control Environment	1. Audit trail 2. Separation of duties 3. Management review and accountability 4. Compliance with internal accounting controls 5. Accuracy of information	_____ _____ _____ _____ _____ _____ _____ _____ _____ _____ _____ _____ Subtotal _____

4. Senior Management/
   Management
   Committee Controls

   1. Senior management's concern & awareness of the area _____
   2. Internal audit coverage   _____
   3. External audit coverage   _____
   4. Resolution of previous findings   _____
                                                   Subtotal   _____

5. Experience
   and Training

   1. Experience of management   _____
   2. Training   _____
   3. Delegation of duties   _____
   4. Experience of staff   _____
                                                   Subtotal   _____

Completed by _____   Total Risk _____

Reviewed by _____   Date _____

Figure 3.E.2
Company E: Zero-Base Budget

Scheduled Audits	(5 Employees) Increment 1	(6 Employees) Increment 2	(7 Employees) Increment 3	(8 Employees) Increment 4
1.	xxx	xxx	xxx	xxx
2.	xxx	xxx	xxx	xxx
3.	xxx	xxx	xxx	xxx
4.	xxx	xxx	xxx	xxx
5.	xxx	xxx	xxx	xxx
6.	xxx	xxx	xxx	xxx
7.	xxx	xxx	xxx	xxx
8.	xxx	xxx	xxx	xxx
9.	xxx	xxx	xxx	xxx
10.	xxx	xxx	xxx	xxx
11.	xxx	xxx	xxx	xxx
12.	xxx	xxx	xxx	xxx
	x,xxx hours			
13.		xxx	xxx	xxx
14.		xxx	xxx	xxx
15.		xxx	xxx	xxx
16.		xxx	xxx	xxx
17.		xxx	xxx	xxx
18.		xxx	xxx	xxx
19.		xxx	xxx	xxx
20.		xxx	xxx	xxx
		x,xxx hours		
21.			xxx	xxx
22.			xxx	xxx
23.			xxx	xxx
24.			xxx	xxx
25.			xxx	xxx
26.			xxx	xxx
27.			xxx	xxx
28.			xxx	xxx
29.			xxx	xxx
30.			xxx	xxx
31.			xxx	xxx
32.			xxx	xxx
			x,xxx hours	
33.				xxx
34.				xxx
35.				xxx
36.				xxx
37.				xxx
38.				xxx
39.				xxx
40.				xxx
41.				xxx
42.				xxx
				x,xxx hours

Gantt chart is used to schedule each auditor's activities over a 13-week period, including training activities.

F Company

1.0 Company's Background

F Company is a high-technology multinational manufacturing organization with 50 major product lines. It was founded at the turn of the century and currently employs more than 90 thousand people in its more than 150 operating units throughout the world.

1.1 Financial Highlights

Consolidated financial statements for 1981 show sales revenues in excess of $6 billion on assets of about $5 billion. Research and development activities accounted for about 5 percent of each sales dollar. The company's shares are listed on major stock exchanges throughout the world, and its external auditors are P Company, a "big eight" public accounting firm.

1.2 Management Style

The company's operating units are semi-independent profit centers organized into 50 product groups which are themselves organized into four major lines of business according to their technological similarities. Although operating units have autonomy in manufacturing, marketing, and research, other activities such as financial, legal, data processing, and other non-product-related functions are centralized at the company's headquarters. Individual operating-unit heads are housed at corporate headquarters.

1.3 Control Atmosphere

The control atmosphere at F Company is quite stringent. In particular, tight financial control is exercised from headquarters over operating units. The company's financial statements carry an assertion by management as follows:

> Established accounting procedures and related systems of internal control *provide* reasonable assurance that assets are safeguarded, that books and records properly reflect all transactions, and that policies and procedures are implemented by qualified personnel. *Internal auditors continually review the accounting and control systems.* (emphasis added)

2.0 Role and Responsibilities of the Internal Audit Department

2.1 Organizational Position, Department Structure, Size, and Personnel

The internal audit department is organizationally under the control of the vice president of finance. On a quarterly basis, meetings are held with the audit committee, which reviews the department's annual work plan and budget and highlights of the most recent audit findings and important upcoming developments.

The director of internal audit is responsible for setting overall goals and objectives for the department, international coordination with external auditors, public relations, and strategic planning.

Two assistant directors report to the director of internal audit. They are charged with domestic and international audit-administration responsibilities. The discussion that follows is based upon the procedures followed by the domestic audit group, which has 45 auditors and three clerical staff members.

Four supervisors report to the assistant director of domestic audit, each assigned a group of audits as their specific area of responsibility.

Although not formally stated, the department views part of its role as a developer of managerial personnel. Indeed, on the average, 70 percent of its annual turnover of staff results in internal transfers to line-management functions.

Personnel are hired out of college, primarily from accounting and increasingly from MIS programs. Comprehensive training programs are provided by the department, and a career-development plan exists to provide promotion opportunities within the department.

2.2 Cost Structure and Charge-out Policy

Departmental costs of about $3 million may be broken down as follows:

Salaries and benefits	76%
Travel	14%
Training and miscellaneous	5%
Facilities	5%
	100%

All costs are charged out to operating units in proportion to their sales revenues.

2.3 Mandate or Charter and Audit Orientation

There is no formal charter outlining the mandate or responsibility of the internal audit department. A memorandum from the vice president of finance to the director of internal audit serves to summarize the role, authority, and responsibility of the internal audit department as follows:

As director you are responsible for directing and coordinating financial and operational internal audit activities in F Company and its subsidiaries worldwide. This includes whatever reviews are necessary to determine that:

- Efficient and ethical business practices are followed.
- Internal accounting controls are adequate.
- Accounting and management information is accurately prepared.
- Company policies and procedures are followed.
- Assets are adequately safeguarded and effectively used.

In all these reviews, the department is expected to assist line and staff management in the discharge of responsibilities and to report its findings and recommendations to them. It is also expected to work closely with the outside auditors and to keep them fully apprised of its findings.

You report administratively to my office, vice president of finance, and with me you have a strong functional reporting responsibility to the board of directors through their audit committee. It should be emphasized that, whenever you deem it appropriate to do so in light of the matters being reviewed, you may report directly to and/or solicit guidance directly from the chairman of the board, the president, the vice president, legal affairs, or the chairman of the audit committee.

The department has a strong operational audit orientation which gradually developed over a 30-year period. It is free to audit whatever it chooses and as frequently as it chooses; consequently, audits vary considerably in objectives, scope, and frequency. Little statistical testing is performed. The emphasis is on problem identification and analysis. Most audits consist of certain mandatory steps pertaining to financial review and evaluation of financial controls and tests of adherence to significant company policies. In addition, checklists of potential problems are used to help identify inefficiencies in operations. When problem areas are identified at the operating unit level, they are analyzed from the company-wide perspective. Thereafter, evaluations of potential cost savings are performed and recommendations made. Only supportable and "hard" savings are included, although typically this is only a part of the total possible improvement.

To illustrate this approach, the following are major areas where significant recommendations were made recently (i.e., significant savings):

- Cash-flow improvements.
- Inventory reductions.
- Direct cash recoveries from customers.
- Reduction of unnecessary costs.
- Administrative efficiencies.

Generally, audits involve an all-inclusive examination of the administrative and accounting functions performed by the organizations being audited. Reviews of reliability and integrity of other financial and operational information generated – including the means used to identify, measure, classify, and report – are performed. In addition, activities of the organizations are reviewed for compliance with applicable policies, procedures, laws, and regulations. Another important part of each audit is the verification of the adequacy of the system of controls designed to safeguard those corporate assets entrusted to the organization being audited. Corporate resources (human, financial, and capital) are examined to ensure they are economically and efficiently used. Finally, operations are reviewed to verify that the results are consistent with the goals and objectives established for the organization.

Audits generally include three phases:

- Preliminary audit work at headquarters.
- Fieldwork at the location.
- Follow-up report.

The intensity of audits varies from complete audits to limited-scope audits which are restricted to review and evaluation of a few of the most important potentially problematic areas.

2.4 Relations with External Auditors

External auditors receive copies of all the reports issued by the internal audit department. However, less than 1 percent of the department's time is specifically allocated to assist the external auditors' year-end work. Indeed, because of the extensive operational audit activities of the internal audit department, external auditors are charged with performing the minimal audit required to express an opinion on the financial statements.

2.5 Audit Techniques
Formal audit programs exist for four major recurring audit areas, including branch-manufacturing facilities, administration, branch order/entry and distribution operations, and data-center operations. These are updated on an ongoing basis. Other audits (e.g., staff functions) are carried out less frequently, and audit programs are developed anew each time the audit is to be carried out.

The department has its own terminal and printer and can access company data bases through its time-sharing facility, permitting wide-ranging types of analyses to be carried out.

3.0 Planning and Coordinating Activities

3.1 Planning Overview
The internal audit director is part of F Company's top management echelon, which includes all divisional vice presidents and other executives. Consequently, he is privy to corporate plans and forecasts with one-, three-, and 5-year horizons. As a result of his continuous participation and interaction with top management, the department encounters few surprises. In fact, the department is virtually always involved whenever significant changes to accounting systems and procedures are implemented in the operating units and often carries out special assignments on behalf of management in strategic areas.

All audits are performed on a cyclic basis that ranges from two to five years with each individual audit having its own cycle rate based on the size and complexity of the function, the potential exposure to loss, the results of prior audits, and the effects of current changes on the operation of the function. All audits in the population are recorded by a computerized system that maintains audit histories and aids in the planning effort.

Annually, computer lists of audits within each supervisor's area of responsibility are produced. These lists are reviewed by the supervisors and updated. Then, current data such as employee counts, inventory values, sales, and inventory demand are entered into the system, updating the existing information for each audit location. The supervisors use this information, along with their combined knowledge of past audit results and current changes within the various organizations, to evaluate the risks and establish the cycle rates of each audit. In addition, they estimate the number of weeks to budget for each audit. After being reviewed, lists are generated of all audits due in the coming year and for future years based on cycle rates.

3.2 Audit-Portfolio Management

Identification of Auditable Units. About 550 audit units have been identified. These fall into about ten categories. For example, there are 150 units in the plant category, 90 in the distribution-center category, and so on. Virtually all the units represent physical locations rather than financial categories. Annually, computer lists of audits within each supervisor's area of responsibility are produced. These lists are reviewed by the supervisors' knowledge of the operations. Knowledge of new locations is gained through the supervisors' periodic contacts with management personnel within the assigned areas of responsibility and from various company publications which highlight new acquisitions or expansions.

Various items of information about audit units are maintained by computer:

- Location name and identification number.
- Audit manager.
- Cycle rate (i.e., frequency of audit).
- Last date audited.
- Scope of audit.
- Audit time in weeks.
- Travel information including audit team's size and weekend commuting data.
- Decision data (discussed in the following subsection).
- Comments and other information.

Evaluation of Audit-Risk-Exposure Concern. Each year audit units are arranged into audit-frequency categories that serve to group audits into coverage cycles varying from two to five years. Audit scope, staffing, and time estimates are determined. Although no formal system is used for making these decisions, a number of variables influence the decisions. In particular, the "decision data" currently being used includes:

- Last date audited.
- Total number (by type) of employees in the audit unit.
- Inventory (by type) on hand in the location.
- Total sales.
- Various comments.

Preparation of the Audit Coverage Cycle and the Work Plan. A computerized set of procedures is used to manage the inventory of auditable units. Each manager receives a list of audits which he manages. Managers prepare lists of potential audit teams and estimate time requirements to complete audits. Also, a tentative schedule of audits is prepared, taking into account this information as well as the professional development requirements of the individual auditors. The managers then get together and arrive at a final master plan for the department.

Once general agreement is reached concerning cycle rates and audit weeks, the supervisors review the master schedules and compare the revised cycle rates to the date each audit was last completed. From this review, lists are generated of all audits due in the coming year. These lists are reviewed, and some minor adjustments are made to provide a proper mix of audits and to equalize the work and the travel schedules between years. This establishes the final audit population for the coming year. There may be minor variations in completing the audits due to unforeseen scheduling problems, but these changes to the annual schedule are relatively minor in comparison to the total number of audits performed.

3.3 Personnel Management, Coordination, and Development

To be promoted, auditors must demonstrate competence in several areas; for example, the ability to run major audits, supervise several staff members, and perform audits of major out-of-town facilities. These types of considerations are built into the assignment of audit responsibilities.

Audit schedules cover periods of ten to thirteen weeks. In preparing these schedules, department management initially considers employees' personal plans.

After consulting with the various audit managers and supervisors about the progress and anticipated completion times of their audits, management separately lists all the available employees, indicating the dates they are available to begin new audits. Also listed for each employee are individual goal requirements, available travel time, and other special considerations. The next step is to sort the employees into in-charge and non-in-charge groups, listing each employee chronologically by date of availability.

All audit activities are closely supervised. For each audit, there is an in-charge auditor assigned to plan, coordinate, and supervise it. In each instance, the in-charge auditor has had some experience in performing the particular type of audit assigned. These in-charge auditors are responsible for the day-to-day supervision and direction of the work of all juniors assigned to the audit. In addition, there is also a coordinator, supervisor, or manager assigned to monitor the work. Their responsibilities include coordinating auditing activities with those in charge, advising the auditors as to appropriate procedures and supervising the preparation of findings and reports.

Each junior auditor's performance is formally evaluated by the in-charge auditor at the completion of the audit. A written evaluation sheet (see Figure 3.F.1) is prepared by the in-charge auditor, discussed with the junior auditor, and submitted to management to be placed in the employee's file. Each evaluation form must be signed by the in-charge, junior, and supervisor. A similar procedure is used to evaluate the in-charge auditor's performance on each audit by the supervisor responsible for the audit. In these evaluation sessions, each employee's performance is reviewed; and plans are discussed concerning the employee's further development.

Individuals keep track of their time which is summarized and listed on an audit-control sheet by the auditor in charge upon completion of the audit. In addition to recording actual time, recommendations for future audits are recorded as well.

A formalized training program exists and is supervised by one of the audit managers. It includes formal training sessions for all levels of staff from juniors to experienced managers. For 1981, 126 weeks of staff training were budgeted in the annual schedule. This training budget consists of applicable orientation programs for new auditors and an ongoing or continual training program for all employees established at a rate of 5 percent of each employee's available time.

Figure 3.F.1
Company F: Internal Auditor's Appraisal Report

Appraisal of	Location Audited	Date Reported	
		From	To
Major Job Responsibilities During This Audit –		Attained	Not Attained

Performance factors	Requirements are: B = below, M = met, E = exceeded, F = far exceeded	B	M	E	F
Knowledge of job	Knowledge of company procedures				
	Preparation of work papers				
Problem solving	Reliability of work performed				
	Recognition of significant audit facts				
	Work is creative				
Communication	Oral presentation				
	Report writing				
Planning	Completes work on time				
	Organization and execution of work plan				
	Resourcefulness displayed in attacking problem				
Working with people	Ability to work well with other members of team				
	Ability to secure cooperation from auditee				
	Tact and courtesy in contacts with auditee				
Additional Considerations	Stability and maturity				
	Management attitude				
	Motivation and drive				
Overall Performance Level	This is not an arithmetical average. Give your opinion stressing the most important factors. Balance strengths against weaknesses. Do not use sliding scale.				

Explain reasons for B, E, or F ratings in detail.

Do you feel that this person is capable of conducting and supervising an audit of this type? Yes ☐ No☐ Explain.	Rater
	Ratee
	Reviewed by

G Company

1.0 Company's Background

G Company is a diversified financial services company with two main lines of business: life insurance and mutual funds management. It employs about 2,000 people and has 3,500 agents throughout the country. Its clientele primarily involves individual investors and policy holders. Within its two main product lines, it offers a variety of financial services and products.

1.1 Financial Highlights
G Company is the largest subsidiary of its parent-holding company with 1981 revenues exceeding $1 billion on assets of about $3.5 billion and managed funds of about $8 billion. Its auditors are O Company, a "big eight" public accounting firm.

1.2 Management Style
G Company is highly centralized with virtually all its non-sales personnel located at its headquarters. It serves its clients through 185 divisional offices throughout the country. The company uses product lines as a basis for organization of its operations.

1.3 Control Atmosphere
The company is in a highly regulated industry. SEC's state-insurance examiners and state-regulatory authorities greatly influence the policies and procedures in force. In addition, the nature of financial services dictates the necessity for strict financial controls. Currently, no statement about the system of internal control appears in either G Company's or its parent's financial statements.

2.0 Role and Responsibilities of the Internal Audit Department

2.1 Organizational Position, Department Structure, Size, and Personnel
The internal audit department at G Company consists of 30 professional and five clerical staff members. It is organized into

three audit groups: EDP, financial, and operational. The director of the internal audit department reports to the senior vice president of finance as well as to the audit committee of the parent company and the audit committee of affiliated companies. The latter reporting relationship is through the parent company's controller who acts as a liaison between the parent company's audit committee and the internal auditors of all the subsidiaries.

The financial audit group is the largest of the three groups with about half of the department's staff. Its organization reflects the product-oriented organization of G Company. The operational audit group is quite small with only two members. The EDP audit group has eight members: seven staff and a manager. The group managers report to the section manager who, along with the EDP audit manager, reports to the director of internal audit.

The department's staff experience ranges from eight months to 20 years at various levels of audit responsibility. A professional audit orientation is emphasized. The department's junior-staff members are management trainees assigned to the department for an eight-month assignment as part of a company-wide-management-training program. The department averages a 33 percent turnover annually.

2.2 Cost Structure and Charge-out Policy

The department's budget of $900,000 may be broken down as follows:

Salaries	70%
Travel	1%
Training	1%
Facilities	28%
	100%

Costs are charged out, based upon the audit time incurred, at a current rate of about $35 per hour.

2.3 Mandate or Charter and Audit Orientation

The primary orientation of the department is toward control and procedures auditing, although a small operational auditing group exists as well. The internal audit charter is derived from the company-management guide which outlines the duties and responsibilities of the director of internal audit. It requires:
• Having an internal audit program that is adequate to protect

the major assets of the company.
- Conducting reviews of various operations to determine effectiveness and efficiency of management.
- Determining that company policies are observed.
- Controlling issuance and revisions to disbursement-approval manuals which assist management with its controls.
- Reporting to the appropriate level of management significant items disclosed by audits.
- Ensuring effective personnel administration and programs to evaluate and train potential management personnel for the company.
- Directing special investigations for alleged misappropriations.
- Ensuring audits of nonassociated enterprises for compliance with contractual agreements or to determine control over company assets in their custody.
- Coordinating programs with external examiners to attain corporate objectives.
- Reviewing, approving, or rejecting proposed systems and procedures for internal control concepts (manual or data processing).
- Determining that staff members research new methods in the field of internal auditing.

Audits have essentially two phases. At the beginning of each year, controls and procedures within audit units are reviewed and evaluated. Then, periodically throughout the year, depending upon the established audit frequency, verification procedures are performed.

2.4 Relations with External Auditors

The department works very closely with external auditors to avoid audit overlaps and to achieve audit-related cost savings whenever possible. The external auditors rely on the working papers of the internal auditors in several key areas and have virtually all their EDP audit work done by the department's EDP audit group. A semiannual status report and an annual summary of selected activities and findings are prepared for the audit committees outlining the activities of the internal audit department.

2.5 Audit Techniques

Formal audit programs exist for all recurring audits. The discretionary audits and special projects are relatively unstructured. In addition to widespread use of audit software (i.e., Mark IV), integrated test facilities exist. A transaction-selection system automatically selects input transactions for audit reviews.

3.0 Planning and Coordinating Activities

3.1 Planning Overview

Long-range planning for the department is incorporated within the five-year plan of the finance department. In addition, the company's five-year plan is examined annually so that audit management can anticipate new products, growth areas, acquisitions, and new systems-development projects. The audit-time budget is prepared for two years based upon the prior year's results; i.e., actual time spent on various audits and audit findings. The planning framework is based upon audit managers' knowledge of the various auditable units and their staffs.

At the beginning of each year, audits are judgmentally assigned an audit frequency. Of the 120 identified auditable units, about 90 are of a recurring type and are performed monthly, quarterly, semiannually, or annually. The other 30 or more units have discretionary frequencies.

The financial audit groups tend to specialize along product lines. Scheduling audits and work assignments occurs within subgroups.

3.2 Audit-Portfolio Management

Identification of Auditable Units. Audit units represent accounts in the company's chart of accounts which have been grouped into cycles based upon the company's segment reporting for 10K purposes and similar to AICPA's transaction-cycle approach for organizing audit units. About 120 audit units have been identified with this approach.

When an account represents some balance across a number of affiliated companies, the auditable unit is considered from the corporate-wide perspective. Audit planning and execution is performed accordingly.

Evaluation of Audit-Risk-Exposure Concern. Unlike the other departments participating in this study, G Company's internal audit concentrates on assessing the importance of particular audit units in a subjective rather than objective manner,

112

although the plan is to move toward a more objective risk-evaluation system.

Several criteria are typically used by managers to establish audit priorities. These include the liquidity of assets in a particular area, the statutory obligations which must be met by the company, and stewardship aspects of accounting properly for customers' funds on deposit with the company. These factors and past experience with the specific areas determine the audit importance assigned to a given audit.

Preparation of the Audit Coverage Cycle and the Work Plan. The audit approach at G Company is unique among the cases studied. Unlike the others which cycle audits over fairly long periods of three to five years, G Company's audits are often cycled within a year. Although the planning is carried out annually, the audit work is subdivided into portions performed monthly or quarterly. Planning the audit frequency is a key decision made every year. These decisions are made subjectively. The audit plan is then discussed with division controllers who often provide additional comments and perspective for this part of the planning process.

Although the frequency of audit units varies, the phases are essentially the same. At the beginning of the year, operating procedures and controls are reviewed and evaluated for each area; then throughout the year and depending upon the frequency set, a number of financial audits are performed.

3.3 Personnel Management, Coordination, and Development

An automated time and work-in-progress reporting system is used to keep track of auditors' activities. Each auditor fills out a weekly time report that is keyed to the audit assignment.

Most audits are carried out by auditors individually with the exception of systems-development audits, wherein a team approach is often used that combines an EDP auditor and a financial auditor into a team. Control reviews are typically assigned to more experienced auditors, whereas financial audits are done by less experienced auditors. Junior auditors are evaluated twice annually, and seniors are evaluted annually. Also annually, two or more two-to-five-day seminars are conducted. On-the-job training forms the mainstay of the professional development approach by G Company's internal audit group.

H Company

1.0 Company's Background

H Company is a retailing company founded at the turn of the century. It employs almost 190 thousand people at its 2,000 locations throughout the United States and Europe.

1.1 Financial Highlights

Consolidated 1981 financial statements indicate sales revenues of about $12 billion on assets of about $6 billion. The company's shares are listed on the New York Stock Exchange as well as certain European exchanges. Its external auditors are O company, one of the "big eight" public accounting firms.

1.2 Management Style

The company's operations are widely distributed throughout the United States and Europe. Strong procedural controls and extensive profit-sharing arrangements serve to maintain control over the local operations (see the next subsection).

1.3 Control Atmosphere

Control procedures have evolved over 80 years and have been audited for 60 years, making them rather strongly entrenched thoughout the company. The company's 1981 financial statements state:

> The company's system of internal accounting controls and procedures is supported by written policies and guidelines and supplemented by a staff of internal auditors. This system is designed to provide reasonable assurance at suitable cost that assets are safeguarded and that transactions are executed in accordance with appropriate authorization and are recorded and reported properly. The system is continually reviewed, evaluated, and (when appropriate) modified to accommodate current conditions. Emphasis is placed on the careful selection, training, and development of professional managers.
>
> An organizational alignment that is premised upon appropriate delegation of authority and division of responsibility is fundamental to the system. Communication programs are aimed at assuring that established procedures, policies, and guidelines are disseminated and understood throughout the company.

2.0 Role and Responsibilities of the Internal Audit Department

2.1 Organizational Position, Department Structure, Size, and Personnel

The internal audit department reports directly to the chairman of the board and also to the audit committee of the board with which meetings are held three times annually. The director of internal audit is a vice president of H Company. It is quite large with a staff in excess of 150 professionals, about 20 clerical personnel, and an annual budget of about $7.5 million.

The department is subdivided into four main groups: EDP audit (25 employees); corporate audit (20 employees); field audit (100 employees); and professional practices, personnel, and administration (5 employees). Audit personnel are geographically distributed throughout the country in five regions and in areas within each region.

In the field-audit group, there are five regional audit managers. The regional audit managers have two to three area-audit managers reporting to them, and each area-audit manager has a staff of about five auditors (one senior auditor and four other auditors). The EDP audit group is distributed in four locations, mirroring the distribution of the corporate systems-development and data-processing organization at four regional sites.

The corporate audit group is split and located at two main sites.

The professional practices, personnel, and administration group is housed at corporate headquarters and charged with enhancing the planning and coordinating of all audit activities and with developing professional practices, techniques and audit procedures, and similar administrative responsibilities.

Personnel are quite experienced and well educated. Virtually all have college degrees; 33 percent are CIAs; and 20 percent are CPAs. The average auditing experience in the department as a whole is about seven years, despite the average annual turnover of 25 percent. The main (and about equal in importance) recruiting sources are colleges, other organizations, and other operating units.

2.2 Cost Structure and Charge-out Policy

The department's budget breakdown is appropximately as follows:

Salaries and benefits	70%
Travel	14%
Training	1%
Facilities and other	15%
	100%

No cost-charge-out system is used.

2.3 Mandate or Charter and Audit Orientation

H Company's policy concerning auditing is stated in its policy manual as follows:

Auditing will be conducted to evaluate and report objectively on the effectiveness of accounting, financial, administrative, and operating controls to support the optimal management utilization of company resources and to assist in protecting the rights and interest of the company's stockholders, members of the board of directors, customers, associates, creditors, and the general public.

Auditing activities conducted internally focus on assuring the adequacy of accounting, financial, administrative, and operating controls and procedures; compliance with such controls and procedures; and their proper application in support of overall management control. Auditing shall evaluate the company's procedures to protect its assets and to insure the preparation of fair and reliable financial reports to management, members of the board of directors, stockholders, government agencies and legislative bodies, creditors, and the general public.

2.4 Relations with External Auditors

Of all the companies studied, H Company's internal audit department had the closest relations with external auditors. Annually, a coordinated audit plan is prepared for the audit committee jointly by the internal audit department and external auditors, outlining the strategies of the various audits in each area, the reports to be issued, a summary of the respective audit teams, and costs (see Figure 3.H.1).

The department's share of joint activities involves about 11,000 hours of work. This accounts for about 5 percent of the department's audit time. The following exerpt from the joint statement by the two groups is indicative of the close cooperation be-

Figure 3.H.1

Company H: Coordinated Audit Plan and Strategy for H Company and Its External Auditors' O Company

Activity	Planned 1981 Audit Costs			Prior Year's Audit Costs		
	External Auditor	Internal Auditor	Total	External Auditor	Internal Auditor	Total
Stores	$	$	$	$	$	$
_____						
_____						
etc.	___	___	___	___	___	___
Stores Subtotal	___	___	___	___	___	___
Catalog						
_____						
_____						
etc.	___	___	___	___	___	___
Catalog Subtotal	___	___	___	___	___	___
Fin. Serv.						
_____						
_____						
etc.	___	___	___	___	___	___
Fin. Serv. Subtotal	___	___	___	___	___	___
Sup. Act.						
_____						
_____						
etc.	___	___	___	___	___	___
Sup. Act. Subtotal	___	___	___	___	___	___
	$___	$___	$___	$___	$___	$___

tween them:

Internal audit activities for 1981, exclusive of its assistance to O Company as part of its annual examination, were selected based upon specific evaluation criteria which were developed to surface high-priority areas that should be reviewed. These criteria were applied against the inventory of auditable activities maintained by internal audit to determine the areas that should be audited during fiscal 1981.

Based upon our review of the total scope of audit work currently performed for the entire company, we feel that the audit plan contemplated by O Company and internal audit is compatible and provides a high degree of efficiency and cost-benefit relationship; at the same time, it satisfies management's objectives regarding the utilization and safeguarding of assets and the professional responsibilities of both internal and external auditors.

The report is signed by both the director of internal audit and O Company's audit partner in charge of the H Company audit.

2.5 Audit Techniques

Formal audit programs exist for all audits. Audit software is used extensively for analytical purposes.

3.0 Planning Activities

3.1 Planning Overview

Planning activities are primarily carried out within the main departmental divisions. Recently, extensive effort has been made to coordinate the plans of corporate audit, EDP audit, and field-audit groups to ensure that the annual audit plan covers company-wide priorities.

In the EDP audit and the field-audit groups, long-range planning has been largely abandoned in favor of annual planning activities. Although the EDP audit group knows the number of audits it will have during the next five years and how it will allocate its time among systems under development, data-processing facilities, etc., it is felt that, because of the dynamics of system development, planning specific audits beyond the current year is not warranted. The EDP audit group feels that such planning wastes a good deal of effort. The corporate audit group, however, plans its activities over a five-year period.

As for store audits performed by the field-audit group, although a five-year "cap" is in effect (i.e., requiring at least one audit during that period for each location), the department prefers to evaluate the stores on an annual basis to determine each year's priority of stores to audit.

Planning generally consists of a three-tier approach. First, management by objectives is used to define specific targets and goals to be achieved by individuals at all levels in the audit department. The specific standards, which vary according to the individual's role in the department, are detailed in a performance-review guide; for example, audit managers' goals are primarily administrative in nature, whereas auditors' goals are oriented toward audit work. The second tier of planning involves the separate evaluation of specific audit priorities by each of the three audit groups. The third tier involves coordination of the audit activities planned by the three audit groups.

Planning and coordinating are increasingly being performed with the aid of computer-assisted tools, including microcomputers and time-sharing services. Of the companies studied, H Company's internal audit department was the only one experimenting with microcomputers, including interregional communications through linked microcomputers for personnel-time-record entry from geographically dispersed offices to the centralized personnel-administration group at headquarters and for preparing coordinated departmental plans.

3.2 Audit-Portfolio Management

Identification of Auditable Units. Three sets of audit inventories are maintained independently by the three subdivisions of the internal audit department. The EDP audit group examines the systems and data-processing group's plans and status reports of projects in progress and selects items to audit. In 1981, for example, 33 audit units were identified. The corporate audit group manages a portfolio of about 350 audit units of a diverse nature. The field-audit group is charged with audits of about 1,700 stores.

Evaluation of Audit-Risk-Exposure Concern. The three groups have different methods of evaluating risk-exposure concern related to their units. The EDP audit group uses a subjective evaluation approach. The corporate audit group uses 25 criteria (listed in Figure 3.H.2) for rating the importance of the audit units on a three-point system: high, medium, and low concern.

The store-audit priorities are assessed by regional audit

Figure 3.H.2
Company H: Selection Criteria for Corporate Audits

1. Nature of activity: financial versus service support
2. Financial significance
3. Purchasing or buying function
4. Receives or disburses cash
5. Rate of growth
6. Maturity of the activity
7. Direct impact on profit and loss
8. Indirect impact on profit and loss
9. Impact of new systems or systems changes
10. Reliability of management-information systems
11. Budget variance and/or operating trends
12. Expiration of right of audit
13. Presence of documented operating procedures
14. Impact on customer service
15. Concerns expressed by management
16. Previous audit history
17. Receives external audit coverage
18. Receives no external audit coverage
19. Monitoring practices of the operating department
20. Presence of compensating controls
21. Type of contractual arrangements with outsiders
22. Special arrangements with suppliers
23. Public disclosure issues and sensitive areas
24. Exposure resulting from governmental regulations
25. Potential for fraud or conflict of interest

managers according to a relatively complex scheme which combines four separate ratings:

- Evaluation of operating information.
- Evaluations by store management.
- Prior audit rating.
- Period of time since prior audit.

Worksheets and rating instructions are provided for each of these areas. Appendixes C, D, and E include sample worksheets to illustrate the comprehensiveness of this assessment approach. An overall rating form is used to bring together and summarize the overall assessment of each audit unit (see Figure 3.H.3).

Preparation of the Audit Coverage Cycle and the Work Plan. There are three plans prepared. Each year the professional practices group assists in coordinating these sets of plans. This is important to ensure staff availability, to ensure that planning is carried out from a company-wide perspective, and to ensure that agreement is reached on the audits planned and priorities assigned. Although the entire year's work is usually determined at the outset of the year, scheduling audits is done for one quarter at a time.

Store audits are typically scheduled for eight man-weeks, the larger stores being audited by teams. The audits are relatively standardized. Barring difficulties, each consists of 13 standard modules.

Corporate audits are planned over a five-year period with audit-frequency assignments based on the priority evaluation described above. Nonstore audits consist of four phases for which completion date and budgeted hours are estimated: preliminary survey, fieldwork, report writing, and report finalization.

3.3 Personnel Management, Coordination, and Development

Management by objectives is used at all levels of the department to ensure congruence between the planned activities and the performance of personnel at all levels. Different goals are set for staff at different levels, as previously indicated. Quarterly audit-activity reports provide acutal-versus-planned statistics for the quarter and the year to date. In addition, brief highlights of major audits are provided. The reports are sent to the director of internal audit, the chairman of the board, and the audit committee.

Figure 3.H.3
Company H: Rating for Stores/Units on Two-Year-Planning Standard

Unit No. _____   Total Weighted Ratings _____

Type of Unit _____   Date Completed _____

Location _____   Completed by _____

Years Since Last Audit		Prior Audit Rating (see worksheet)		Operating Information (see worksheet)		Management Evaluation (see worksheet)	
Years	Weighted Rating	Last Audit Rating	Weighted Rating	Priority	Weighted Rating	Priority	Weighted Rating
1	30	4	20	Low	30	Low	20
	29	(no correc-	19		29		19
	28	tive action	18		28		18
	27	required)	17		27		17
	26		16		26		16
	25	3	15		25		15
	24		14		24		14
	23		13		23		13
	22		12		22		12
	21		11		21		11
	20	2	10		20	Moderate	10
	19		9		19		9
	18		8		18		8
	17		7		17		7
	16		6		16		6
2	15	1	5	Average	15		5
	14		4		14		4
	13		3		13		3
	12		2		12		2
	11		1		11		1
	10	0	0		10	High	0
	9	(unsatis-			9		
	8	factory			8		
	7	conditions)			7		
	6				6		
3	5				5		
	4				4		
	3				3		
	2				2		
	1				1		
4	0			High	0		

Circle the weighted rating that corresponds to the number of years since the last audit. You may choose to consider months at your option.	Circle the weighted rating that most closely corresponds to the rating on the last rating guide and/or the conditions described in the last audit report.	Circle the weighted rating that corresponds to the rating arrived at by completion of the operating information worksheet.	Circle the weighted rating that most closely corresponds to the rating given the store/unit by management.

122

Annual evaluations, based upon a comparison of objectives achieved against those planned, are made and summarized in annual reports. Considerable emphasis is placed upon training and development, although this is primarily on-the-job training; for example, auditors have been temporarily transferred to systems for one-year assignments. In addition, the company offers a variety of training programs in human-relations skills. The professional practices group coordinates the development of department-wide seminars.

I Company

1.0 Company's Background

I Company is a petroleum company. It is one of the largest petroleum companies in the United States and is engaged in two main lines of business: (1) petroleum exploration, production, refining, and marketing and (2) chemical production and distribution.

1.1 Financial Highlights

I Company reported sales of about $16 billion on assets of about $11 billion in 1981 and has about 35,000 employees worldwide. Its stock is listed on the New York Stock Exchange as well as several other exchanges. Its external auditors are Q Company, one of the "big eight" public accounting firms.

1.2 Management Style

The company is strongly centralized with a large corporate staff. There is an emerging trend toward decentralization through the establishment of profit centers. No statement appears in the company's annual report about either the system of internal accounting control or the internal audit department.

2.0 Role and Responsibilities of the Internal Audit Department

2.1 Organizational Position, Department Structure, Size, and Personnel

I Company's internal audit department reports to the executive vice president of finance from whom it receives general administrative direction. Moreover, the director of internal audit is an officer of the company. Functionally, the director of internal audit reports to the audit committee of the board of directors which has the authority to direct reviews and reports on any aspect of the company's business and affairs. Formal meetings are held semiannually, but there is open access to the audit committee chairman at all other times.

The department has approximately 110 employees (about 100 professional and ten clerical personnel subdivided into three main groups): systems and EDP auditing (8), planning and research (3), and corporate audit (99). The corporate audit group is further subdivided into four audit groups mirroring the corporate structure: internal operations (16), petroleum products and chemicals (39), corporate (22), and natural resources (22). The department staff's total audit experience falls into the following categories:

0 to 2 years	19%
3 to 5 years	28%
6 to 10 years	41%
11 years or more	22%
	100%

Ninety percent of the staff have at least one college degree. However, only about 20 percent have professional designations (primarily CPA).

2.2 Cost Structure and Charge-out Policy

The department's 1981 budget was about $6.8 million, and its cost structure may be broken down as follows:

Salaries and benefits	80%
Travel	15%
Training (external only)	1%
Miscellaneous (facilities, etc.)	4%
	100%

Virtually all the department's training is in-house.

Except for special projects and some investigative costs, no charge-out system is used.

2.3 Mandate or Charter and Audit Orientation

The internal audit charter is a three-page document approved by the executive committee of the board of directors. It covers the function, scope, authority, organizational philosophy, reporting relationships, and duties of the internal audit department. The charter emphasizes that there are other units within the company with responsibility for specialized inspection, auditing, and internal control-monitoring activities and requires coordination of the internal audit department's activities with these units to avoid significant duplication and overlapping of efforts.

The *Standards* serves as general guidelines to the internal audit department in performing its functions under the authority prescribed in its charter. The charter requires that internal audit coordinate its audit activities with those of the company's external auditors and that staff members provide audit assistance to external auditors as approved by the audit committee.

The orientation of the department is toward financial audits and includes review and evaluation of internal controls and tests of compliance with prescribed company policies. Operational auditing is de-emphasized due primarily to the technical nature of most of the company's operations and the limited technical expertise of internal auditors.

2.4 Relations with External Auditors

The internal audit department enjoys good working relations with external auditors and provides direct assistance to them as well as taking direct responsibility for certain audits. These amount to about 5,000 hours or 5 percent of available departmental time. Typically, external audit planning does not cover as long a time horizon as that of internal audit. However, recently, long-range joint planning and coordinating has been used to increase the opportunities for direct-responsibility audits as part of the ongoing work effort of the internal audit department.

2.5 Audit Techniques

The department does not use preprinted audit programs. It feels that, since the objectives and scope of audits vary, a "canned" approach based on preprinted audit programs is undesirable. An internal quality-assurance program is used which involves checklists, reviews by supervisors, and a separate quality-review program (covering 5-10 percent of audit work). Audit software (e.g., DYL280, SAS, Mark IV) is used primarily by computer-audit specialists.

3.0 Planning and Coordinating Activities

3.1 Planning Overview

Planning occurs at four levels. Long-range planning is carried out over a three-year horizon, and an audit schedule for that period is prepared. The first year of the three-year plan is the basis for audit-committee involvement. Audits are scheduled semiannually, and individual audit planning is quite important since no preprinted guidelines are used.

Long-range planning is used for identifying audit candidates and determining top management's priorities and concerns. All managers in charge of audit areas carry out long-range planning for the areas independently. This involves review of management's six-year strategic plan, discussions with management, and transformation of key findings into audit plans. For example, areas of growth/expansion might be highlighted; corporate concerns such as safety, equipment maintenance, and personnel practices might prompt new audit units to be defined or others to be emphasized; regulatory factors might lead to emphasis of certain audits, and so on.

The long-range plan is revised yearly with one year dropped and one year added. A formal planning meeting is held annually to coordinate the work plans of the individual groups, and a consolidated one-year plan is prepared for review by the audit committee. Semiannually, group managers prepare lists of audits to perform and give them to supervisors who schedule staff accordingly. Audit objectives are specified in long-range and annual plans. These vary from cycle to cycle. Audits are of a nonrecurring nature. Consequently, a good deal of procedural planning is required prior to each audit.

3.2 Audit-Portfolio Management

Identification of Auditable Units. Six definitions of audit unit serve as the basis for identifying auditable units. These include: transaction cycles, corporate staff functions, large data centers and applicable systems, new systems-development projects, construction projects in progress, and completed capital projects. Special control sheets are designed to facilitate the identification and the evaluation of audit units. Managers complete these control sheets which serve as a compendium of audits, re-

Figure 3.I.1
Company I: Evaluation of Audit Units

Risk Factors	Risk Level				
	1	2	3	4	5
1. Revenues					
2. Assets					
3. Operating budget					
4. Capital budget					
5. Public exposure					
6. Known problem areas creating high audit or business risk					
7. Management or audit committee directives					
8. Geographic location					
9. Rate of growth in entity					
10. Management's problems in entity					
11. Liquidity of assets					
12. Volume of transactions					
13. Materiality of accounts or transactions					
14. Statutory or contractual requirements					
15. Past audit experience					
16. Stability of entity practices					
17. Stability of entity procedures					
18. Stability of personnel					
19. Extent of regulatory control					
20. Political atmosphere*					
21. Business environment*					
Total					

*Especially critical in foreign operations.

lated indices of concern, planned objectives to be pursued in the audits, and expected timing of audits within the three-year-planing cycle.

Evaluation of Risk-Exposure Concern. For each field location, a risk-evaluation matrix is filled out, depending upon which set of audit units and related considerations is appropriate. In some cases, this may be more than one set. The matrix, illustrated in Figure 3.I.1, contains a list of considerations down the left-hand side and cells with values from one to five across the top, one representing low risk and exposure and five representing heavy risk and exposure. Managers simply mark the scores for each consideration by checking the appropriate cell. Then the total number of items checked for each column is prepared. High-point totals in the heavy-exposure (i.e., four and five) columns generally indicate that unit should be scheduled for audit within the next planning period. Other considerations also may come into play. Currently, little formal guidance exists for assigning point values and making the evaluations and plans.

The purpose of using the matrix is for encouraging documentation of judgments and consideration of important risk factors rather than providing a formal, uniform model for determining audit priority of units of the audit universe.

Preparation of the Audit Coverage Cycle and the Work Plan. Three groups of audit objectives have been identified for use in preparing audit plans: systems objectives, operational objectives, and special objectives. These are further subdivided, making a total of seven audit objectives. At the same time that risk-exposure concern is evaluated for each audit unit, a subset of audit objectives taken from the seven objectives mentioned and listed in Figure 3.I.2 is specified for the audit. This is done in conjunction with the risk-exposure-concern evaluation which prompted the audit in the first place.

A coordination meeting is held to ensure agreement by the groups on the three-year plan with emphasis on the first year of the plan. Interdependencies, particularly when EDP matters are concerned, are settled; and the plan is sent to the audit committee. The planning and research group is responsible for monitoring and coordinating the planning process which takes about four months.

Figure 3.I.2
Company I: Audit Objectives

System Objectives

1. Review and evaluation of systems and controls, both manual and EDP, that authorize, identify, process, classify, and report financial information.

2. Review of controls established to ensure compliance with important policies, laws, regulations, etc.

3. Review of controls established for safeguarding assets.

4. Substantiation and evaluation of assets and transactions, including testing of account balances.

Operational Objectives

5. Appraisal of programs and systems (control processes) used to assess the economy and the efficiency with which resources are employed in operations.

6. Review of operations or programs to determine whether results are consistent with established plans, objectives, and goals.

Special Objectives

7. This includes special requests from management, gathering information for filing claims, investigating fraud, and meeting statutory requirements.

3.3 Personnel Management, Coordination, and Development

Several means are used for managing personnel: two evaluation systems, a formal training program, and a detailed time-keeping system. The department practices a skill-evaluation program which provides feedback and guidance to audit personnel. An evaluation form is completed after every audit exceeding 80 hours. These forms are tabulated and serve as the basis for the annual company-wide performance-progress review.

A formal training program is in force. It aims at developing specific audit skills and more general business skills (emphasized in roughly equal proportions). Staff training includes formal courses, on-the-job training, and self-study professional development.

The department's policy manual contains a suggested program of courses and seminars for each level of audit staff, falling into three main sections: audit skills, supervisory/management-communication skills, and specialized skills. Within each section, specific courses and/or seminars are itemized and listed as being either required or recommended.

A project-control system is used to keep track of personnel activity and audit status. Biweekly time sheets are part of the company-payroll system. A generalized software package (i.e., DYL 280) is used to extract departmental time records. The project-control system (PC70) is used to gather and print biweekly reports, including staff-utilization statistics, time by audit and by audit phase within the audit unit, and audit status. Actual-to-budget comparisons are also included.

Summary

In this chapter, a number of different companies have been reviewed. This review provides an insight into the state of the art in planning and coordinating of internal audit department activities. Such a review provides a basis for ecclectically combining the best aspects of the methods and practices observed into a single, unified approach. This synthesis can then serve as a guide to auditors seeking to establish new, or improve upon current, planning practices to support their activities within their organizations.

Of the departments that were studied, it should be recognized that they were sought out because they professed, or were considered by their peers, to have particularly good planning systems in effect. Consequently, it is likely that the practices described here are better than average and not necessarily representative of actual practices in widespread use. Indeed, as pointed out in chapters 1 and 2, there are reasons to suppose that planning practices can stand a good deal of improvement. It is noteworthy that each department appears to emphasize particular features of planning, but that none of the departments has a uniformly strong comprehensive planning and coordinating system in force.

A Company's internal audit department (IAD) has a professional management orientation and de-emphasizes professional auditing skills. It does, however, have a rather sophisticated audit-portfolio management system for its size. All its planning is done without computer assistance.

B Company's IAD emphasizes professional auditing in a very traditional vein, has a very large computerized inventory of auditable units, but has a very simple basis for evaluating audit-risk-exposure concern. This is not a criticism. Indeed, it may be a strength. It has not been demonstrated that a complex scheme produces better evaluations than a simple one. It has been shown, however, that simple schemes are easier to understand and work with.

C Company's IAD has a management-training orientation similar to A's, but it is 15 times as large as A Company's IAD. A well-developed management-by-objectives approach is used in planning activities and evaluating performance at all levels of the department. The audit-portfolio management scheme is computerized; however, it is falling into disrepair/disuse because of its complexity (i.e., 20 different sets of weights for seven factors). Although the approach has theoretical merit, this alone does not appear to be enough to make the scheme useable.

D Company's IAD bears, for the most part, little similarity to the previous three companies' IADs. It has sufficient personnel to audit each unit each year as well as participate in new developments on a continuing basis. Although each operating unit must be audited within a given period, considerable latitude exists in the context, scope, and approach used in audit projects. More so than the other companies, D's business lends itself to a different (i.e., based on a hierarchical breakdown of the business) approach to identifying auditable units; and this is currently being investigated by it. Long-range planning is actively engaged in, particularly planning aimed at technical improvements. A relatively informal and simple audit-portfolio management system is being used, although a more formal and automated approach is in the final stages of development.

E Company's IAD has by far the most detailed risk-exposure-concern-evaluation approach of any of those reviewed. This degree of detail may be warranted by the strict zero-base-budgeting approach which ties department-size decisions to the audit-portfolio management scheme. In this vein, E's IAD can be viewed as having the most integrated planning and coordinating approach of all of the companies examined, since there is a "flow-through" of decisions made at one level to another. In some of the other companies, staffing levels seemed to be relatively independent of audit intensity and coverage decisions. The staff level sometimes determines the coverage rather than the desired coverage determining its level.

F Company's IAD concentrates on operational auditing, using locations as its basis for identifying audit units. Its personnel-management practices seem well developed; however, its audit-priority management system appears to be overly informal for the size of operations involved. The existing computerized audit-inventory management system could probably be readily extended to include a more formal evaluation of audit priorities. In addition, it is surprising that so little formal long-range planning is carried out by F Company's IAD. Moreover, a recent survey[22] found that about 50 percent of the respondents did not prepare formal long-range plans.

G Company's IAD appears to have the least formalized planning and coordinating system of the companies participating in the study. However, it is attempting to use a top-down identification of audit units. It may be that this approach is particularly useful for financial audit-oriented departments.

H Company's IAD is by far the largest and most decentralized of those studied. Consequently, it requires the additional coordination that a decentralized organizational structure necessitates. This coordination activity is evolving. Relatively little long-range planning is carried out by H's IAD, a conscious decision rather than an omission. An intensive degree of coordination of activities between the IAD and external auditors was observed in contrast with some of the other departments studied. Although relatively detailed evaluations of risk-exposure concern are performed, they have only recently been automated.

I Company's IAD has attempted to implement a comprehensive four-tier-planning system built around six definitions of audit units and seven sets of audit objectives. Although guidelines exist for enhancing the risk-evaluation process, the department has resisted formalizing them further.

Footnotes:

[15] A number of big eight accounting firms serve as external auditors. Arthur Young; Coopers and Lybrand; Deloitte Haskins & Sells; Ernst & Whinney; and Peat, Marwick, Mitchell are among them. Touche Ross, Arthur Andersen, and Price Waterhouse clients are not represented.

[16] The Conference Board's survey covered 284 companies: 40 percent with sales exceeding $1 billion, 18 percent with sales in the $500-999 million range, and 40 percent in the $100-500 million range.

[17] The *Survey of Internal Auditing: 1979* contained responses from 497 companies (452 from the United States and Canada, used hereafter as the basis for reported findings). The average sales volume of responding companies was $2.1 billion on average assets of $1.7 billion. They averaged about 16,000 employees, 17 internal auditors (about one per 1,000 employees), and three clerical staff members.

[18] The sizes of the internal audit departments surveyed ranged as follows:

		Conference Board	1978 Survey	IIA's 1979 Survey	Average Dept. Size**
Small	1- 3	18%	18%	23%	3
Medium	4- 6	20%			
	7-10	17%	37%	36%*	7
Large	11-20	17%			
	21-50	17%			
	51 +	6%	40%	41%	40
Overall					20

* IIA's reports figures for four to nine in contrast with The Conference Board's category of four to ten.

**Including clerical support.

[19] See footnote two above.

[20] The *Survey of Internal Auditing: 1979* indicates that only 12 percent of respondent companies have fixed terms of duty for internal auditors. Of those that do, 50 percent have normal terms of ser-

vice of between two to three years, 22 percent have terms of three to five years, and 24 percent have terms of one to two years.

[21]The *Statement of Principles and Standards for Internal Auditing in the Banking Industry* published by the Bank Administration Institute in 1977 emphasizes that "internal auditing is that management function which independently evaluates the adequacy, effectiveness, and efficiency of the systems of control within an organization and the quality of ongoing operations." (See page 6.)

[22]The Tulsa Chapter's survey found that only 56 percent of the Fortune 500 companies surveyed used long-range plans. The local chapter had an even lower percentage reported: 39 percent. The findings indicated that IADs in larger companies generally made more frequent use of long-range plans than their counterparts in smaller companies.

4

Developing
Comprehensive Plans

This chapter provides the reader with an overview of a methodology that might be used in developing a comprehensive set of integrated departmental plans. Based on this section, the next chapter provides more detailed specifications pertaining to the approach suggested here for developing plans. This chapter draws upon the case studies discussed, writings discussed in Chapter 2 and others to be discussed here, the *Standards* , and the researcher's personal experience in developing and assisting in developing comprehensive departmental planning and coordinating systems.

According to Albrecht, the most important aspect of a plan is a clear statement of what results are being planned, how these results will be achieved, the quality and quantity of resources needed to execute the plan, and their manner of deployment.

Once a commitment to a written plan is made, the department must live by it; therefore, the plan constrains the department's behavior. It governs what audits are to be carried out, what resources in terms of personnel are to be committed, and how they are to be used. It also governs the sequence of activities by a series of schedules and prescriptions. Although few plans are so rigid that they cannot be modified, once a plan is made, it becomes a precedent which is and should be difficult to overcome (Blumenthal, 1969). Consequently, planning activities should be undertaken with care. Moreover, performance evaluations should be made at least on the basis of adherence to plans; otherwise, the planning process and its results (the plans) could hardly remain credible for very long.

In this chapter, the planning framework outlined in Chapter 2 is subdivided into six main components (and several subcomponents) linked in a step-by-step outline of a proposed comprehensive planning approach (see Figure 4.0.1) as follows:

1.0 The Role, Responsibility, and Approach of the Internal Audit Department
1.1 Management's Expectations
1.2 Professional Standards
1.3 Coordination with External Auditors and other Interested Parties
1.4 The Internal Audit Charter
1.5 Long-Range Plans and Policies to Govern Departmental Activities
2.0 Facilities and Procedures Management
2.1 The Audit Framework
2.2 Criteria for Determining Audit Scope and Priorities
2.3 Cyclic Audit Coverage
3.0 Audit-Portfolio Management
3.1 Inventory of Auditable Units
3.2 Risk-Exposure-Concern Evaluation
3.3 Priority Ranking
4.0 Personnel-Skill Management and Development
4.1 Plan of Organization, Supervision, and Evaluation
4.2 Audit-Time Requirements
4.3 Audit-Staff Requirements
4.4 Training and Development
5.0 Planning and Budgeting
5.1 Preparing the Ideal Long-Range Audit-Coverage Plan
5.2 Budgeting and Resource Allocation
5.3 Preparing the Annual Work Plan
6.0 Work Scheduling and Performance Monitoring
6.1 Work Assignment
6.2 Work Scheduling
6.3 Work Monitoring
6.4 Performance Evaluation

A brief overview of these phases is presented below and should be read in conjunction with Figure 4.0.1.

Phase 1. Management's goals, professional standards, and other requirements such as coordination with external auditors should govern the definition of the role, responsibility, and audit approach of the internal audit department. A clear statement of these should be documented and codified in the department's charter or mandate. Long-range planning should help guide the change and evolution of this statement as these become warranted.

Phase 2. The charter should guide departmental policies in

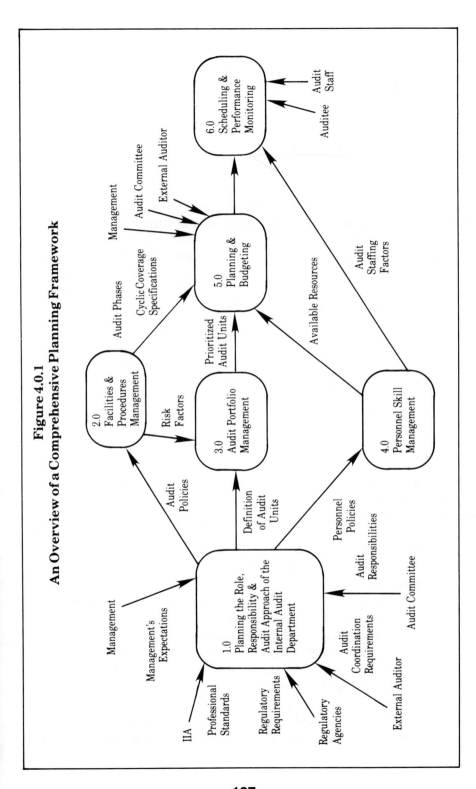

Figure 4.0.1
An Overview of a Comprehensive Planning Framework

137

the areas of defining a suitable audit framework, appropriate criteria for determining audit scope and audit priorities, a useful and appropriate definition of what is an auditable unit, and policies in the areas of personnel management (i.e., organization, supervision and evaluation, staffing, and training and development).

Phase 3. The audit-portfolio management procedures should be fully congruent with the departmental policies established to govern them. The term "audit-portfolio management" is used to emphasize the fact that the internal auditor fulfills a role analogous to that of the stock-portfolio manager, who evaluates stocks on the basis of their perceived risk-reward attributes, matches them to the risk-reward attributes of his/her clients, and collects them in a portfolio to hold. Likewise, the internal auditor must attempt to balance the risks associated with the portfolio of auditable units of the organization so as to be consistent with management's desired level of risk. Conceptually, this is straightforward. Practically, it is an extremely difficult challenge for any internal audit department. Auditable activities reflecting the audit framework and definitions of auditable units should be identified, inventoried, and controlled. Periodically, these inventories should be reassessed and ranked by their audit priority according to the most recent information available.

Phase 4. Personnel must be managed in accordance with the policies established. The overriding goal is to ensure an adequate supply of professional "resources" with the appropriate mix of skills to permit fulfillment of audit responsibilities with relatively little compromise.

Presumably, audit personnel are hired to help fulfill the department's role in achieving the audit goals of the organization. Audits are not assigned merely to keep audit personnel busy. Consequently, active pursuit of appropriate skills commensurate with the audit activities of the department is an important aspect of departmental planning and coordinating activities. This would include a program of internal training and long-term development as well as recruiting activities within an appropriate organizational setting and effective measures for performance review and evaluation.

Phase 5. Given an appropriate identification of audit tasks and the personnel skills available, planning and budgeting can be carried out in a relatively straightforward manner. Ultimately, the goal of this phase is to arrive at an appropriate work plan for the year.

Phase 6. Assigning and scheduling audits go together. The goal is to match skills to specific audits at appropriately scheduled times so as to best utilize the available resources of the department. A timekeeping or time-estimating system should be used to gather information about audit-time relationships, thereby facilitating the preparation of a reasonable cyclic audit-coverage plan with reasonable annual work-plan components as well as to permit work monitoring and performance evaluation.

This view of comprehensive planning is consistent with the *Standards.* Section 520 requires that the director of internal audit establish plans to carry out the responsibilities of the internal audit department and that these plans be consistent with the department's charter and with the goals of the organization.

Interestingly, the *Standards* does not seem to view the department's charter as representing an outcome of a planning process; hence, a plan of the department's role, purpose, authority, and responsibility. At any rate, it suggests that the planning process should include the establishment of goals, audit-work schedules, staffing plans, financial budgets, and activity reports (sections 520.02 to 520.06). As will be seen subsequently, the view of planning expressed herein is rather comprehensive and encompasses the view expressed by the *Standards* as well as other relevant aspects of departmental planning.

1.0 The Role, Responsibility, and Approach of the Internal Audit Department

1.1 Management's Expectations
What are management's expectations of internal audit? The answer is not clear. Some companies report significant top-management involvement in directing the activities of the internal audit department. On the other hand, substantial budgetary allocations are made to many internal auditing departments.

Management often chooses to highlight internal audit activities in the annual report to shareholders. On the other hand, criticisms are often levelled at the expertise of the internal audit department, particularly in technically involved operational auditing and EDP auditing areas. In some organizations, the internal audit department is a highly placed function. In others, the department is viewed primarily as a means of controlling another "necessary evil" — external audit costs— or satisfying outside agencies such as the SEC, state regulatory agencies, and so on.

Increasingly, the relationships among internal audit, management, and the board of directors are changing. Internal audit is receiving the attention of top management. It will be argued here that such increased attention should be channeled more specifically than appears to have been hitherto done.

It is pointless to involve management in most audit-planning decisions; however, there are several areas in which top-management involvement is either unavoidable or absolutely essential. Management's participation in the budgeting process is unavoidable; consequently, the emphasis here should be to demonstrate to management what the planned budget allocation to the internal audit department can achieve in terms of audit coverage.

Management's participation in directing the activities of the internal audit department has been downplayed. This is understandable. After all, there are many important groups within organizations competing for management's attention. Nonetheless, periodic involvement by top management in helping to set guidelines for the deployment of departmental resources is desirable. In particular, management should be involved in establishing the explicit criteria which will determine the audit coverage to be provided. Without such involvement, the priority decisions used to plan audit coverage may be out of step with corporate-wide goals and expectations.

A 1978 Conference Board study (Macchiaverna, 1978, p. 7) reported:

> Virtually all of the senior corporate executives interviewed maintained that internal auditing's most important activity is providing management with an independent check on the adequacy and effectiveness of corporate control systems. Many derive comfort from knowing that internal auditing will discover weaknesses in controls or inadequate policies and procedures and bring them to management's attention before they cause serious problems.

For a variety of reasons, it is not always the case that management's most important concerns and goals are recognized by internal audit. Internal audit priorities may not be understood by management or may simply not reflect management's well-considered requirements because of miscommunication, lack of explicit statements, and so on.

A biennial exercise, in which top management participates, for establishing and/or reevaluating criteria for determining audit priorities for audit-planning decisions will be most useful. The time demands of this exercise are modest, and at least three techniques are available to permit its implementation: strategy-set transformation, Delphi, and analytical hierarchy process. These are discussed in Chapter 6. The important consequence of engaging in such an exercise is the improved integration of internal audit-planning decisions into the overall corporate-wide scheme of things.

1.2 Professional Standards

Internal audit professionals share with other employed professionals, such as legal counsellors, accountants, and psychologists, certain problems (or opportunities, depending upon one's view of the situation). As an employee group, it is dependent upon and constrained by management; however, it also has the benefit of the guidance and training provided by its professional governance bodies as well as obligations to abide by professional standards and code of ethics. Sometimes, such dual responsibilities may lead to tensions; but by and large, they are easily resolved.

In the planning area, professional standards impose responsibilities upon internal auditors which may not be fully appreciated by management unless care is taken to involve management in the planning process. Professional standards for planning were discussed in chapters 1 and 2. The planning approach discussed here is fully consistent with the *Standards* and elaborates upon them in certain key areas.

1.3 Coordination with External Auditors

As emphasized by Mautz *et alii*, few units of a company have relationships with outside groups as the relationship between internal and external auditors. In more than 85 percent of the companies studied in this extensive 1980 study titled *Internal Control in U.S. Corporations*, internal audit provides some or all of the following types of assistance to external auditors:

- Complete responsibility for auditing one or more parts of the organization (e.g., manufacturing plants, EDP).
- Complete responsibility for auditing one or more accounts or

types of transactions (e.g., transaction tests, inventory audits).
- General assistance (e.g., clerical help, accounts receivable circularization).

A major consideration in the extensive involvement of internal auditors with external auditors is the reduction of external audit fees. Aside from this concern, there are many areas of mutual interest and opportunities for cooperation. These can be best explored through joint long-term planning and coordinating.[23] But this may require a rethinking by external auditors of their approach, since they rarely plan over the same time horizon as internal auditors, who typically plan two to five years ahead.

A 1980 study by Barrett and Brink made essentially the same points and emphasized the need for improved coordination through joint planning. Clearly, achieving a partnership arrangement in terms of work sharing between internal and external auditors requires coordination of the long-range-planning effort and possibly even involvement of the audit committee.

1.4 The Internal Audit Charter

The basis for departmental planning activities is found in the internal audit department's charter which should outline the present responsibilities and authority of the internal audit function.[24] (See Appendix F and IIA's recent monograph *Developing a Charter for an Internal Audit Function.*) It should also set out the auditing standards considered appropriate for discharging these responsibilities together with rules of professional conduct for the internal audit staff such as:
- A statement of responsibilities of the internal audit department.
- A statement of authority and reporting responsibilities of the internal audit department.
- A statement of the internal audit department's policy regarding work-plan coordination with external auditors.
- Rules of professional conduct.
- Auditing standards governing the conduct of audit work.

1.5 Long-Range Plans and Policies to Govern Departmental Activities

Long-range plans for an internal audit department should consider long-term work policies, long-term (interperiod) work-balancing plans, and long-term resource-development plans.

Work Policies. Together with the character-setting policies contained in the charter of the department, work policies are explicit guidelines used to define the audit-planning process. These policies can, in fact, be viewed as the implementation of the approach contemplated in the departmental charter; hence, they should be consistent with it. Specific policies are required in five key areas:

- Risk-type definitions.
- Specification of audit approach.
- Audit-cycling approach.
- Definition of audit-unit categories and audit units within categories.
- Personnel management and development policy as it will affect specific work assignments.

Interperiod Work Balancing. No department can increase or decrease its staff on short notice or at will. Regardless of the evaluations of audit-unit importance, pragmatic decisions must be made in terms of providing a balanced and stable workload for the departmental staff over a period of two to five years.

Resource Development. The personnel resources of an internal audit department are fluid in the sense that staff members progress in terms of their professional growth and experience. On one hand, this is desirable. On the other hand, it requires a comprehension by the department management of the fluidity of the staff and appropriate planning at both ends of the "escalator." Empty slots are constantly being created, and others are constantly being filled. Appropriate planning and coordinating are required to ensure that this movement takes place orderly.

2.0 Facilities and Procedures Management

2.1 The Audit Framework

Consistent with the charter, an audit framework should be developed for planning and performing audits in a comprehensive manner that will integrate the audit of manual financial or operating procedures whenever carried out with the computer systems that support them. The purpose of this audit framework is to prevent severe audit shortcomings potentially resulting from the failure to coordinate manual and EDP audits and to subdivide all audits into the same phases for purposes of further planning. The audit framework should consist of a number of organized phases covering the following activities:

- Planning.
- Documentation of the important activities performed by each auditable unit, including relevant aspects of procedures carried out at centralized computer facilities.
- Review and evaluation of controls and operating procedures, including relevant general and application controls in the EDP area.
- Verification of compliance (i.e., adherence to prescribed policies).
- Substantiation (i.e., verification of transactions and balances) or, in the case of operational audits, detailed tests of operations.
- Report of findings.

The interrelationship of these phases is discussed briefly below.

Planning. Proper planning ensures that audit efforts are directed at relevant aspects of the organization's activities, commensurate with their importance.

The planning phase includes basic preaudit planning to determine which accounting procedures, functional activities, and computer systems should be subjected to audit; the audit phases to be covered during the audit; and the order in which these phases should be executed and to what degree of intensity.

Additional planning may involve developing or revising periodically specific audit programs for each area to be reviewed. Each audit program should state precisely the objectives of the audit; the specific audit techniques (e.g., computer-assisted audit techniques, statistical sampling, questionnaires, and tabular schedules) that should be used to achieve the objectives; timing and staffing the audit; the required degree of audit coverage; and the budgeted time to complete the audit.

Effective coordination between the activities of internal auditors and those of the auditees and other parties (e.g., external auditors) requires regular planning meetings between the parties. Coordination should cover such matters as the nature and the extent of audit work to perform as well as methods and procedures, timing, resolution of audit findings, and follow-up arrangements.

Documentation. Audit documentation is the process of determining and recording in an organized manner the practices and procedures within a particular activity as well as the audit procedure executed. In contrast with recording corporate policies and procedures or general systems documentation, audit documentation usually focuses only on those aspects that have control or audit implications. During the documentation phase of an audit, techniques such as flowcharts, internal control questionnaires, and narratives could be used to cover both manual and computer operations.

Audit documentation provides the means for recording the behavior of the processes within an activity. It also provides audit supervisors with a basis for evaluating the decisions and the conclusions of the audit staff and the resulting reports to management. Initial audit documentation of an activity may require a considerable investment of time and effort. In subsequent audits, documentation efforts may be reduced unless extensive system changes take place.

Review and Evaluation. Review and evaluation of a particular business activity provide the means by which auditors determine the existence and adequacy of internal control and other procedures. Assessments of identified control strengths and/or weaknesses are then used to determine the degree of additional audit effort required.

Verification of Compliance. The evaluation of controls identifies the strengths and/or potential weaknesses in a given area. Before drawing conclusions about the adequacy of internal controls, auditors must verify that the identified controls have functioned as prescribed on a continuous and regular basis. Any identified control weaknesses require further investigation to determine whether in fact errors or irregularities did occur. In this phase of the work, every important control or operating procedure on which management places reliance should be tested to ensure that it has functioned in a continuous and effective manner. Testing can be performed on a judgmental or statistical basis but should be extensive enough to provide adequate assurance regarding the operational quality of the procedure.

All findings require proper documentation. Deviations from policies should be examined to determine their frequency and cause. Conclusions should be based on the results of the tests performed. Whenever possible, findings should be stated in quantitative terms.

Substantiation and Tests of Operations. Even if a system of internal control appeared to be effective and reliable, there would still be inherent limitations precluding absolute assurance that the financial records accurately represent the facts at a particular point in time. Such limitations include:

● Management's usual requirement that a control be cost-effective.

● Most controls tend to be directed at regularly recurring types of transactions and not at unusual transactions.

● Human error.

● Varying efficiency with volume of transactions and staff changes.

● Collusion to circumvent controls which are dependent upon segregation of duties.

● Abuse of authority by employees responsible for exercising control.

These considerations are particularly important in areas involving liquid assets. In a financial audit, tests are designed to corroborate the information in the financial records by means such as (1) examining third-party documentary evidence (e.g., vouching of payments against suppliers' invoices), (2) mailing account-verification notices to customers and suppliers, and (3) observing the physical existence of assets by counting cash, securities, and inventories.

In an operational audit, tests are designed to permit specific conclusions to be drawn about the quality of the activity or operation being audited by means such as (1) detailed scrutiny of classes of transactions pertaining to the activities of interest and (2) analyses to permit evaluations of the activities from the standpoint of efficiency and effectiveness.

Reporting. The objective of reporting is to communicate the audit results to the appropriate levels of management. The content of a report must be rationally related to the extent of audit work performed and the quality of audit evidence examined. Internal audit reports might be directed to:

● Top management whenever audit findings indicate a need for immediate corporate action (e.g., when changes are required to strengthen weak procedures or when widespread failure to follow corporate policy creates a serious control weakness).

● Appropriate line management for corrective action (e.g., when weaknesses or deviations are isolated to a particular function).

Reporting may take several formats:

Discussion Notes

After completing an audit or a major phase of a large audit, auditors might report informally to the appropriate line manager with a summary of findings, recording these in discussion notes and discussing them. This approach provides auditors and line managers with the opportunity to voice their opinions and to reach common conclusions.

Audit Reports

As with discussion notes, formal audit reports are normally issued at the completion of an audit or a major phase of it. They tell recipients about the scope of the audit (e.g., what was covered and to what extent), an opinion based on the results of the audit (both positive and negative findings), and a summary of suggestions or recommendations when applicable.

Report Follow-up

In all instances when internal auditors have reported findings or recommended improvements, a timely follow-up is essential to ensure that appropriate action has been or will be taken.

Departmental Activity Reports

Periodically, status reports summarizing the internal audit department's activities should be prepared and issued to management. These reports should cover the objectives of departmental audit work carried out during the period, the extent of audit coverage, and a summary of positive and negative findings.

An appropriate definition of auditing phases has important consequences for estimating audit-time requirements and for planning audits over a long-range time horizon. Briefly, it is suggested that audit *phases*, rather than audits, are the appropriate basis for estimating time requirements in many circumstances. In addition, audit *phases*, rather than audits, are the appropriate basis for scheduling audit coverage on a cyclic basis. Although the phases discussed above may not be universally aplicable, they are well known and useful for illustrating the planning concepts presented here.

2.2 Criteria for Determining Audit Scope and Priorities

Although the generally accepted view of internal auditing defines it as a control device which functions by measuring and evaluating the effectiveness of other controls, it has been suggested that, in addition to this retrospective function, internal auditing can also have prospective effects; that is, internal auditing can act as a motivator by encouraging better design and implementation of control procedures and better adherence to prescribed policies and procedures by auditee personnel. It also deters actions leading to poor practices, irregularities, and fraud.

Indeed, it has been suggested that the anticipation of being audited is often more powerful than the actual audit itself and that less auditing is necessary than is conventionally practiced so long as audits are performed periodically and are effective when carried out. Audits may be viewed as a means of deterring compliance deviations and evaluating and correcting control flaws and failures once their deterioration is discovered.

Preventive Effects. Churchill emphasized the preventive aspect of audits. He argued that, since anticipatory actions occur before auditors arrive, there may be no perceptible effect of their visits (i.e., auditors might not be able to observe or report these effects). Nonetheless, the preventive effects of auditing may be more significant than any of the actual findings of the audit or the recommendations that auditors make.

Detective-Corrective Effects. Barefield discusses the corrective impact of audits and describes two components of that impact. First, during the conduct of the audit, the auditor may uncover errors due to improperly performed tasks and may inform the auditee that he/she must correct the errors that resulted. Second, the audit report may cause the auditee to change the way in which certain tasks are carried out, either voluntarily or by directives of superiors.

Barefield suggests that the ultimate objective of a theory of internal auditing is an explanation of the impact of different audit plans on the quality of internal control. He defines an audit plan as a specification of audit frequency, audit extensiveness, and audit timing for each auditable unit within an organization. This corresponds to only one level of the planning hierarchy previously identified – the audit-coverage plan:

• Audit frequency is defined as the number of audits performed during some specified time period.

• Audit extensiveness is the amount of audit effort expended during a given audit.

• Audit timing is the point(s) during the specified planning period at which an audit is performed.

This view is used in establishing a relationship between the internal audit-planning activities that are visible to the auditee and auditee's behavior. The effects of other departmental planning activities upon the audit department's relationship with top management and other audit-planning activities internal to the audit function, not visible to the auditee, are not considered.

Barefield's premise is that alternative audit plans or schedules of audit frequency, extensiveness (i.e., intensity), and timing have important implications for the auditee's behavior and influence the quality of internal control.

2.2.1 Conditional Investigation by Auditors

In conventional approaches for planning what, when, and how much to audit, it is assumed that all auditable units will be audited at least so often during some period. However, a less conventional approach, conditional investigation, makes these aspects of auditing subject to formal decisions based on predicted consequences of carrying out or not carrying out a given audit. There are three main policy alternatives available for such decisions:

Random-Audit Frequency. On the assumption that the deterrent-preventive aspects of audits are generally more important than specific audits, this policy aims at being unpredictable. Auditees cannot guess when and to what extent they will be audited and are motivated to maintain their procedures at reasonable levels. However, to maintain their expectations of being audited, some audits must be carried out each period and must be effective (i.e., find errors and flaws) so as to maintain their deterrent effect. In addition, sufficient penalties and rewards, hinging upon the outcome of the audit, must exist to provide adequate incentives to auditees. There are many reasons why such a policy might be rejected. First, it is based upon a relatively narrow view of auditee motivation. Second, it does not highlight the important service role of audits and auditors aimed at improving control practices. Third, such a policy is very difficult to justify to management.

Fixed Audit Frequency. A fixed frequency policy is based on the implicit assumption that there are natural frequencies associated with audit units. The problem is to find the "right" fixed frequency for each audit unit. This approach is followed by many internal audit departments, although frequencies may be adjusted periodicallly (i.e., if unusual events so require, a prespecified frequency might be ignored).

149

Conditional Audit Frequency. Under a conditional audit approach, all auditable units (either financial or operating entities) might be monitored continuously for signs of abnormal activity. Audits are only scheduled when units exhibit evidence of impaired controls. The reasoning behind this approach may be that each auditable unit represents an economic activity of interest or that controls exist to help optimize the functioning of the economic activities by maximizing profit or minimizing costs due to fraud, errors, or inefficiencies. Thus, the quality of the economic activity depends to some degree (not necessarily entirely) upon the continuous functioning of controls.

Continuous functioning of controls can be interpreted as continuous compliance with control procedures. When compliance deteriorates, this affects the quality of the economic activity. Thus, abnormal economic activity may be an indicator of control failure. By monitoring various indicators of economic activity, the internal auditor might be alerted to control problems.

Compliance with controls is assumed to deteriorate naturally over time unless appropriate action is taken at some appropriate point in time to restore compliance to its proper level. There are many intervening factors which affect the rate of deterioration. Audits are viewed as being instrumental in helping to restore compliance to its proper level. The extent of this restorative effect will depend on a variety of factors including the auditor's skill and the characteristics of the auditable unit.

Although there are costs associated with the deterioration of economic activity, there are also costs associated with auditing such as those of evaluating controls and correcting flaws and failures. In addition, there is a cost associated with the continuous monitoring of auditable units. The auditor's role may be defined as minimizing the total expected costs with respect to the intensity of effort and length of time between successive audits of each auditable unit (i.e., to audit as little and as infrequently as possible but often enough to minimize the deleterious economic effects upon the corporation due to significant deterioriation of controls).

Mathematical models and techniques exist for carrying out the computations necessary for appropriately balancing these considerations; however, their application to realistic internal audit situations has not been demonstrated except in extremely simplified settings (see Hughes, 1974 and 1977).

In order to monitor the functioning of controls in auditable units, auditable units must be appropriately defined and inventoried; and an appropriate set of indicators must be developed to permit auditors to recognize a significant deterioration in activities and controls within them. This monitoring process is conceptualy similar to analytical review procedures applied on a frequent basis.

One of the problems in monitoring the indicators is that they tend to naturally fluctuate from period to period. These fluctuations may or may not represent actual deterioration of controls. In some instances, they may reflect the effects of temporary events and other "normal" operating circumstances rather than long-term control failures. Since auditors cannot know for certain whether the fluctuation is a temporary aberration or an indicator of actual deterioration of controls requiring an audit without actually performing an audit and incurring the cost of that audit, they must play a "guessing game."

A number of techniques have been proposed to help make this guessing game more scientific.[25] Although the suggestions have concentrated on mechanistic, economic processes atypical of many activities taking place in commonly audited processes, they do provide insight into a more rigorous methodology for scheduling audits than has hitherto been used by the internal auditing profession. Chapter 6 contains additional discussion of these techniques.

2.2.2 Criteria for Evaluating Risk-Exposure Concern

Wilson and Ranson provide a discussion along the lines of that above. They describe a mathematical model for setting audit frequency so that the subjective judgments commonly exercised in this regard may be substantially formalized. They identify four variables – size, risk, management quality, and cost of auditing – which may be used to construct a scale against which to measure the relative urgency of auditing specific units.

Size. Wilson and Ranson assume that the bigger the audit unit in terms of "dollar throughput" (i.e., the amount of the company's resources over which the audit unit exercises some control), the greater the potential losses owing to poor control.

Risk. The more risky the operation, the greater the *expected* losses, a function of the potential losses and the probability of things going wrong. Wilson and Ranson's method of risk assessment will be discussed later along with methods of risk assessment proposed by others.

Management Quality. Immediately after an audit, expected losses should drop. Typically, it is assumed that they drop to zero and then begin to rise back to their "normal" level (see Figure 4.2.1). The speed of their return to their old level (as represented by the steepness of the pattern of expected losses over time and the frequency assigned to an audit) depends upon the quality of management. This parameter must be estimated to permit the pattern of expected losses to be anticipated and for the mathematical model to be constructed.

Cost of Auditing. The final ingredient in the model is the cost of carrying out the audit. The two heaviest costs would likely be personnel time and travel expenses. The key step in implementing this approach involves developing criteria to determine the exposure risks for each auditable unit. The purpose of this procedure is to assist in establishing priorities for the frequency and extent of auditing. Choosing risk factors or other indicators reflecting audit concern is not a trivial task. There are many candidates, as was evident in the case studies previously discussed. Whatever the criteria selected, a uniform table of exposure considerations should be developed to measure the potential risks for each auditable unit or process so that they may be compared and ranked in order of desirable audit priority. This exercise should take into consideration at least those risks which relate to:

● The intrinsic qualities of the auditable unit (e.g., cash on hand will have a high exposure risk from the point of view of theft; and the billing process, if not properly controlled, could be a source of significant lost revenue).

● The probability that the system of internal control may fail to prevent or detect errors or irregularities.

● The probability that the audit tests may fail to detect weaknesses or problems.

Section 520.04 of the *Standards* suggests that the criteria used for setting priorities should include the date and results of the last audit; financial exposure; potential loss and risk; requests by management; major changes in operations, programs, systems, and controls; opportunities to achieve operating benefits; and changes and capabilities of audit staff. However, a larger subset of criteria might be drawn from the list provided by Patton *et alii* included here as figures 4.2.2 and 4.2.3 from the case study materials in Chapter 3 or from some of the articles cited here.

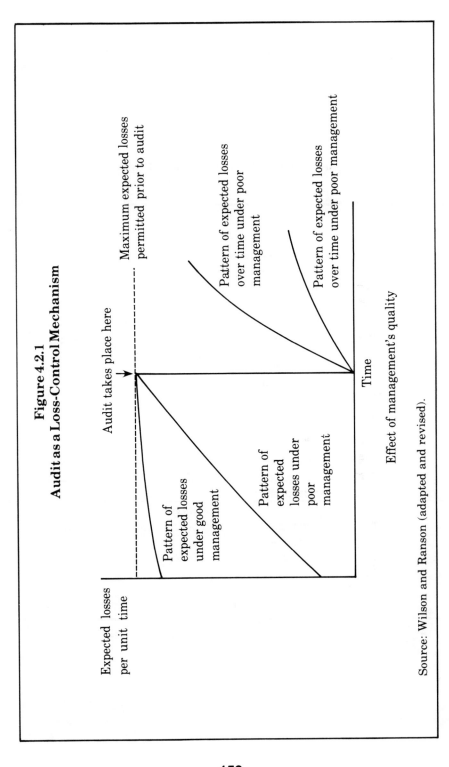

Figure 4.2.1
Audit as a Loss-Control Mechanism

Source: Wilson and Ranson (adapted and revised).

Figure 4.2.2
Most Commonly Cited Risk-Exposure-Concern Factors

Factor Ranking	Factor
1.	Quality of internal control system
2.	Competence of management
3.	Integrity of management
4.	Size of unit (revenues, assets)
5.	Recent change in accounting system
6.	Complexity of operations
7.	Recent change in key personnel
8.	Liquidity of assets
9.	Deteriorating economic condition of unit
10.	Rapid growth
11.	Extent of computerized data processing
12.	Time since last audit
13.	Pressure on management to meet objectives
14.	Extent of governmental regulation
15.	Level of employee morale
16.	Audit plans of independent auditors
17.	Political exposure and adverse publicity
18.	Need to maintain independence of internal audit department
19.	Distance from main office

Source: Patton group.

Figure 4.2.3
Analysis of Ten Most-Cited Risk Factors by Industry

Factor Ranking	Banking and Insurance	Manufacturing	Other
1.	Quality of internal control	Quality of internal control	Quality of internal control
2.	Competence of management	Competence of management	Competence of management
3.	Integrity of management	Integrity of management	Integrity of management
4.	Recent change in accounting system	Size of unit	Recent change in accounting system
5.	Size of unit	Deteriorating economic position	Complexity of operations
6.	Liquidity of assets	Complexity of operations	Liquidity of assets
7.	Change in key personnel	Change in key personnel	Size of unit
8.	Complexity of operations	Recent change in accounting system	Deteriorating economic position
9.	Rapid growth	Rapid growth	Change in key personnel
10.	Governmental regulation	Pressure on management to meet objectives	Rapid growth

Source: Patton group.

2.3 Cyclic Audit Coverage

Most internal audit departments cannot audit every important audit unit every year. Consequently, some rational basis for determining periodicity of audits for each audit unit is required. As pointed out above, several alternatives are available such as random cycles, fixed cycles based on mathematical models, and cycles based on judgment with or without decision aids. The optimal audit frequency should balance the expected losses if an audit does not take place against the cost of performing the audit.

Figure 4.2.4 is a graphical example of the concept of optimally balancing the risk of not auditing and audit-related costs under three different qualities of management. For example, for category B, the optimal audit frequency under average management is about every two years. Under poor management, the frequency increases to about every 1.3 years, whereas under good management, the frequency decreases to once every four years. Refer to Wilson and Ranson for additional discussion of their approach.

3.0 Audit-Portfolio Management

3.1 Inventory of Auditable Units

An inventory of all significant auditable units should be compiled. For each main category of audit activity being considered (e.g., operational audits, financial audits, systems-development audits, and security reviews), an appropriate definition of auditable unit is required; and a systematic identification of all such units within each category is essential.

Most writings in this field emphasize the need for systematic identification of auditable units but convey the notion that the definition of auditable units is irrelevant. It is my contention that the definition of what constitutes an auditable unit or process powerfully determines the magnitude of the internal audit department's contribution to the organization. Certain definitions open up new opportunities, whereas others merely encourage maintenance of the status quo. For example, the simple definition of an auditable unit as including its computer systems rather than defining it as two separate audit projects – a manual audit and a computer audit – can enhance the audit process but may also call for a significant upgrading of the audit personnel's skills with all the attendant repercussions.

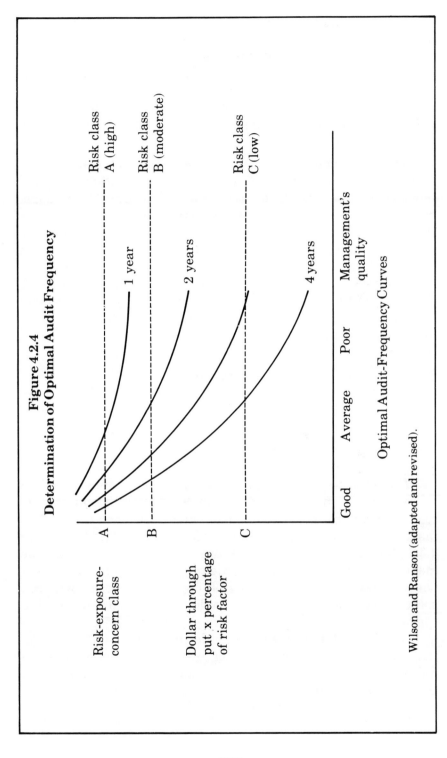

**Figure 4.2.4
Determination of Optimal Audit Frequency**

Risk-exposure-concern class

Dollar through put x percentage of risk factor

Risk class A (high)

Risk class B (moderate)

Risk class C (low)

A

B

C

1 year

2 years

4 years

Good   Average   Poor   Management's quality

Optimal Audit-Frequency Curves

Wilson and Ranson (adapted and revised).

When a company's financial systems are relatively central-ized, an opportunity exists to implement a top-down audit per-spective oriented around the financial information systems rather than around the locations of data entry. In widely diver-sified industries, this will be quite difficult to do unless unifying traits of products or markets permit the identification of a hierar-chical relationship extending from corporate management down to line functions.

This can be done by undertaking analyses of business objec-tives, management processes, organizational relationships, and information systems. Also, interviews with corporate manage-ment can help lend a top-down structure to organizational ac-tivities. Interviews with other organizations may sometimes be useful and may provide insight into the hierarchical structure of one's own organization. The key is to avoid listing an overabun-dance of small, isolated audit projects and to emphasize, instead, the integrating aspects of various units, thus perceiving more clearly the value of an operating activity and the value of an audit of that activity.

3.2 Risk-Exposure-Concern Evaluation

Using the audit framework and the criteria (factors) de-veloped for evaluating auditable units as to their "concern" index, a methodical evaluation must be made and validated. Two approaches for doing this have been proposed: direct assessment and pairwise comparison.

Direct Assessment. Under the direct assessment method for each factor, an evaluation of its importance with a magnitude scale perhaps ranging from 1 percent to 100 percent must be made. This can be done by using the format illustrated in Figure 4.3.1. Next, for each auditable unit, an assessment might be made by using an importance scale ranging from one to ten with one representing the lowest possible degree of concern[26] with re-spect to each factor for that auditable unit and ten representing the highest degree of concern (see Figure 4.3.2). The assessments for each auditable unit will be made through a combination of judgmental and objective data. For example, the quality of inter-nal control may be a subjective assessment, whereas the size of the unit based on unit revenues, expenditures, or assets will rep-resent an objective assessment.

Figure 4.3.1
Evaluating Risk-Exposure-Concern Factors

Factor	Importance 1% to 100%
1.	_____
	1 100
2.	_____
	1 100
3.	_____
	1 100
4.	_____
	1 100
5.	_____
	1 100
Total	

Figurè 4.3.2
Evaluating Risk-Exposure Concern of Audit Units

Audit Units	Factor 1 Weight (W_1)		Factor 2 Weight (W_2)		Factor 3 Weight (W_3)		Factor 4 Weight (W_4)		Factor 5 Weight (W_5)	
	Raw Score (RS_n)	Weighted Score	Raw Score	Weighted Score	Raw Score	Weighted Score	Raw Score	Weighted Score	Raw Score	Weighted Score
1	1 to 10	$RS_1 x W_1$	1 to 10	$RS_1 x W_2$	1 to 10	$RS_1 x W_3$	1 to 10	$RS_1 x W_4$	1 to 10	$RS_1 x W_5$
2	1 to 10	$RS_2 x W_1$	1 to 10	$RS_2 x W_2$	1 to 10	$RS_2 x W_3$	1 to 10	$RS_2 x W_4$	1 to 10	$RS_2 x W_5$
3	1 to 10	$RS_3 x W_1$	1 to 10	$RS_3 x W_2$	1 to 10	$RS_3 x W_3$	1 to 10	$RS_3 x W_4$	1 to 10	$RS_3 x W_5$
4	1 to 10	$RS_4 x W_1$	1 to 10	$RS_4 x W_2$	1 to 10	$RS_4 x W_3$	1 to 10	$RS_4 x W_4$	1 to 10	$RS_4 x W_5$

Pairwise Comparison. The Patton group suggests a rigorous approach for evaluating risk-exposure concern based on a method developed by Saaty : the analytical hierarchy process (discussed in chapter 6). The first step involves gathering information about auditors' attitudes about the importance of various factors. Under this approach, auditors compare all possible pairs of risk-exposure-concern factors – one pair at a time – and assign numbers from one to nine to the more important factor. This number indicates their judgments about the degree of concern attached to one factor relative to the other. When this is carried out for each pair of factors, a set of weights can be derived mathematically from the list of pairwise ratings representing a numerical measure of factor importance for each factor.

Since the importance of a factor depends upon the context which auditors are considering, auditors will have different magnitudes of concern with regard to the same factor when evaluating different auditable units. A second step is, thus, required; it is essentially a repetition of the first step except that, for each risk factor, all pairs of auditable units are compared one pair at a time and that a number from one to nine is assigned to the one with greater risk. When this has been done for all possible pairs of auditable units for one factor, the same process is repeated for another factor, and so on, until all factors have been covered.

This two-step approach can yield a good scale for setting priorities. Unfortunately, it can be applied only in restricted circumstances when relatively few factors and audit units are to be evaluated. Consider, for example, an organization with 500 auditable units wishing to use ten key risk factors for priority ranking. Step one would require 90 comparisons. Step two would require 2,495,000 comparisons requiring more than ten man-years to carry out.[27]

In contrast, the direct-assessment method introduced earlier would, if carried out in two steps, require only 5,010 comparisons[28] (i.e., first rating the ten factors on a scale of 1-100 and then rating each auditable unit on each of the ten factors. This represents one man-week with the same assumptions as earlier, a more modest demand upon planning time.

Direct assessment is the commonly used method, as indicated by the case studies in Chapter 3. The risk is that a poorer scale might result; however, this has not been demonstrated. Prudence suggests the adoption of a less costly method such as scaling discussed in Chapter 6.

It should be pointed out that, as the number of auditable units decreases, the pairwise method becomes increasingly attractive. For example, for a department with 150 auditable units, it would take about six man-weeks to accomplish an evaluation. Although this is still costly, it is an exponential reduction in cost far greater than the reduction in number of audit units.

The pairwise-comparison method is usefully applied when audit units fall into natural categories such as ten divisions. In this case, both methods could be used. Pairwise comparison could be used to assess the audit importance of the divisions, and direct assessment could be used to evaluate the audit importance of specific audit units. If the number of units in a particular category is small, pairwise comparison could also be efficiently applied within the category. Additional discussion of this technique may be found in Chapter 6.

Regardless of the method used, it is important to define clear guidelines for evaluating each factor properly such as that presented in Appendix B. A way of validating the ratings might be to have three senior auditors go through the process independently, correlate their ratings, and identify areas of strong disagreement. These should be discussed and a consensus reached. When no significant differences remain, an average score might be computed to arrive at the final rating.

Wilson and Ranson provide a different method for assessing the risk related to a particular auditable unit. They suggest that each auditable unit's "throughput dollars" be determined and that these be analyzed and classified into "kinds" of dollars processed. Some of the categories they suggest include:

- Administrative expense.
- Value of materials used.
- Capital expenditures planned.
- Liquid assets handled.
- Company funds spent (e.g., taxes, advertising, insurance).
- Transactions posted in the accounts.

To each of these categories, an estimated loss factor is assigned representing a standard percentage of throughput dollars in that category typically considered at risk due to possible mismanagement. Once this is done, each factor is reevaluated on a unit by unit basis for all auditable units to determine whether the loss factor should be increased or decreased, depending upon criteria such as the complexity of the activities of the unit, quality of supervision, stringency of prescribed policies and procedures and their degree of enforcement, visibility of errors made by unit personnel, and potential usefulness of the internal auditor's contribution.

Once a consensus is reached as to the percentages for each category for each unit, the percentage at risk is multiplied by the throughput dollars in the category. The results for all categories are summed, arriving at the risk of loss estimated for the auditable unit. When this is systematically carried out for all auditable units, the resultant risk-of-loss rating represents a relative factor for ranking the auditable units according to the concern magnitudes evoked by them.

3.3 Priority Ranking

Once units are "measured" as to their audit importance, a priority ranking is a relatively straightforward exercise. Simply sort the units in order of decreasing magnitude of the risk-exposure-concern index. Nevertheless, rarely can such a straightforward procedure be applied. A number of considerations can influence the priority rankings:

- At any specific point in time, some lower priority items can be more urgent that some higher priority items.
- Items of varying priorities might be best handled at the same time for either effectiveness or efficiency reasons.
- There may be more items in a specific priority category than resources in terms of audit personnel available.
- There may be personnel-assignment factors which figure prominently in the scheduling of audits despite a given priority ranking.
- Management sometimes encourages periodic audits of low priority areas according to some minimal frequency.

For these and other possible reasons, the simple priority ranking only serves as a starting point rather than the de-facto audit plan. Departures from systematically determined priorities should be explained and documented. These justifications should be defensible and explicit. If a department finds itself departing frequently from its objective-priority setting system, it should reconsider the methods it uses. It may be that, for different definitions of auditable units, different priority-setting schemes are required.

4.0 Personnel-Skill Management and Development

4.1 Plan of Organization, Supervision, and Evaluation

A plan of organization and procedural arrangements must be coordinated to provide effective guiding and monitoring for staff activities and to serve as a basis for evaluating performance and providing feedback. There are two main aspects to such coordinated procedures. First, it is important to elicit and receive feedback from outside a department. Second, it is essential to implement an adequate system of performance review and evaluation on an ongoing basis within the department.

External feedback can play an important role in keeping the department in line organizationally and professionally. A planned program of feedback elicitation must be a multilevel program corresponding to the planning hierarchy. Four levels of external feedback are considered here:

- Top-management reviews of the quality of an audit department's activities are carried out infrequently but comprehensively. This type of review can be carried out by a specially appointed internal task force, a team of external consultants, or by a peer review team (see Anderson, 1982).
- Regular top-management reviews of audit coverage and important findings by the department as well as progress made toward meeting predefined departmental goals and objectives are noted.
- External auditors' comments on work of internal auditors upon which reliance is often placed are evident.
- There is feedback from auditees with regard to value for money of audit services (i.e., when a charge-out system is used and the audit objectives are geared toward cost savings and other improvements in procedures).

To permit these levels of feedback, specific arrangements must be in place to not merely permit but to seek out and require evaluative feedback. For example, a periodic quality-assurance-review policy might be embedded within a department's charter. Periodic (e.g., quarterly) meetings with top management might be formally required. An annual evaluation report from external auditors should be required, summarizing their involvement with the internal audit department and important findings and conclusions with respect to its work which was reviewed. Finally, a charge-out scheme might motivate responses by auditees. Unfortunately, it would likely only elicit a response when a degree of dissatisfaction was present. Thus, this type of arrangement might be bolstered by requiring written comments or replies to all major findings and recommendations contained in audit reports.

An effective system for internal supervision, evaluation, and feedback has four elements associated with it:

● An effective plan of organization with an appropriate set of job descriptions.

● A plan of supervisory work review, evaluation, and feedback.

● Procedural guidelines incorporated in a departmental manual.

● A scheduling/monitoring system to permit close supervision of personnel on an ongoing basis.

The plan of organization must provide room for career advancement, an appropriate assignment of responsibilities, and a limited span of control so that each auditor receives an adequate amount of personal attention, supervision, and feedback.

Two types of organizational plans are popular in internal audit organizations. The "pool" concept permits audit supervisors to draw upon a central pool of auditors as required. The advantages of this approach are that it provides internal auditors with a broad exposure to a variety of audits and also provides supervisors the opportunity to draw upon the specific skills they need without regard to team boundaries. The disadvantages are that auditors may not get enough personal attention over a long-enough period to develop good audit skills and may not obtain the same depth of experience as they might in a team-oriented organization.

The "team" concept requires that a department be subdivided into groups of about seven auditors under the direction of a supervisor and with explicitly defined audit project assignments. Auditors remain on the same team for one to two years, depending upon the organization, and then rotate to another team. They benefit from continuity of contact with their supervisor, their fellow team members, and the auditee.

The team approach is really feasible only for large departments. Small and medium-size departments virtually always use the pool approach. To minimize the disadvantages inherent in the pool concept, some simple compensating arrangements might be made. For example, a detailed evaluation of auditor performance might be required upon completing every audit project (see Figure 3.F.1). A file of such evaluations can provide the continuity that might otherwise be missing under this plan of organization. Close attention to scheduling audit assignments with specific individuals in mind, rather than man-hours, can also contribute to a planned development of professional audit depth in the department.

A well-documented set of procedural guidelines incorporated into a departmental manual is another form of supervision, albeit impersonal in nature. Procedural guidelines can encourage the integration of manual and EDP audit phases into a coherent whole and can provide an auditor with the perspective necessary to understand the relationship between a particular audit and the goals of the internal audit department. To this end, the audit manual should contain the department's charter, rules of professional conduct, standards for carrying out audits and reporting findings, and a description of the internal audit department and its organizational structure. Also, it should include descriptions of the major auditable units and their significance as well as detailed programs and general guidelines for their use.

A monitoring system must be in effect for scheduling, reporting, recording, and summarizing an audit department's activities timely. The availability of such a system, whether manual or computerized, facilitates ongoing planning and scheduling for upcoming activities, review of the status of audits in progress, and the assessment of the degree of success in attaining predefined goals such as comparisons of actual audit time against budgeted time, comparisons of start and completion dates to scheduled dates, proportion of billable time, absenteeism, travel targets, and so on (see Levinston, 1977).

4.2 Audit-Time Requirements

For each audit phase of each audit unit, a time estimate by required skill level should be prepared. When a timekeeping system is maintained, past records might be used. Otherwise, rough guesses will be necessary. Eventually, as time reports are gathered, the data for estimating time requirements should become more precise. In some cases, additional estimates for travel time may be necessary.

Figure 4.4.1 shows a format for estimating time requirements for each auditable unit by audit phase.[29] The subtotals and totals provide a basis for estimating personnel-skill requirements for carrying out planned audits as well as for cyclical scheduling of audit activities. These will be discussed subsequently.

A number of alternative approaches have been suggested. For example, Davidson described a criteria-matrix approach for project selection and time allocation. Under this approach, a project-ranking scheme similar to that previously outlined is described; however, rather than estimating audit-time requirements in advance as a basis for scheduling audits, Davidson's approach allocates all audit time available to individual audit projects in proportion to their combined rating over all the criteria used for ranking priorities. In other words, if the ratings over all groups add up to 100 and if a project's score is 13, it will get 13 percent of the total department's available audit time. Although some aspects of the approach are commendable, it has a number of flaws. The most prominent is the unsupportable assumption that the combined score, reflecting importance of the audit, also reflects the amount of audit time that should be or needs to be spent in a given area.

The Patton group suggests that units with greater potential losses should receive more resources. There is, however, no necessary or demonstrated relationship between the size of the concern index and the audit time required. Indeed, some audit areas with a high concern magnitude might be easily audited with a minimal time requirement. Conversely, some audits with relatively lower payoffs might absorb larger amounts of audit time. There are diminishing returns from additional time allocations to audits beyond some threshold. These make an allocation such as the one proposed by Davidson potentially inefficient.

The Patton group circumvents this problem with a simple adjustment which takes into account the diminishing returns as audits are prolonged. They suggest dividing the combined concern index for each auditable unit by the share of audit resources that it would consume. By repeatedly changing the intensity of the audits and the share of departmental resources consumed by each unit, an auditor can find the optimal allocation of departmental resources to all auditable units.

The difficulty with this approach is that, while it is computa-

Figure 4.4.1
Estimated Audit-Time Requirements by Audit Phase

Auditable Units	Planning & Supervision	Documentation	Review & Evaluation	Compliance Tests	Detailed Tests	Reporting	Total
Audit unit 1	X	X	X	X	X	X	X
Audit unit 2	X	X	X	X	X	X	X
Audit unit 3	X	X	X	X	X	X	X
• • •							
Total (man-hours)	500	1,000	2,500	2,000	3,000	1,000	10,000
Skill level	High	Moderate	Moderate	Low	Low	Moderate	

Time-Requirements Summary

Required skill level: High 500
Moderate 4,500
Low 5,000

Total (man-hours) 10,000

tionally sound, it is not realistic. The approach assumes that all man-hours are identical and readily allocated among different audits. This may not be the case. Specialized training, experience, and professional status differ among individuals. Audit-skill and effort requirements differ among auditable units. Neglecting these important factors can lead to poorly planned audit activities and limits the usefulness of the Patton group's approach, although with appropriate modifications it can be used within subplans.

Morehead and Myers outline a formal method for determining and revising on an ongoing basis the time requirements for each audit. Their method revolves around two charts. The first chart (see Figure 4.4.2) is a table with entries outlining the important determinants of how much time is required for each audit. This chart is used to develop an audit's "complexity" score. The second chart (see Figure 4.4.3) is a linear relationship between scores on the first chart and audit time, empirically developed on the basis of past experience (i.e., data from previous audits). The second chart serves as a basis for estimating the time requirements for each audit as a function of its score on the first chart. Thus, a two step procedure is recommended by them:

• For each audit, fill out chart one and compute each audit's complexity score and estimate the relationship between the complexity score and audit time. This results in chart two.

• For each new audit, look up the estimated audit time (on the vertical axis) that corresponds to its current complexity score (on the horizontal axis).

Morehead and Myers suggest that chart one may help estimate the time requirements for each phase of the audit in addition to its role in estimating total time. For example, they relate the complexity elements in chart one to three audit phases – familiarization, fieldwork, and reporting – although other phase definitions could be used. Each phase receives a time budget in proportion to the sum of the complexity scores computed for its associated complexity elements relative to the total complexity score computed for the audit. Although the particular elements within chart one could be changed as specific circumstances warrant, this approach may be a useful procedure for developing reasonable audit-time estimates. Additional discussion of this approach is provided in Chapter 6.

Audit Title: Audit Unit ABC

Audit Time: 480 hours

Figure 4.4.2
Estimating Complexity Levels of Audits

Complexity Factors	Overall Weight	Guidelines for Estimating Complexity					Estimated Audit Complexity
		Level 1	Level 2	Level 3	Level 4	Level 5	
Percentage of Information availability	20%	20 100%-80%	40 79%-60%	60 59%-40%	80 39%-20%	100 Under 20%	40
Documented Procedures	10%	10	20	30	40	50	20
Prior knowledge	15%	15 Previous exposure/experienced auditor	30	45	60	75 Unfamiliar area/inexperienced auditor	30
Degree of cooperation	10%	10 Excellent	20 Good	30 Average	40 Fair	50 Poor	30
Complexity to understand	15%	15 Simple	30	45	60	75 Complex	45
Number of auditor's interfaces	10%	10 0-5	20 6-10	30 11-15	40 16-20	50 Over 20	30
Report writing and follow-up	15%	15 Compliance-type rec./min. follow-up	30	45	60	75 Mgmt. type rec./considerable follow-up	45
Number of auditee's interfaces	5%	5 Little contact with others	10	15	20	25 Many contacts	20
	100%	100	200	300	400	500	260

Summary: Complexity 260
Time 480

Source: Adapted from Morehead and Myers.

Figure 4.4.3
Estimating the Relationship Between Audit Time Required and Complexity

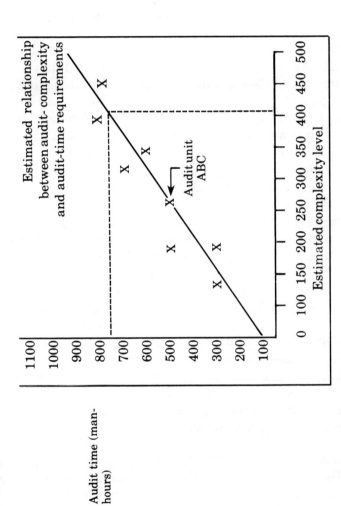

Source: Adapted from Morehead and Myers.

4.3 Audit Staff Requirements

Once the cyclic audit plan is prepared, it may reveal a shortfall between the required audit-skill hours and the available skill hours. Plans will be required to adjust for the shortfall. If insufficient hours are available in the department, recruiting will be required from inside or outside the organization, the audit plan will have to be scaled down (i.e., fewer units audited or a longer cyclic plan developed), or subcontracting portions of the work may be a viable alternative.

If there are sufficient total hours but they do not comprise the appropriate skill-level mix, a program of training and personnel development will be required to bring skills to the necessary level, the audit plan will have to be revised to permit more emphasis upon audits with lower skill requirements, or portions of audits might be contracted out.

In planning for staff requirements, it is necessary to outline the skill requirements pertaining to each audit phase. Figure 4.4.1 is illustrative of this analysis. Next, an inventory of personnel skills available must be referenced or prepared. Then, skill requirements must be matched against skill availability.

Once a matching of skills and audit phases is performed, the "ideal" cyclic audit-coverage plan may be formulated in implementable terms, taking into consideration the personnel skills currently available and projected, which are the main constraint to be taken into account in the cyclic work plan.

Figure 4.4.4 is an example of a personnel-skill-requirement projection based on the cyclic coverage plan. It illustrates a shortfall analysis of this plan. The ideal cyclic coverage plan and the shortfall analysis provide a basis for approaching corporate management for additional resources or for an authorized scaling down of departmental activities.

4.4 Training and Development

Because business activities and internal auditing are of a dynamic nature, it is essential that the knowledge and the skills of the audit staff be continuously maintained at levels consistent with the requirements of audit assignments that they undertake. This means that a predetermined portion of each auditor's available time should be allotted to professional training and development.

Franklin warns that, as an organization grows and changes,

Figure 4.4.4
Analysis of Staff-Resource Requirements in Man-Hours

Staff Classification	Currently Available	Year 1 Require-ments	Year 1 Short-fall	Year 2 Require-ments	Year 2 Short-fall	Year 3 Require-ments	Year 3 Short-fall
Assistant auditor							
Auditor							
Senior auditor							
EDP auditor							
Senior EDP auditor							
Total							

people who were once competent may become obsolete, if not outright incompetent. They may be promoted into positions of greater responsibility not only for their own work but also the work of others. Although training cannot compensate for the lack of adequate auditing procedures and inappropriate job responsibilities, it can enhance the development of professional and managerial skills. However, he asserts:

> What many organizations pass off as training programs are nothing more than a crazy quilt of training patches randomly and independently applied over the years as various crises occurred without any overall objective. (Franklin, 1981, p. 42)

Franklin offers a number of reasons for the neglect and the failure of training and developing activities:

- Good managers are not necessarily good teachers.
- The consequences of poor training do not show up immediately but later (on the job) and may not be attributed to poor training.
- Training needs of professionals are often poorly understood.
- Actionable concepts are not taught.
- Ineffective or incorrect training methods are used.

It is outside the scope of this study to present a comprehensive training and developing program. However, it is useful to outline a framework for such a program coordinated with the previously described audit framework as an example of a planned approach to implementing a coherent and relevant series of training programs. Each element of this program should be geared to a particular *entry* level of skill and should aim at achieving a particular *exit* level of skill. Generally, audit personnel will be assigned to courses on the basis of their auditing knowledge, experience, and the skill requirements of future audits.

Certain courses will be common to all members of the department. Their primary purpose is to provide a common understanding of the department's standards and techniques. Beyond this, however, some staff members will specialize in areas such as EDP auditing or statistical auditing. In addition, supervisory level training will be provided to assist supervisors or potential supervisors in developing their managerial skills.

To be effective, the courses must be job relevant and tailored to the needs of the department and its members. Courses may be obtained through external sources. In larger departments, some

174

courses could be developed internally. For example, refer to Rainey and Lynch for a description of JCPenney Company's approach to setting up management training for its audit department.

In addition to in-house-development programs, attendance at seminars and other professional courses might be encouraged. These often provide exposure to new and job-relevant audit techniques.[30]

5.0 Planning and Budgeting

5.1 Preparing the Ideal Long-Range Audit-Coverage Plan

Because the concern magnitudes of some auditable units will be very high while others will be very low, the audit of all units on an annual basis may not be the most cost-effective approach. A more realisitic approach might, over some time horizon, direct greater audit frequency or depth of coverage to the audit units with higher concern magnitudes and less audit attention to those with lower degrees of concern.

One way of using concern magnitudes for determining the degree of audit intensity warranted by various auditable units might be as follows (see Figure 4.5.1):

Step 1
Prepare an ordered list of auditable units ordered by magnitude of concern.
Step 2
On the basis of the rankings, subdivide the list into suitable cyclic audit-coverage and depth-of-coverage categories such as (a) units requiring a complete audit each year, (b) units requiring a visit each year but not necessarily a complete audit (specify the type of audit required), (c) units requiring a complete audit every second year, and (d) units requiring a visit every second year but not necessarily a complete audit (specify the type of audit required). Continue this process until all auditable units are assigned an audit frequency and a depth of coverage and note that this could be done with a mathematical approach or judgmentally.

The entire population of auditable units would thus be subdivided into a number of categories. If, for example, a three-year cycle were used, at least three categories would be required: (a) category X would represent audits to be carried out each year; (b)

Figure 4.5.1
Assigning Audit Units to Cyclic Coverage Categories and Levels of Audit Intensity

Audit Units in Order of Importance	X (Annually) Complete	X (Annually) Partial	Y (Biennially) Complete	Y (Biennially) Partial	Z (Triennially) Complete	Z (Triennially) Partial
1.	X					
2.	X					
3.	X					
4.		X				
5.		X				
6.		X				
7.		X				
8.			X			
9.			X			
10.			X			
11.				X		
12.				X		
13.				X		
14.				X		
15.				X		
16.				X		
17.					X	
18.					X	
19.						X
20.						X

category Y would represent audits to be carried out once every two years; and (c) category Z would represent audits to be carried out once every three years. The category cutoffs could depend upon both the concern index and the time requirements for each audit.

These categories could be further divided into subcategories (see Figure 4.5.2). Although each auditable unit would be audited at least once during the three-year cycle, not all units would require a full (i.e., six-phase) audit. This is particularly true of units in the lower concern categories. Thus, a long-range plan might require a full audit of all category X units but only partial audits of Y and Z units. Categories Y and Z might be split into subcategories Y_1, Y_2, Z_1, and Z_2. Category Y_1 units would be audited every second year but would receive a complete audit. Category Y_2 units would be audited every second year but would receive only a compliance audit and not a full six-phase audit. Similarly, category Z_1 would receive a full audit but only once in three years, whereas category Z_2 audits would be partial triennial audits.

It should be noted that units will not remain in the same category forever. They will move in and out of categories on the basis of periodic reevaluations of concern magnitudes.

Step 3

Prepare a list of audits by category showing cumulative audit-time requirements as illustrated by Figure 4.5.3.

Step 4

Extrapolate the plan to the lowest common-factor year. For example, if a three-year cycle is used, a six-year-planning horizon must be used, since in year six all the plans coincide (i.e., the annual, biennial, and triennial plans will fall into the year-six work plan.

Step 5

Extrapolate personnel-skill resource availability over the same time horizon. This requires that current personnel skills be inventoried and that the time path of departmental personnel skills be projected through a process of evaluating and predicting the anticipated progress and tenure for each auditor over the time horizon.

Step 6

Match audit-coverage plans against personnel-time availability and identify personnel-skill shortfalls or excesses as illustrated in the previous section (see Figure 4.4.4).

Figure 4.5.2
Cyclic Audit-Coverage Plan

Priority Category	Audit Cycle	Audit Phase	Cycle 1 — Year 1	Cycle 1 — Year 2	Cycle 1 — Year 3	Cycle 2 — Year 4	Cycle 2 — Year 5	Cycle 2 — Year 6
X	Annual	Planning	X	X	X	X	X	X
		Documentation	X	X	X	X	X	X
		Review & evaluation	X	X	X	X	X	X
		Compliance	X	X	X	X	X	X
		Substantiation	X	X	X	X	X	X
		Reporting	X	X	X	X	X	X
Y1	Biennial, full	Planning	X		X		X	
		Documentation	X		X		X	
		Review & evaluation	X		X		X	
		Compliance	X		X		X	
		Substantiation	X		X		X	
		Reporting	X		X		X	
Y2	Biennial, partial	Planning	X		X		X	
		Documentation						
		Review & evaluation	X				X	
		Compliance	X		X			
		Substantiation						
		Reporting	X		X		X	
Z1	Triennial, full	Planning		X				X
		Documentation		X				X
		Review & evaluation		X				X
		Compliance		X				X
		Substantiation		X				X
		Reporting		X				X
Z2	Triennial, partial	Planning		X				X
		Documentation		X				X
		Review & evaluation		X				
		Compliance						X
		Substantiation						
		Reporting		X				X

Figure 4.5.3
Approach for Analyzing Staff Requirements for a Cyclical Audit-Coverage Plan*

Priority Category	Auditable Units	Planning	Documentation	Review & Evaluation	Compliance	Substantiation	Reporting	Totals
X	___	X	X	X	X	X	X	X
	___	X	X	X	X	X	X	X
	___	X	X	X	X	X	X	X
	___	X	X	X	X	X	X	X
	___	X	X	X	X	X	X	X
Category X	Subtotals	1.0	1.0	1.5	2.5	5.0	1.0	12.0
Y1	etc.							
Category Y1	Subtotals	___	___	___	___	___	___	___
Y2	etc.							
Category Y2	Subtotals	___	___	___	___	___	___	___
Z1	etc.							
Category Z1	Subtotals	___	___	___	___	___	___	___
Z2	etc.							
Category Z2	Subtotals	___	___	___	___	___	___	___
	Grand Totals	4.0	5.5	8.5	17.5	15.0	3.5	54.0

*In man-years.

Step 7

Iterate, through steps two to six, balancing the workload over the coverage cycle guided by the concern ratings for auditable units and the skill, progress, and tenure ratings for audit personnel.

Step 8

If significant shortfalls still exist, present the plan to management for authorization to fill the gaps. This may be done through: (a) expansion of the department, (b) contracting for temporary services from external sources such as external auditors or management consultants, (c) shifting projects to other departments and task forces within the organization, and (d) cutbacks in audit coverage.

Step 9

If significant excess time is available, the planned audit coverage may be expanded, additional special projects may be undertaken, or departmental growth may be reduced.

Neumann outlines the work-package-risk-analysis procedure (WRAP). He claims that this procedure is useful for setting priorities and for eliminating the need to cycle audits arbitrarily on a one-, two-, or three-year cycle. It uses the concept of expected savings per audit hour to establish relative priorities. Where the concept of savings is not appropriate, expected risk per audit hours is suggested as a substitute. And audit priorities are not set on the basis of absolute magnitudes rather on the basis of the payoff per audit hour invested in the audit project.

Blumenthal warns that large payoff areas are not always the best candidates for auditing first. He emphasizes that urgency is at least as important a criterion for setting priorities and that payoffs do not necessarily reflect urgency. Where an analysis is performed so as to provide payoff figures by audit phase, it may help identify diminishing returns to scale. But this may not be possible to do in many situations.

Perhaps the most useful information provided by an analysis based on payoff per audit hour might result from a comparison of rankings based on absolute size of the concern magnitudes and rankings based on payoff per hour. This comparison might be helpful during the iteration process, described above, aimed at balancing personnel availability and audit-project requirements.

5.2 Budgeting and Resource Allocation

Assuming that resources are limited, it is not possible to simply assign all the resources necessary to achieve the ideal long-range audit-coverage plan. A process of budgeting and resource allocation must exist. To the extent that a well-defined, systematic, and reasonable process exists for budgeting and resource allocation, the resource limitation can be appropriately taken into consideration. However, in the absence of a systematic budgeting and resource-allocation process, the effects of resource constraints might haphazardly and improperly fall upon various areas of internal audit responsibility.

To be effective, the resource-allocation process must be firmly based upon the approved objectives set for the internal audit department. It should specify a set of appropriate assumptions consistent with those of corporate management. Finally, it should outline alternatives to permit the judicious selection of the most appropriate package of audits.

The budget process typically involves a number of budget types and varying degrees of participation. For example, three main types include fixed budgets, flexible budgets, and zero-base budgets.

A fixed budget may specify the authorized staffing level of the internal audit department, including the maximal number and the skill levels of staff authorized for the department. Even within such a budget, there is room for resource-mix planning and evaluation of mix packages based upon audit requirements.

A flexible budget permits adjustment of the department staff and facilities on the basis of company growth. In such a budgeting environment, growth areas will be highlighted and earmarked for special audit attention, including audit-resource development through training, recruiting, and facilities planning (e.g., special software, etc.).

Zero-base budgeting requires the periodic (often annual) reevaluation of planned audit activities and related staffing levels. If not carefully considered and practiced, this budgeting approach may hamper the development of long-term stability and professional capabilities in the internal audit department. In recognition of the potential negative consequences of this budgeting approach, modifications might be made to the frequency of the rigorous zero-base-budgeting process (i.e., requiring a rigorous reevaluation every three to five years and modest reevaluations during intervening periods). Zero-base budgeting is discussed in Chapter 6.

5.3 Preparing the Annual Work Plan

At some point in time, it is necessary to set the targets and fix the resources for the coming year to permit development of specific plans. This rarely can be done for one year at a time. A preferable approach in planning for the current year is to take into account the year beyond. This approach can provide insight into work-shifting opportunities and constraints.

The current year plan must take into account not just the desired audit coverage but also the available resources in terms of skills and man-hours available or anticipated to be available during the year.

Often, special consideration must be given to coordination of work with external auditors, both as to timing and resource requirements.

The actual work plan should be presented to the audit committee and compared against the ideal work plan to provide a perspective upon the audit-coverage trade-offs made and to highlight important coverage cutbacks. Once the general degree of coverage is planned and approved, a more detailed planning phase is reached involving the assignment of audits to specific periods and individuals.

6.0 Work Scheduling and Performance Monitoring

6.1 Work Assignment

Assuming that audits are not completely homogenous and that there is not perfect substitutability among auditors as regards audit assignments, an important part of the scheduling process involves the appropriate matching of auditors and audit tasks. Matching must take into account on-the-job-training and development factors as well as employee-time availability and specialized skills. Work assignments involve matching audit skills to audit tasks: matching audit personnel to audits.

Audits can be subdivided into specific phases or tasks. For example, audit planning may be a separate task from audit documentation, which is a separate task from control testing or transaction checking. These separable tasks may be assigned to personnel best equipped and available to carry them out. Appropriate assignments of skills to audit tasks will help the department achieve improved efficiency levels as well as increased quality of audits owing to appropriate matching of audit requirements and personnel skills. In addition to the skills-availability factor, an important staffing factor involves developing staff skills and giving assignments of increasing responsibility to capable audit personnel.

Whereas each issue can be resolved one at a time, the optimal solution requires the simultaneous resolution of several considerations. Particularly in large audit departments, work assignments require a good deal of planning effort and may be enhanced through automated aids. Such aids are rarely used. Consequently, relatively unrefined procedures are typically used for assigning personnel to audits. It is not known whether substantial improvements will result if automated quantitative tools are available and used. In Chapter 6, this issue is covered in more detail, and quantitative tools are suggested to permit more refined solutions to the work-assignment problem.

6.2 Work Scheduling

Based on preferred matching of auditors and audit units, a specific time slot must be assigned to each audit. Scheduling audits can be problematic, especially when there are many auditors, many small audit units with inflexible timing criteria, and restrictive auditor-skill requirements. In such cases, network models, Gantt charts, and linear programming may serve as effective aids. These tools are discussed in Chapter 6.

In contrast with work assignments that match audit requirements with specific personnel skills, work scheduling involves assigning audits to specific time slots. Although at first glance this may not seem to be a difficult problem, several factors may complicate this aspect of audit planning.

Audits must be scheduled within a restricted time. Typically, there are more audits than slots when time is limited to a short period such as from three to six months. Auditees also may place restrictions or requests that will affect scheduling. Furthermore, personnel factors such as vacations, illness, training, and so on, may intervene. Finally, the same person may be required on several audits. But a person is not a divisible commodity and can only be in one place at a specific point in time. In contrast, audits are subdivisible into smaller phases. Thus, planning by audit phase, rather than by person or audit, may lead to efficiencies in personnel assignment and scheduling.

Because of all of these considerations, the scheduling issue, like the work-assignment issue, becomes quite complicated as a department increases in size. This is not to say that scheduling is impossible but that it becomes increasingly difficult to carry out efficient scheduling within the constraints described above. There are quantitative techniques for enhancing the work-scheduling process. These are described in detail in Chapter 6.

6.3 Work Monitoring

Plans require feedback mechanisms. A time-tracking system is a necessity to permit feedback regarding both the effectiveness of planning and the performance of individuals.[31]

There is no substitute for personal supervision and review as part of the monitoring activity. Typically, this aspect of monitoring is delegated to various levels within the audit department. In the absence of such personal involvement, work-status reports and time analyses fulfill a key role in providing feedback about planned activities and progress toward achieving work plans. In particular, potential deficiencies in plans can be identified early and corrected.

6.4 Performance Evaluation

The consensus seems to be that auditors should be evaluated upon completion of each assignment. Such evaluations are aimed primarily at encouraging the development of the specific skills which are deemed to be desirable attributes of professional auditors. In addition, semiannual or annual evaluations based on fulfilling prespecified duties, responsibilities, and objectives are considered to be valuable by many internal audit departments.

Summary

This chapter has outlined a multiphase, comprehensive planning system. Key planning phases and their interrelationships have been identified, and their essential attributes have been described. The discussion herein portrays planning and coordinating of internal audit activities as a difficult, time-consuming network of activities. This is not, however, an academic exercise. The chapter also reflects current practices. Its main contribution is that it distills observed practices into a unified whole and provides a potentially useful framework for conceptually integrating planning practices.

It may appear that an overwhelming amount of attention has been paid to elements of planning. This is the purpose of this research study, and it must be emphasized that – implicitly or explicitly, more or less formally, manually or with the aid of automated tools – these are the planning activities in which internal auditing departments actually engage.

This chapter should be considered an overview of the planning process. It omits a great amount of supporting detail which, for the sake of completeness and for those contemplating enhancements to their own planning and coordinating activities, is included in the next two chapters that may be properly considered appendices of this chapter.

Chapter 5 examines planning activities, judgments, decisions, and information flows involved in the planning and coordinating of internal auditing functions. For those who are not interested in detail, Chapter 5 may be omitted.

Chapter 6 expands upon several of the planning techniques touched upon in previous chapters. It may be considered in the nature of an expanded reference or glossary, outlining the characteristics, advantages, and disadvantages of specific techniques used or recommended for enhancing planning and coordinating activities.

Footnotes:

[23]See M.H. Barrett and V.Z. Brink's *Evaluating Internal/External Audit Services and Relations,* The Institute of Internal Auditors, 1980.

[24]Most respondents to the *Survey of Internal Auditing: 1979* (69 percent) indicated that they had a formal audit charter (small, 58 percent; medium, 68 percent; large, 77 percent) and that they required complete adherence to the *Standards for the Professional Practice of Internal Auditing* (73 percent). A smaller number of these had integrated these standards into their audit manuals:

Size of Department

	Small	Medium	Large	Overall
Requires adherence to Standards	76%	73%	71%	73%
Integrated into audit manual	30%	37%	47%	39%

[25]See R.S. Kaplan, "Application of Quantitative Models in Managerial Accounting: A State of the Art Survey," *Bayer Lecture Series: 1976-1977,* University of Wisconsin, 1977, pp. 17-71; R.S.

Kaplan, "The Significance and Investigation of Cost-Variance Survey and Extensions," *Journal of Accountancy Research,* Autumn 1975, pp. 311-337; R.P. Magee, "A Simulation Analysis of Alternative Cost-Variance Investigation Models," *Accounting Review,* July 1976, pp. 529-544; and R.P. Magee and J.W. Dickhaut, "Effects of Compensation Plans on Heuristics in Cost-Variance Investigation," *Journal of Accounting Research,* Autumn 1978, pp. 294-314.

[26]It is generally inadvisable to use zero, since it eliminates from any further consideration whatever is multiplied by it. Consequently, zero should only be used for *nonapplicable* factors but *not* for improbable factors.

[27]90 = 10 x 9 possible pairs if order matters (typically it would ensure reliablilty).

2,495,000 = 10 factors (500 x 499) if order matters as above.

$$10 \text{ man-years} = \frac{(2,495,000 + 90) \div}{(250 \text{ working days} \quad x\ 8\,hrs\ x\ 60\,min\ x\ 2}$$
comparisons per minute)

[28]5,010 = 10 + (500)(10). Note that this and the computations above are for illustrative purposes only. The assumptions made may not be realistic.

[29]This is an unrefined analysis for illustrative purposes. A refined analysis requires additional cumulative columns for other skill categories.

[30]The *Survey of Internal Auditing: 1979* indicates the following as main sources of formal training programs for members of internal audit staffs (ranked by order of popularity):

1. IIA seminars
2. Professional publications
3. Company training program
4. University courses
5. AICPA and CPA review courses
6. American Management Association
7. DP vendors and manufacturers
8. Other (e.g., Bank Administration Institute; external audit firms's programs)

[31]As reported in the *Survey of Internal Auditing: 1979*:

	Size of Department			
	Small	**Medium**	**Large**	**Overall**
Time budgets prepared	77%	85%	95%	87%
Broken down by component parts	25%	36%	63%	44%
Detailed time reports	45%	74%	87%	72%

5

A Structured Analysis for a Comprehensive Audit-Planning System

While the previous chapters established a conceptual foundation for a comprehensive audit-planning system, this chapter provides detailed specifications in terms of processes and data flows as well as required data stores. There are a great number of systems-analysis techniques available for developing such specifications. The approach taken here is structured systems analysis. The specific tools used include data-flow diagrams, a data dictionary, structured English, Leighton diagrams, and logical data-structure diagrams.

In the ensuing sections, the salient features of these techniques will be discussed. An overview of the system will be provided and followed by detailed comprehensive audit-planning-system (CAPS) specifications. The structure of this chapter is as follows:

1.0 Structured Systems Analysis
    1.1 Leighton Diagrams
    1.2 Data Flow Diagrams
    1.3 Structured English
    1.4 Logical Data Structures
    1.5 Data Dictionary

2.0 Systems Specifications for CAPS
    2.1 Systems Overview
    2.2 Data-Flow Diagrams and Process Descriptions in Structured English
    2.3 Logical Data-Structure Diagrams
    2.4 Data Dictionary

This chapter is a very detailed analysis of features which were previously discussed at a conceptual level. The purpose of this analysis is to provide details which may be important to personnel involved in maintaining or enhancing internal audit-planning systems.

It is not expected that everything included here will be of value to any one person or organization. It is hoped that the analysis is sufficiently comprehensive and that it contains some information of value to most interested parties. Without a doubt, this chapter will not interest most readers because of its detail and can be safely omitted. Some readers may be interested in skimming the chapter to obtain insight from the diagrams.

Those who may object to the substance of the contents should note that the diagrams merely reflect, in a synthesized and systematic way, the procedures observed in the case studies in Chapter 3. Thus, the contents should not be viewed as a fabrication but an attempt to portray explicitly and accurately the planning activities and information flows involved in planning internal audit activities. Those who are familiar with these activities will not be surprised. Those who are not may be amazed.

1.0 Structured Systems Analysis

De Marco defined structured analyis in terms of the goals it hopes to accomplish:
- To produce a maintainable document outlining a system of interest.
- To reduce the level of complexity by partitioning the system into modules, processes into subprocesses, and so on.
- To use graphic form to help describe the system.
- To differentiate between logical and physical considerations.
- To build a logical system before implementing a physical system.

Although most auditors are familiar with tools such as flowcharting, they are less familiar with those used herein. The flowchart, which has been and is a widely used analytical tool, will not be used here for several reasons.

First, flowcharts may not be highly maintainable because they do not use hierarchial breakdowns of flows and processes. Thus, modifications, especially in the form of adding new processes or decision choices, may require redrawing the flowchart.

Second, because of the absence of effective modular partitioning, flowcharts decline in simplicity as a system grows larger.

Thus, the effectiveness of flowcharts as an analysis tool decreases, especially when the number of options available in each module is large. But this is when an analysis tool is required most.

Third, although flowcharts take into account processes, states, decisions, and directions, their pictorial capabilities have some severe drawbacks. In the words of Gane and Sarson:

> Though one flowchart can be worth a thousand words, it traps the analyst into a commitment; to use the standard flowchart symbols means inevitably that the analyst must commit to a physical implementation of the new system . . . . Until the development of the structured systems analysis tools, there was no way of showing the underlying logical functions and requirements of a system; one very quickly got bogged down in the details of the event or proposed physical implementation.

Thus, flowcharting does not belong to the group of preferred structured analysis tools and will not be used here. Instead, Leighton diagrams, data-flow diagrams, structured English, logical data-structure diagrams, and a data dictionary will be used. Since most auditors are unfamiliar with these techniques, brief descriptions of the techniques are provided below.

1.1 Leighton Diagrams

The objective of this tool is to help communication of primary conceptual issues by depicting major portions or functions of a system and their relationship to one another. As a representation of system architecture, Leighton diagrams highlight the span of control and the relative importance of individual subsystems in the larger scheme of the system. The following are considered to be important attributes of this technique:

- Hierarchic organization of system elements.
- Sequence (precedence) of processes incorporated.
- Priority levels of processes explicitly highlighted.
- Interface with parties outside the system boundaries highlighted.
- User requirements expected to be delivered by system functions highlighted.

1.2 Data-Flow Diagrams (DFDs)

Data-flow diagrams are used to graphically represent a system as a network of processes and the interfaces among them. The construction of a DFD involves a top-down approach to system building. An overall system-data flow is first produced, which is then successively broken down to provide additional details until each subprocess identified performs only one specific function. The goal behind this process of hierarchical subdividing is to ensure that no diagram is too complex to be read or unable to be understood. There are four basic elements in a data-flow diagram:

- Data paths or flows (arrows) that show the directional flow of information.
- Processes (bubbles) that represent the transformations of data.
- Data stores (rectangles) representing data that must be stored for future use by external users or for further processing by the system.
- External entities, sometimes called " data sources and sinks," that represent originators and receivers of data external to the system.

1.3 Structured English

Because the English language is oftentimes ambiguous and inconsistent, the description of systems processes has come to take the form of what is known as "structured English" or psuedocode. Structured English is actually a subset of the English language that makes use of indentation, limited syntax, and limited vocabulary to give concise descriptions of processing steps. The following are the three syntax forms that structured English can take:

- Sequence: declarative sentence one, declarative sentence two, etc.
- Alternation or decision: if . . . then . . . else (or otherwise) . . .
- Iteration: while . . . do . . .

1.4 Logical Data Structures

Although representing data-base structure is a newer area of representation than the activity-oriented schemes, it has grown in importance in recent years. Activity-related schemes are unable to highlight important logical attributes of data. Just as data management has increased in importance, so too have data-base-representation schemes.

The data-analytic technique adopted here is the logical data structure (LDS). According to Carlis and March, an LDS is a union of user views of data which unambiguously shows the underlying semantic structure in the data base in a record-independent form. It is also called a "conceptual model," a "canonical record structure," and an "infological level model." The basic components of a LDS as identified by Carlis and March are as follows:

• An entity represents a generic group of objects about which information is maintained (e.g., audit units, audit personnel, etc).

• Attributes are the characteristics of entities (e.g., name of audit unit).

• A relationship is the structured association between two entities (e.g., audit unit of auditor).

• An identifier is a subset of attributes or relationships whose values are used to uniquely identify instances of the entity (e.g., name of audit unit, employee number, etc).

1.5 Data Dictionary

According to De Marco, a data dictionary is a set of rigorous definitions of all the elements in a DFD and serves to give meaning to the DFD without which it is simply a picture of circles or bubbles. There is no hard and fast rule that must be followed in the construction of a data dictionary. It can be done manually, or it can be automated. There are no requirements as to what the contents of a data dictionary must be. Some guidelines for developing an effective data dictionary are:

• It should provide for different methods of accessing a definition.

• It should have cross-referencing capabilities.

• It should be maintainable for update purposes.

• It should contain no redundancy.

2.0 Systems Specifications for CAPS

2.1 System Overview

Global View of Architecture. The Leighton diagram for CAPS (see Figure 5.1.1) provides an overview of the architecture of the system. The system consists of six main modules whose sequence of execution flows from top to bottom. Planning, responsibility, and audit approach are involved in the first step in developing a comprehensive set of plans for the internal auditing department.

Figure 5.1.1
Global View of the Architecture in a Comprehensive Audit-Planning System

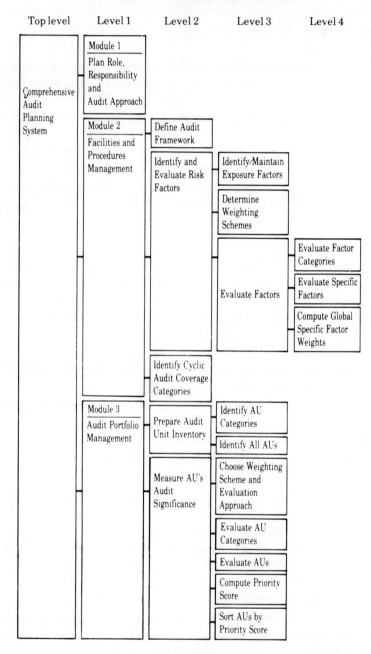

(Continued on Next Page)

Top level	Level 1	Level 2	Level 3	Level 4

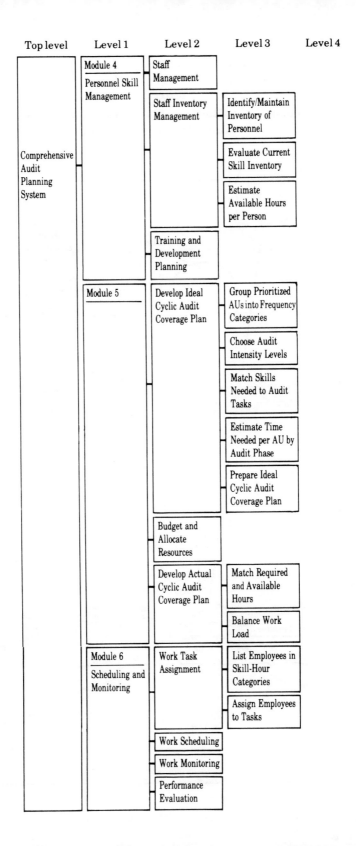

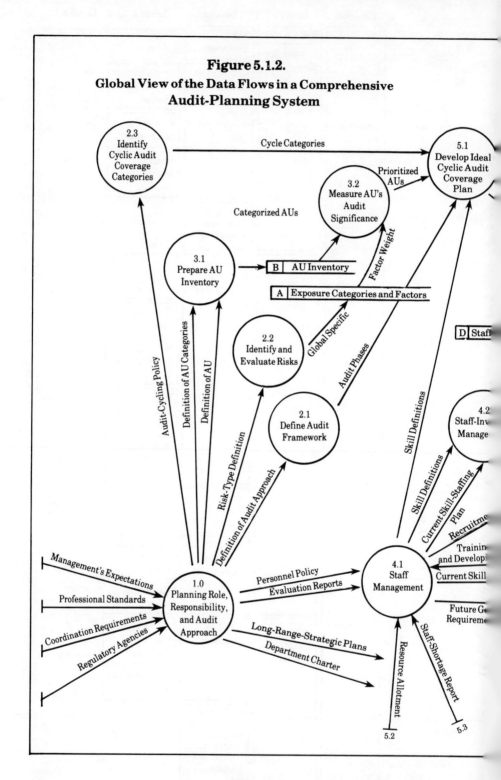

Figure 5.1.2.

Global View of the Data Flows in a Comprehensive Audit-Planning System

194

Figure 5.1.2 (continued)

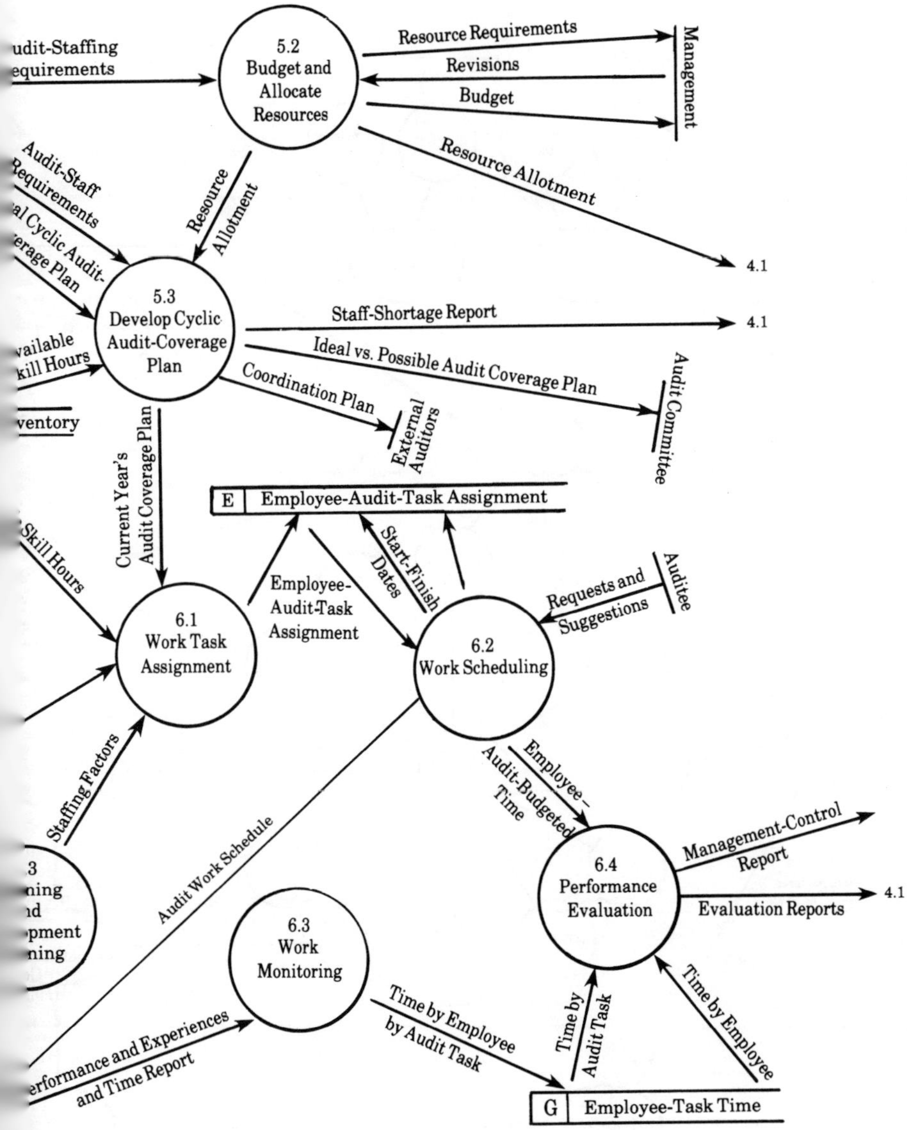

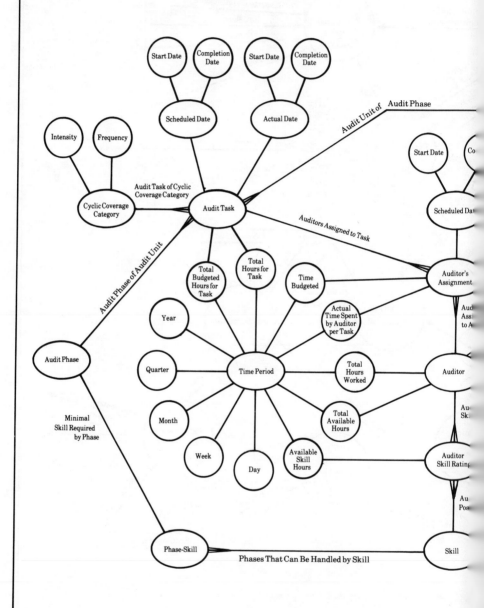

Figure 5.1.3
Global View of the Logical Data Structure
in a Comprehensive Audit-Planning System

Figure 5.1.3
(Continued)

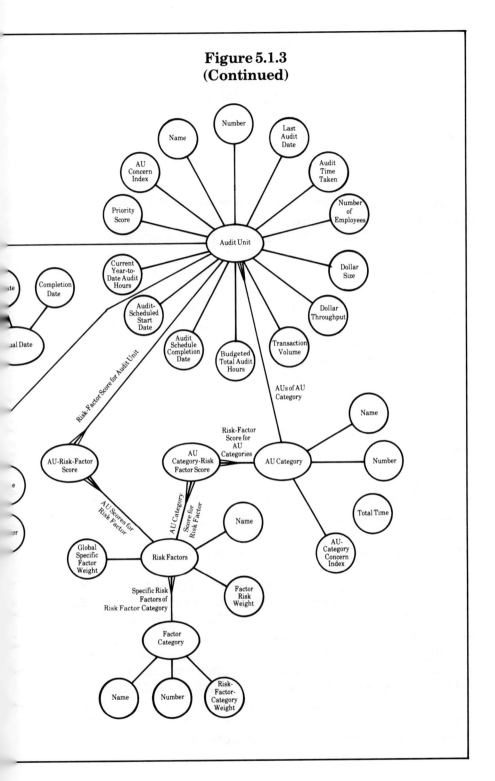

The next major process is facilities and procedures management. This module consists of submodules with the "calling" hierarchy moving from left to right. Thus, this second module calls on three submodules: identify audit framework, identify and evaluate risk factors, and identify cyclic audit-coverage categories. The submodule identify and evaluate risk factors, in turn, calls on three other submodules, and so on.

Typically, input and output are indicated at the extreme right with the source-destination device and nature shown by using standard flowchart-device symbols and arrows; but these are not included in Figure 5.1.1.

Global View of Data Flows. The data-flow diagram for CAPS (see Figure 5.1.2) provides an overview of the network of processes connected by data flows comprising the system. These modules are discussed in section 2.2. This diagram is not intended as a working document; rather, its main purpose is to provide, in one place, a comprehensive layout of the main functions, data flows, data stores, and relationships involved in planning and coordinating activities of internal audit departments. In later sections of this chapter, detailed information about these modules (bubbles), data flows (arrows), and data stores (rectangles) will be provided.

Global View of the Logical Data Structures. This diagram for CAPS (see Figure 5.1.3) identifies the key entities, their attributes, and the logical relationships that underlie the entire system.

The entities here are represented by simple ovals, the attributes by circles, and the relationships by named arcs. To represent many-to-one relationships (e.g., audit-unit-of-audit-unit category), "chicken feet" are added to the appropriate end of an arc.

Many-to-many relationships are not permitted. They are redefined into their component many-to-one relationships; for example, the entity's risk factors have three attributes: name, risk-factor weight, and global-specific-factor weight. They also have a many-to-one relationship with the entity's factor category. This means that for every factor category, there are many risk factors. This relationship is named "specific risk factors of category."

More detailed descriptions of each entity and attribute are contained in the data-structures and data-elements sections of the data dictionary at the end of this chapter.

2.2 Data-Flow Diagrams and Process Descriptions in Structured English

This section contains data-flow diagrams for CAPS. The context diagram (see Figure 5.2.0.1) indicates that the system produces 13 outputs. The level-one diagram (see Figure 5.2.0.2) indicates that six modules comprise the system. Thus, this section is organized into six subsections, one for each module. Each subsection begins with a brief overview. A series of diagrams is provided depicting the essential features of each module such as the names and the identification numbers of the module-component processes (bubbles), the names and the identification numbers of data stores (rectangles), and the names of the data flows between modules and data stores (arrows). Additional information is provided in the data dictionary of the chapter.

Six Modules Follow
Figures 5.2.0.1 and 5.2.0.2

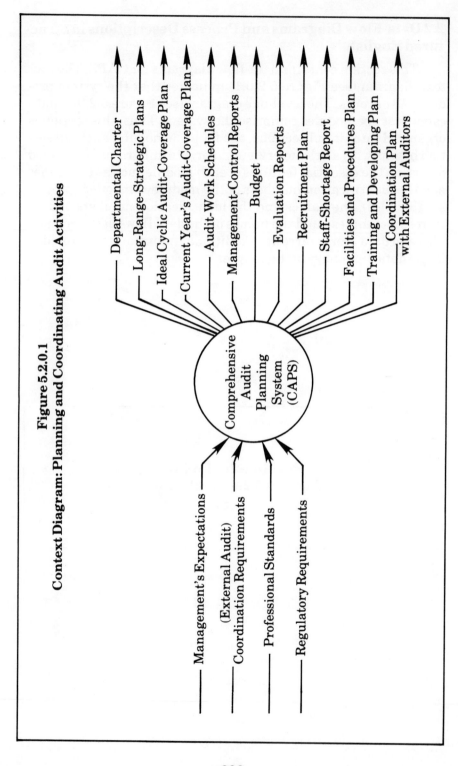

Figure 5.2.0.1
Context Diagram: Planning and Coordinating Audit Activities

Departmental Charter

Long-Range-Strategic Plans

Ideal Cyclic Audit-Coverage Plan

Current Year's Audit-Coverage Plan

Audit-Work Schedules

Management-Control Reports

Budget

Evaluation Reports

Recruitment Plan

Staff-Shortage Report

Facilities and Procedures Plan

Training and Developing Plan

Coordination Plan
with External Auditors

Comprehensive
Audit
Planning
System
(CAPS)

Management's Expectations

(External Audit)
Coordination Requirements

Professional Standards

Regulatory Requirements

Figure 5.2.0.2
Level One: Comprehensive Audit-Planning System

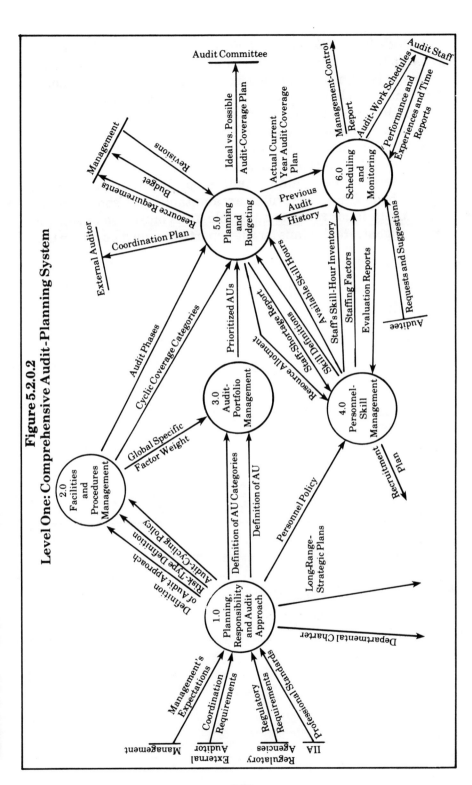

Module 1: Planning, Responsibility, and Audit Approach. In order for the internal audit department's planning activites to be carried out in a consistent and effective manner, a departmental charter must first be developed outlining the responsibilities and the authority of the internal audit function. It should also include rules of professional conduct consistent with those of the accounting and auditing professions to be followed by members of the internal audit staff.

Criteria for determining audit scope and priorities must be established. What constitutes an auditable unit should be defined. Criteria for ranking auditable units must also be set, and long-range strategic plans for the department must be drawn up.

Figure 5.2.1

Module One: Planning, Responsibility, and Audit Approach

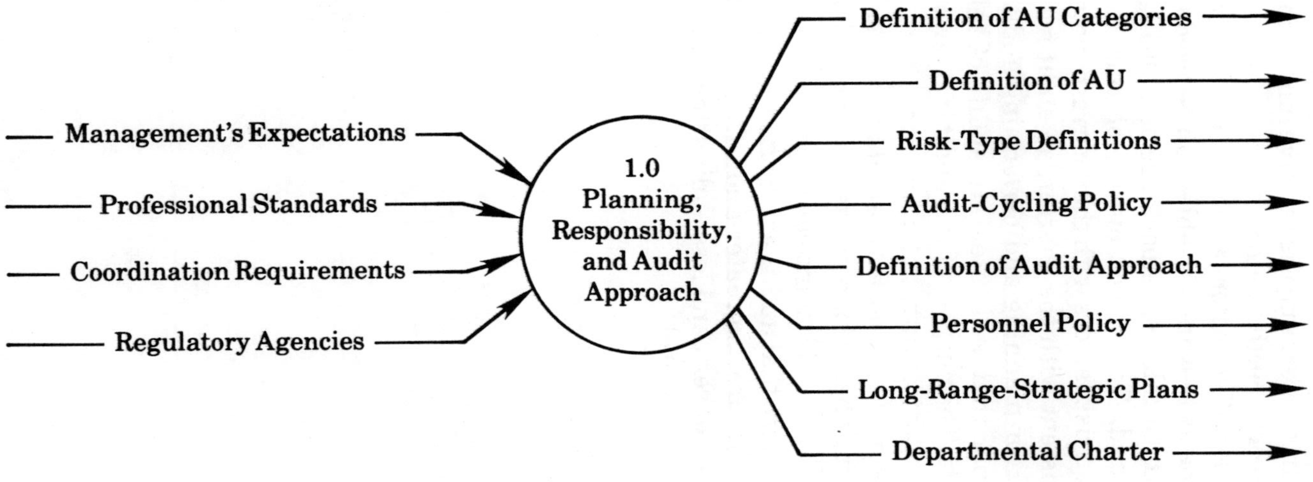

203

Module 2: Facilities and Procedures Management. This module deals primarily with identifying risk factors and their evaluation to determine the relative importance of each category as well as each specific factor.

The identified factors are based on the definition provided in module one as to what variables can be used to construct a scale against which relative importance of auditing specific units can be measured. The major output of this module is a list of categorized risk factors with their corresponding weights.

Consistent with the charter, an audit framework should be developed for planning and performing audits in a comprehensive manner that will integrate audits of related manual and EDP audits. The purpose of this audit framework is to prevent severe audit shortcomings potentially resulting from the failure to coordinate manual and EDP audits and to subdivide all audits into the same phases for purposes of further planning.

Likewise, cyclic audit-coverage categories must be determined to ensure that audits are carried out in a cost-effective way (i.e., one that directs greater audit frequency to the audit units with higher concern and less audit attention to those with lower level of risk/exposure).

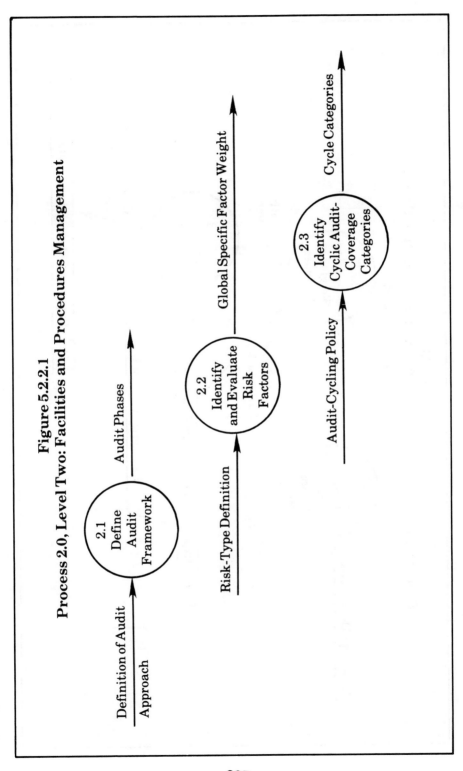

Figure 5.2.2.1
Process 2.0, Level Two: Facilities and Procedures Management

205

Figure 5.2.2.2
Process 2.2, Level Three: Identify and Evaluate Risk Factors

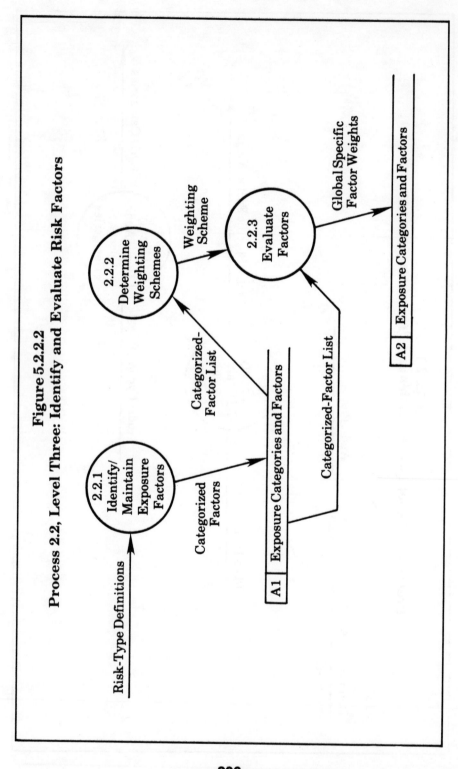

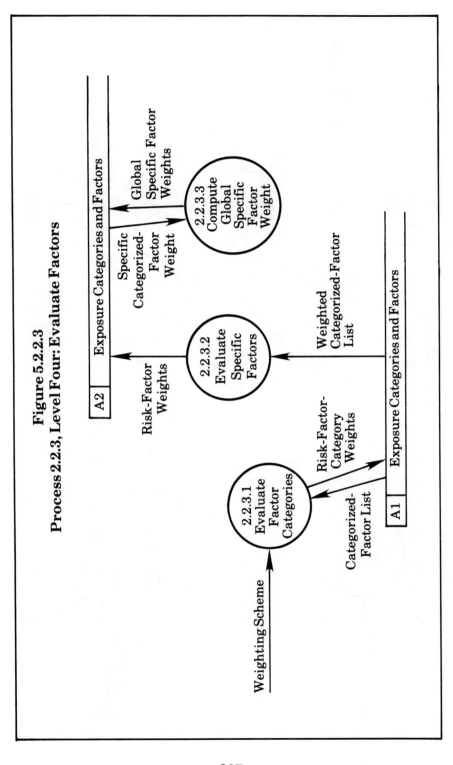

Figure 5.2.2.3
Process 2.2.3, Level Four: Evaluate Factors

Figure 5.2.2.4
Summary of Module Two: Facilities and Procedures Management

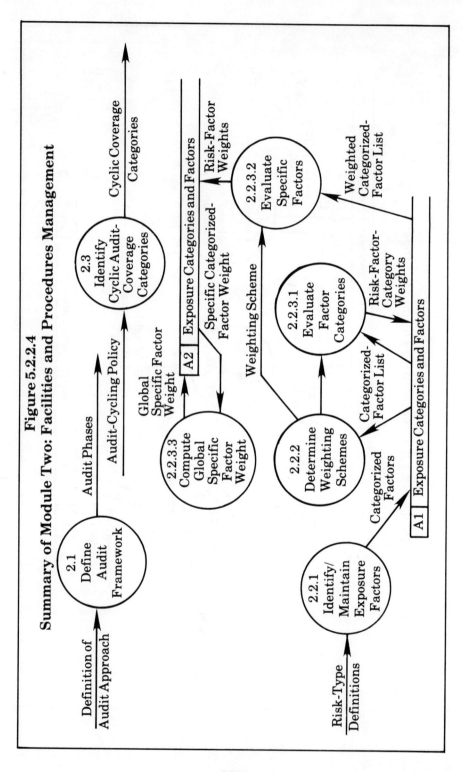

Module 3: Audit-Portfolio Management. The objective of
audit-porfolio managment is to maintain an inventory of all significant audits prioritized in accordance with a unit's concerns.
Based on definitions of audit-unit categories and auditable units,
a systematic identification of these categories and units within
each category is carried out. However, maintaining an inventory
of auditable units is not complete without assessing each unit's
significance relative to the others. Thus, units are measured in
terms of the risk factors identified and weighted in the previous
module.

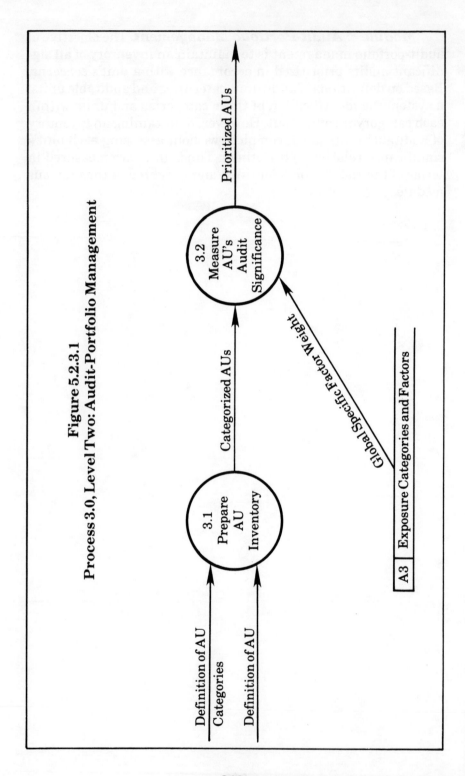

Figure 5.2.3.1
Process 3.0, Level Two: Audit-Portfolio Management

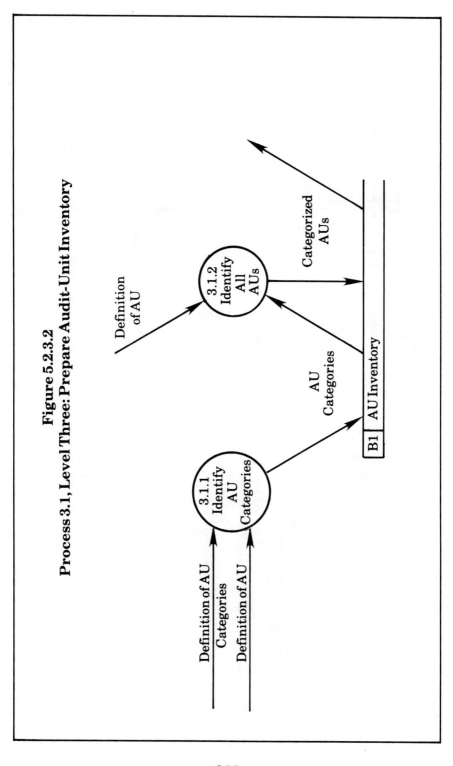

Figure 5.2.3.2
Process 3.1, Level Three: Prepare Audit-Unit Inventory

211

Figure 5.2.3.3
Process 3.2, Level Three: Measure AU's Audit Significance

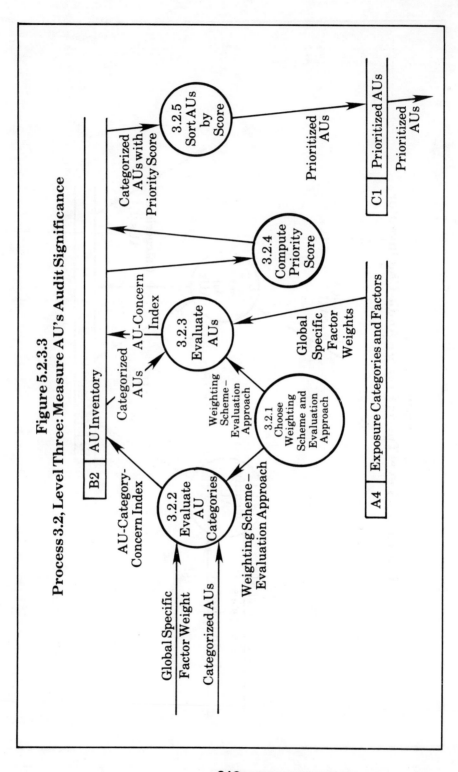

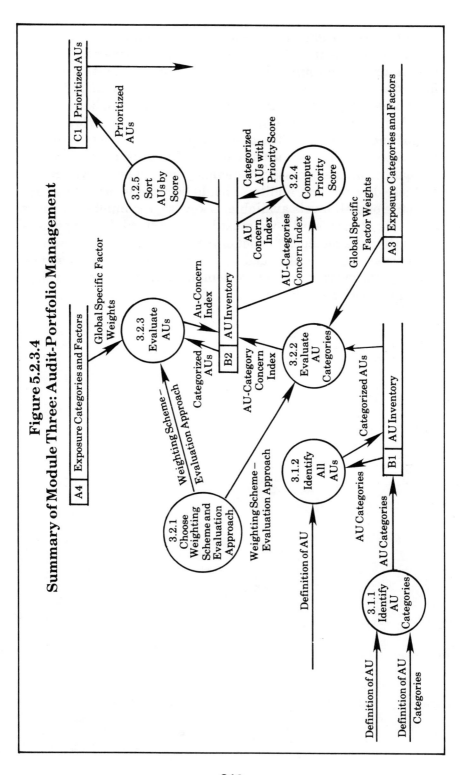

Figure 5.2.3.4
Summary of Module Three: Audit-Portfolio Management

213

Module 4: Personnel-Skill Management. Once the auditable units are identified and prioritized, an assessment of personnel resources determines the extent of audit work that can be performed over a period of time. An inventory of audit personnel must be developed and maintained. Skill levels must be defined.

Written position descriptions should exist for each level of internal audit personnel. The descriptions must provide an indication of the responsibilities at each level of personnel as well as the qualifications necessary for employment at each level. Based on these descriptions, auditors should be rated in order to obtain a profile of skill levels available. Likewise, the number of hours available at each skill level must be determined. Under personnel-skill management, it is not only the present audit-personnel needs that must be attended to but also future requirements. Considering current and future demand, a training and developing plan must be developed.

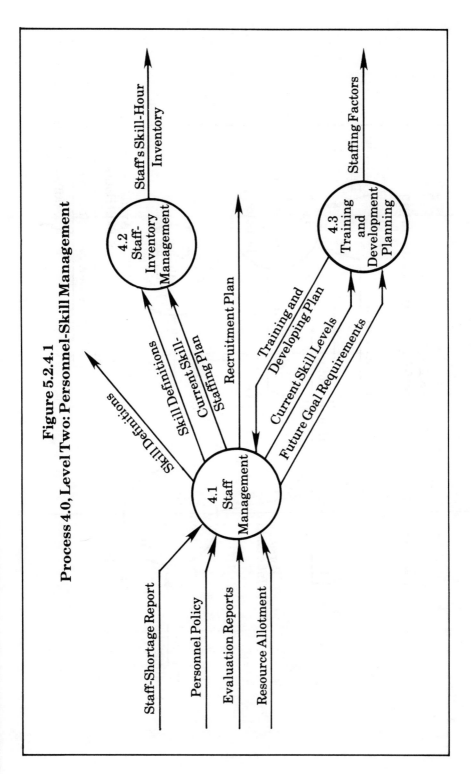

Figure 5.2.4.1
Process 4.0, Level Two: Personnel-Skill Management

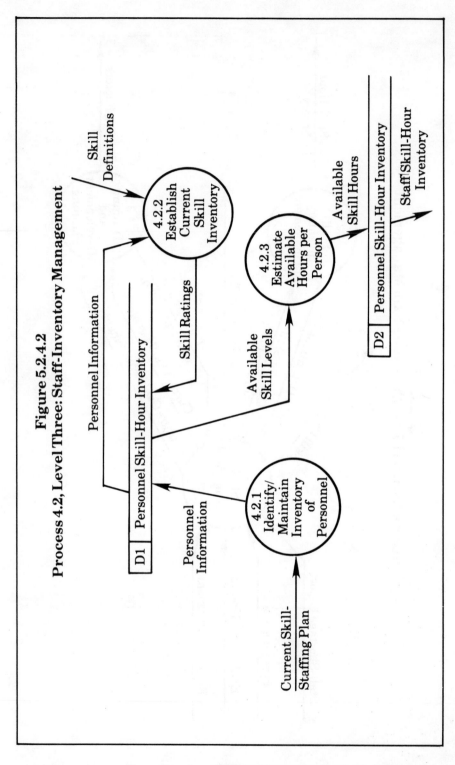

Figure 5.2.4.2
Process 4.2, Level Three: Staff-Inventory Management

216

Figure 5.2.4.3
Summary of Module Four: Personnel-Skill Management

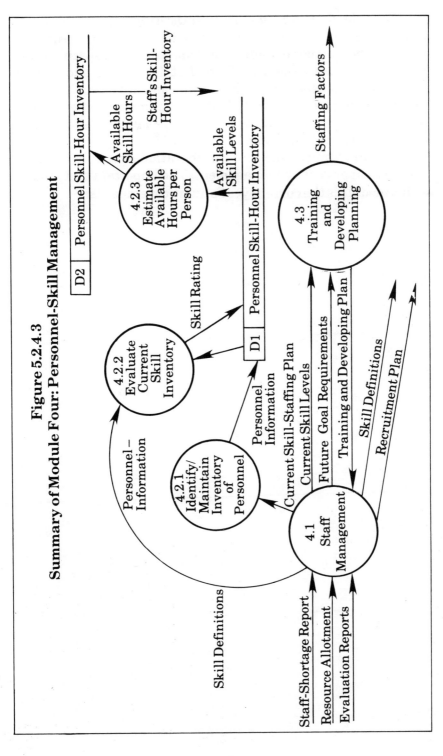

Module 5: Planning and Budgeting. This module accomplishes three objectives. First, it determines audit frequency, which is the number of audits performed during a specified time period for an auditable unit. Second, it determines audit extensiveness or intensity level, which is the amount of audit effort to expend during a given audit. And third, it matches the required personnel resources with the current resource availability in terms of skill levels and time.

Matching must take into consideration available financial resources approved by management. The important end product of this module is the current year's audit-coverage plan.

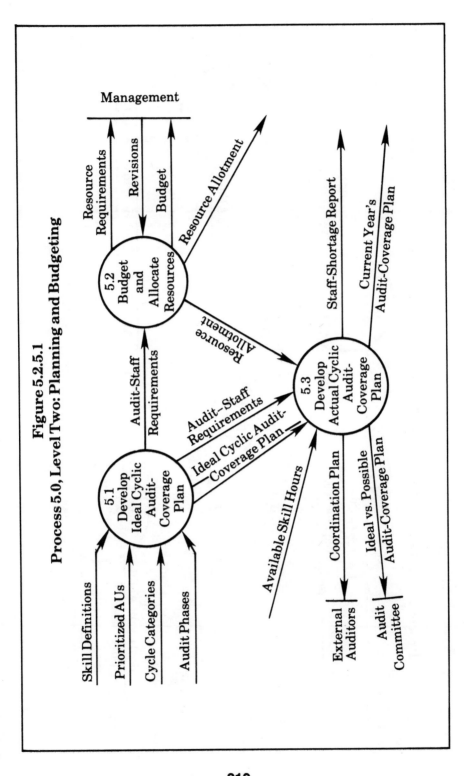

Figure 5.2.5.1
Process 5.0, Level Two: Planning and Budgeting

Management

Resource Requirements

Revisions

Budget

Resource Allotment

5.2
Budget
and
Allocate
Resources

Audit-Staff Requirements

Resource Allotment

Staff-Shortage Report

Current Year's Audit-Coverage Plan

5.3
Develop
Actual Cyclic
Audit-
Coverage
Plan

5.1
Develop
Ideal Cyclic
Audit-
Coverage
Plan

Audit-Staff Requirements

Ideal Cyclic Audit-Coverage Plan

Available Skill Hours

Coordination Plan

Ideal vs. Possible Audit-Coverage Plan

Skill Definitions

Prioritized AUs

Cycle Categories

Audit Phases

External Auditors

Audit Committee

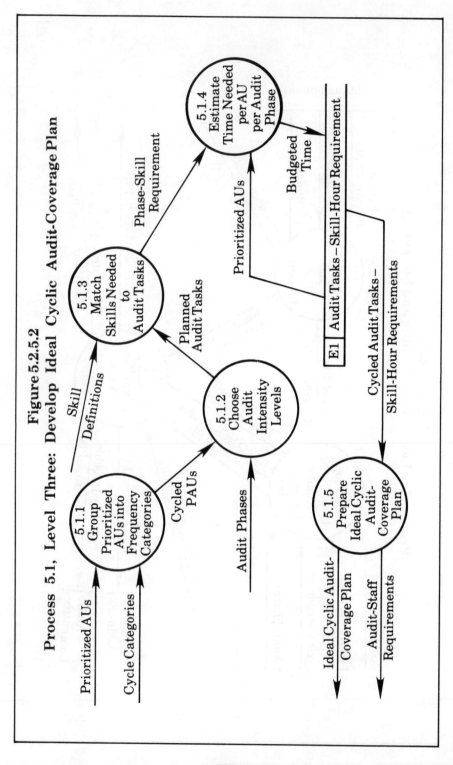

Figure 5.2.5.2
Process 5.1, Level Three: Develop Ideal Cyclic Audit-Coverage Plan

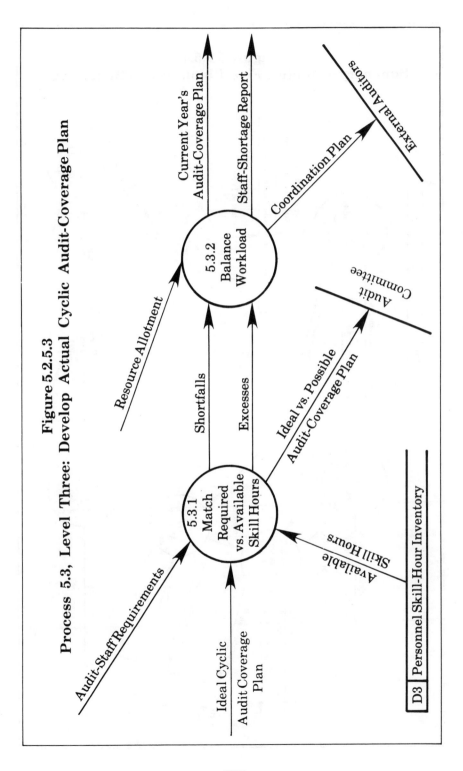

Figure 5.2.5.3
Process 5.3, Level Three: Develop Actual Cyclic Audit-Coverage Plan

221

Figure 5.2.5.4
Summary of Module Five: Planning and Budgeting

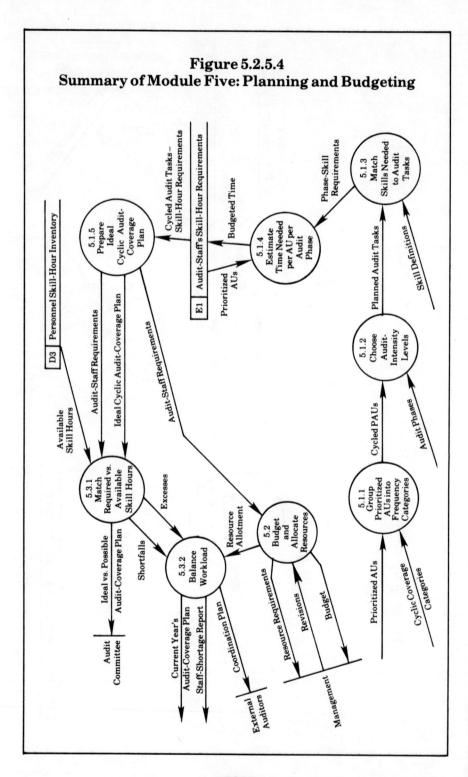

Module 6: Scheduling and Monitoring. This module is concerned with two tasks: scheduling audit work and monitoring its progress and the performance of the audit personnel involved.

Given the current year's audit-coverage plan as well as a list of audit personnel, their skill levels, and their time availability, specific audit staff members can be assigned to a particular audit task as well as start and finish dates, taking into consideration auditees' requests. The time spent on each task by each auditor must be tracked. This serves as a basis for evaluation and control purposes.

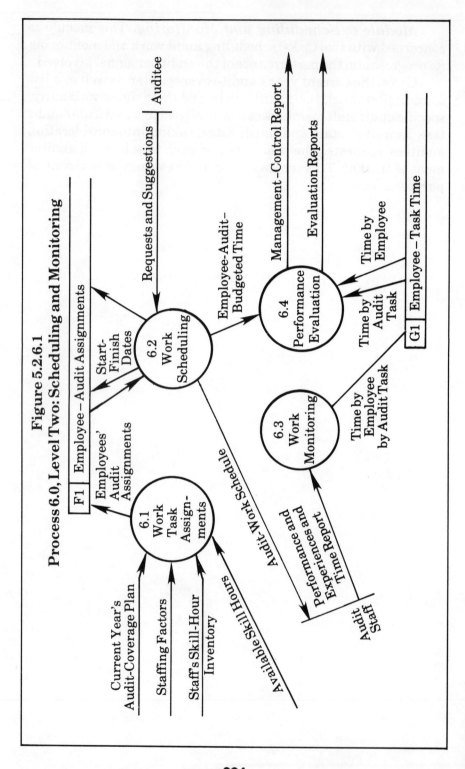

Figure 5.2.6.1
Process 6.0, Level Two: Scheduling and Monitoring

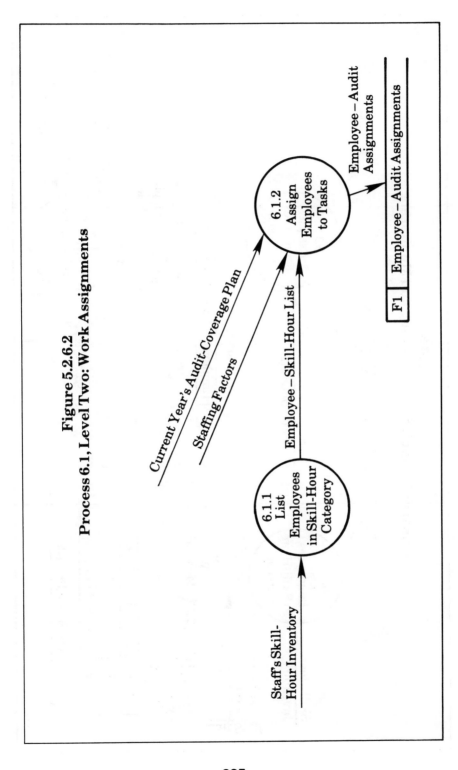

Figure 5.2.6.2
Process 6.1, Level Two: Work Assignments

Figure 5.2.6.3
Summary of Module Six: Scheduling and Monitoring

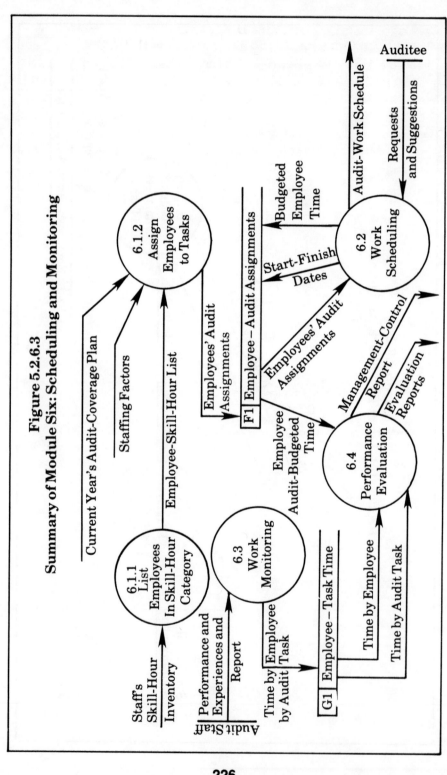

2.3 Logical Data-Structure Diagrams

This section contains LDS diagrams with the six data sets deemed to reflect the information requirements of a system: audit units, risk-exposure-concern factors, personnel skills, audit tasks, auditor-task assignments, and time periods. For each data set, the diagrams indicate the entities (records), attributes (fields), and key relationships comprising the data set. Additional information about the data sets is contained in the data dictionary.

Figure 5.3.1
Data Set 1: Audit Units

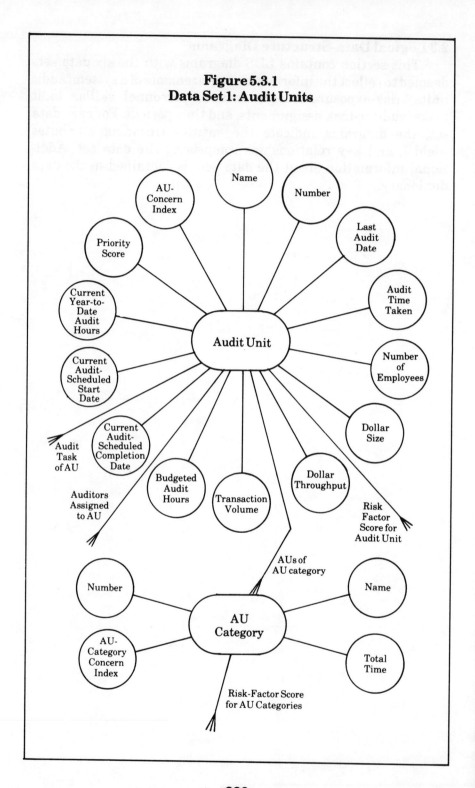

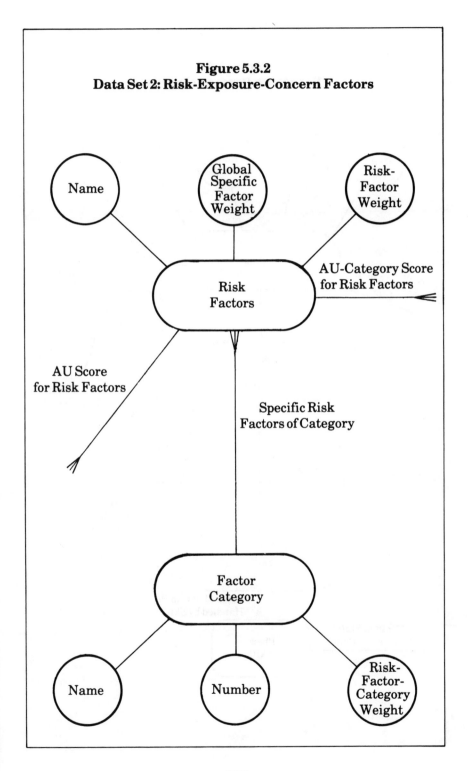

Figure 5.3.2
Data Set 2: Risk-Exposure-Concern Factors

Name

Global
Specific
Factor
Weight

Risk-
Factor
Weight

Risk
Factors

AU-Category Score
for Risk Factors

AU Score
for Risk Factors

Specific Risk
Factors of Category

Factor
Category

Name

Number

Risk-
Factor-
Category
Weight

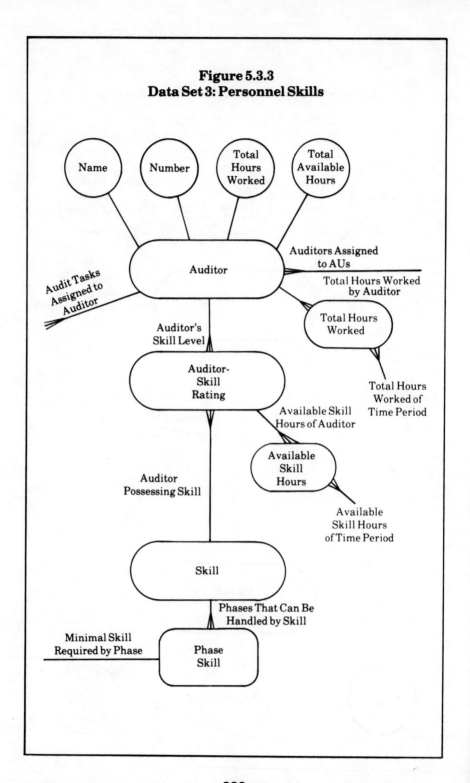

Figure 5.3.3
Data Set 3: Personnel Skills

Name

Number

Total Hours Worked

Total Available Hours

Auditor

Auditors Assigned to AUs

Total Hours Worked by Auditor

Audit Tasks Assigned to Auditor

Auditor's Skill Level

Total Hours Worked

Total Hours Worked of Time Period

Auditor-Skill Rating

Available Skill Hours of Auditor

Auditor Possessing Skill

Available Skill Hours

Available Skill Hours of Time Period

Skill

Phases That Can Be Handled by Skill

Minimal Skill Required by Phase

Phase Skill

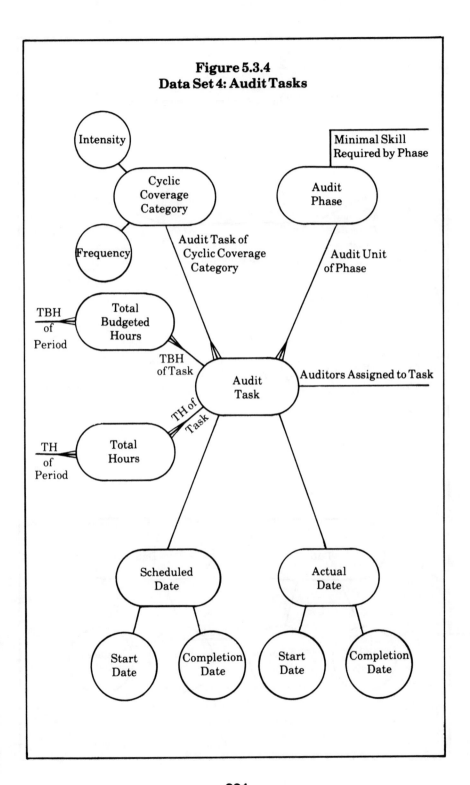

Figure 5.3.4
Data Set 4: Audit Tasks

Intensity

Cyclic Coverage Category

Frequency

Audit Task of Cyclic Coverage Category

Minimal Skill Required by Phase

Audit Phase

Audit Unit of Phase

TBH of Period

Total Budgeted Hours

TBH of Task

Audit Task

Auditors Assigned to Task

TH of Task

TH of Period

Total Hours

Scheduled Date

Actual Date

Start Date

Completion Date

Start Date

Completion Date

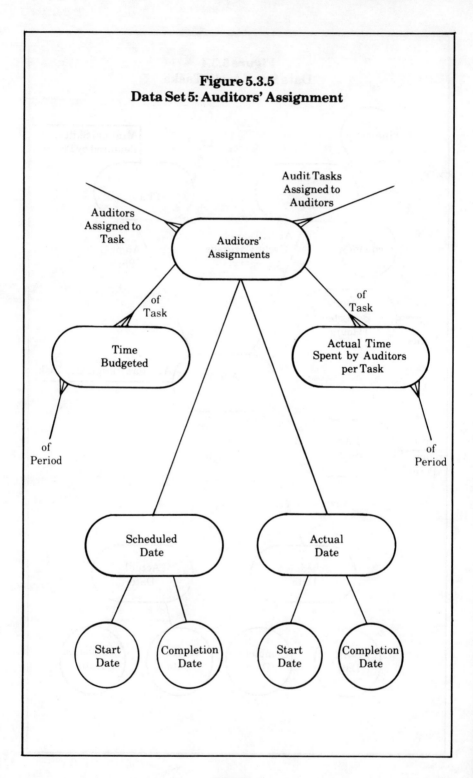

Figure 5.3.5
Data Set 5: Auditors' Assignment

Audit Tasks Assigned to Auditors

Auditors Assigned to Task

Auditors' Assignments

of Task

of Task

Time Budgeted

Actual Time Spent by Auditors per Task

of Period

of Period

Scheduled Date

Actual Date

Start Date

Completion Date

Start Date

Completion Date

Figure 5.3.6
Data Set 6: Time Periods

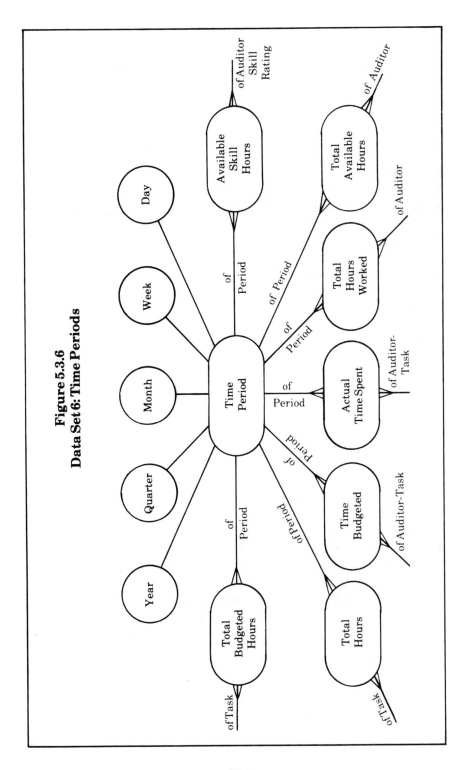

2.4 Data Dictionary

This section contains a data dictionary that provides brief descriptions of processes, flows, data stores, data structures, and data elements previously discussed or diagrammed. Within these categories, the lists are in alphabetical order except for the processes and data stores, which are in numerical order.

For each process, the following information is provided:
- Name of the process.
- Indication that it is a process.
- Reference identifying the process by its number.
- Input (i.e., data flow) to the process with references, when applicable, to the process of their origin.
- Output (i.e., data flow) from the process with references, when applicable, to the process of their destination.
- Description of the process in structured English.

For each data flow, the following information is provided:
- Name of the data flow.
- Indication that it is a data flow.
- Source reference with identification number and name of the process module or submodule (e.g., 5.3.2) or data store (e.g., B1) that the data flow from.
- Destination reference with identification number and name of the module or submodule (e.g., 6.1.2) or data store (e.g., B2) that the data flow into.
- Expanded description of the data flow.

For each data store, the following information is provided:
- Name of the data store.
- Indication that it is a data store and its identifying reference (e.g., A1).
- Contents of the data store and their source.
- Cross-reference summary of all data flow into and data flow out of the data store, including source and destination modules and names of the data flow.

For each data structure, the following information is provided:
- Name of the data structure.
- Indication that it is a data structure.
- Aliases, abbreviations, etc., used to refer to this data structure (if there are any).
- Short description of the data structure.
- Source of the data structure.

234

- Data elements that make up the data structure.
  For data elements, the following is provided:
- Name of the data element.
- Indication that it is a data element.
- Short description of the data element.
- Source of the data element.
- Possible values that this data element might take on.

DATA DICTIONARY FOR COMPREHENSIVE AUDIT-PLANNING SYSTEM

Part 1: Processes

Plan, Responsibility, and Audit Approach	Process Ref: 1.0
Input	**Output**
Management's expectations (MGMT)	2.1 Definition of audit approach
Professional standards (IIA)	2.2.1 Risk-type definitions
Coordination requirements (EXT AUD)	2.3 Audit-cycling policy
Regulatory requirements (REG AG)	3.1.1 Definition of audit-unit categories
	3.1.1 Definition of audit unit
	4.1 Personnel policy, department charter, and long-range strategic plans

Description. Based on management's expectations and taking into consideration coordination requirements with external auditors, professional standards, and regulatory requirements, determine role, responsibility, and approach of the internal audit department. Define long-range goals related to specific operating plans and budgets and accompanied by measurement criteria and targeted dates of accomplishment. Develop departmental charter and develop guidelines to determine audit scope, criteria for prioritization, and personnel policies.

Define Audit Framework	Process Ref: 2.1
Input	**Output**
1.0 Definition of audit approach	5.1.2 Audit phases

Description. Consistent with the defined audit approach, develop an audit framework to ensure coordination of manual and EDP audits to facilitate further planning by subdividing all audits into the same phases.

Identify/Maintain Exposure Factors   **Process Ref: 2.2.1**

Input   **Output**

1.0 Risk-type definitions   A.1 Categorized factors

Description. Given the definition of what variables can be used to construct a scale against which relative importance of auditing specific units can be measured, develop and/or update a list of specific risk factors grouped into general categories. These identified, categorized factors are to be stored in data base.

Determine Weighting Schemes   **Process Ref: 2.2.2**

Input   **Output**

A.1 Categorized factor list   2.2.3.1 Weighting scheme

                                   2.2.3.2 Weighting scheme

Description. Choose a method of measuring the relative significance of each risk-exposure factor. The choices are direct assessment or pairwise comparison.

Evaluate Factor Categories   **Process Ref: 2.2.3.1**

Input   **Output**

2.2.2 Weighting scheme   A.1 Risk-factor-category
                                   weights

                                   A.1 Categorized factor list

Description (Logic Summary). Get categorized factor list from data base (A.1). If chosen method is pairwise comparison, do evaluation by comparing two factor categories at a time. Assign a greater percentage weight to category considered greater in relative importance until all possible pairs compare; otherwise, use direct-assessment method. Do evaluation by assigning precentage wieghts to categories according to importance and store risk-factor-category weights in data base.

Evaluate Specific Factors   **Process Ref: 2.2.3.2**

Input   **Output**

2.2.2 Weighting scheme   A.2 Risk-factor weights

A.1 Exposure categories / factors

Description (Logic Summary). If chosen method is pairwise comparison, do evaluation by comparing two risk factors at a time. Assign greater percentage weight to risk factor considered greater in relative importance until all possible pairs compare; otherwise, use direct-assessment method. Do evaluation by assigning percentage weights to risk factors according to importance and store risk-factor weights in data base.

**Compute Global Specific Factor
  Weight**   **Process Ref: 2.2.3.3**

Input   **Output**
A.2 Specific categorized   A.2 Global
   factor weight   specific factor weights
Description. Multiply every risk-factor weight (process
2.2.3.2) by corresponding risk-factor-category weight (process
2.2.3.1) to get global specific-factor weight (GSFW).

Identify Cyclic Audit-Coverage   Process Ref: 2.3
   Categories

Input   **Output**
1.0 Audit-cycling policy   5.1.1 Cyclic coverage categories
Description. Given an audit-cycling policy, establish the frequency categories for planning audits in time periods such as
years, quarters, months.

Identify Audit-Unit Categories   Process Ref: 3.1.1

Input   **Output**
1.0 Definition of audit-unit   B.1 AU categories
   categories
1.0 Definition of audit-unit
Description. Based on definition of audit-unit (AU) categories
and audit unit, identify the applicable categories to derive a
subset of auditable units from the universe of possible auditable
entities. Store AU categories in data base.

Identify All AUs   Process Ref: 3.1.2

Input   **Output**
B.1 AU categories   B.1 Categorized AUs
Definition. List all auditable units that belong to each of the
identified AU categories from data base B.1 and store them in
data base.

Choose Weighting Scheme and   Process Ref: 3.2.1
   Evaluation Approach

Input   **Output**
————   3.2.2 Weighting scheme –
                                      evaluation approach
                                   3.2.3 Weighting scheme –
                                      evaluating approach

Description. For weighting scheme, choose between pairwise comparison or direct assessment. For evaluation approach, choose between evaluating AUs or AU categories for each factor or evaluating factors for each AU or AU category.

Evaluate AU Categories	**Process Ref: 3.2.2**
Input	**Output**
B.1 Categorized AUs	B.2 AU-category-
A.3 Global specific factor	concern index
weights	
3.2.1 Weighting scheme –	
evaluation approach	

Description (Logic Summary). If chosen method is pairwise comparison and if approach is to evaluate risk factors for each AU category, compare two risk factors at a time and assign weights from an importance scale to each risk factor based on results of comparison until all possible pairs compare. Store weights in data base. Compute AU category-concern index by . . . (procedure not specified, refer to Chapter 6 for additional information); otherwise, evaluate AU categories for each risk factor and compare two AU categories at a time. Assign weights from an importance scale to each AU category based on the results of comparison until all possible pairs compare and store weights.

Compute AU category-concern index by . . . (procedure not specified so refer to Chapter 6; otherwise, choose direct-assessment method.

To evaluate factors for each AU category, assign weights from an importance scale to each AU category for all factors. Compute AU category-concern index by multiplying each weight assigned to each factor by its corresponding GSFW and sum across all factors; otherwise, evaluate AU categories for each factor.

Evaluate by assigning weights from an importance scale to all AU categories for each factor. Compute AU category-concern index by multiplying weight assigned to each AU category by its corresponding GSFW and sum across all factors and store AU category-concern index.

Evaluate AUs	**Process Ref: 3.2.3**
Input	**Output**
B.2 Categorized AUs	B.2 AU-concern index
3.2.1 Weighting scheme –	
evaluation approach	
A.4 GSFW	

Description. If chosen method is pairwise comparison and if approach is to evaluate risk factors for each AU, compare two risk factors at a time and assign weights from an importance scale to each risk factor based on results of comparison until all possible pairs compare. Store weights in data base.

Compute AU-concern index by . . . procedures not specified, refer to Chapter 6 for additional information; otherwise, evaluate AUs for each risk factor, compare two AUs at a time, and assign weights from an importance scale to each AU based on the results of comparison until all possible pairs compare · Store weights.

Compute AU-concern index by . . . procedures not specified, refer to Chapter 6 for additional information; otherwise, choose direct-assessment method.

If approach is to evaluate factors for each AU, do an evaluation by assigning weights from an importance scale to each AU for all factors, compute AU-concern index by multiplying each weight assigned to each factor by its corresponding GSFW, and sum across all factors; otherwise, evaluate AUs for each factor. Do evaluation by assigning weights from an importance scale to each factor.

Compute AU-concern index by multiplying each weight assigned to each AU by its corresponding GSFW, sum across all factors, and store AU-concern index in data base.

Compute Priority Score	**Process Ref: 3.2.4**
Input	**Output**
B.2 AU-concern index	B.2 Categorized AUs with
B.2 AU-category-concern	priority score
index	

Description. Multiply all AU-concern index by the AU-category-concern index of its category and store priority scores in data base.

Sort AUs	**Process Ref: 3.2.5**
Input	**Output**
B.2 Categorized AUs with	C.1 Prioritized AUs
priority score	

Description. Rank categorized AUs in descending order based on their priority scores and store prioritized AUs in data base.

Staff Management	**Process Ref: 4.1**
Input	**Output**
1.0 Personnel policy	4.2.1 Current skill-staffing plan
4.3 Training/developing plan	4.2.2 Skill definitions
5.2 Resource allotment	4.3 Current skill levels

5.3.2 Staff-shortage report   4.3   Future goals/requirements
6.4   Evaluation reports   5.1.3 Skill-definition-recruiting
                                        plan

Description. Develop skill definitions. Consider present and future audit-personnel needs at all levels in relation to trends and expectations.

Identify/Maintain Inventory of   **Process Ref: 4.2.1**
    Personnel

Input   **Output**

4.1 Skill definitions   D.1 Personnel information
4.1 Current skill-staffing plan

Description. Develop an updated list of audit personnel and store pertinent information in data base.

Evaluate Current Skill Inventory   **Process Ref: 4.2.2**
Input   **Output**
D.1 Personnel information   D.1 Skill rating

Description. Assess skill levels of audit personnel based on skill definitions and personnel information and store skills ratings in data base.

Estimate Available Hours per Person   **Process Ref: 4.2.3**
Input   **Output**
D.1 Available skill levels   D.2 Available skill hours

Description. Estimate available number of hours per skill level by estimating the time availability of each audit staff member and store available skill hours in data base.

Training and Developing Planning   **Process Ref: 4.3**
Input   **Outputs**
4.1 Current skill levels   4.1 Training/developing plan
4.1 Future goals/requirements 6.1.2 Staffing factors

Description. Prepare training and developing plan to meet future goals and requirements by taking financial resource constraints into consideration.

Group Prioritized AUs into Frequency   **Process Ref: 5.1.1**
    Categories
Input   **Output**
C.1 Prioritized AUs   5.1.1 Cycled PAUs
2.3 Cyclic coverage categories

Description. On the basis of priority scores, assign AUs to the frequency categories representing audit periods or subperiods of the planning cycle.

Choose Audit-Intensity Levels   **Process Ref: 5.1.2**
Input   **Output**
5.1.1 Cycled PAUs   5.1.3 Planned audit tasks
2.1 Audit phases
Description. For each categorized AU, determine which audit phases will be conducted over each planning period or sub-period.

Match Skills Needed to Audit Tasks   **Process Ref: 5.1.3**
Input   **Output**
4.1 Skill definitions   5.1.4 Phase-skill requirements
5.1.2 Planned audit tasks
Description. Based on given skill definitions, establish the skill levels needed for each audit phase of each auditable unit.

Estimate Time Needed per AU   **Process Ref: 5.1.4**
    per Audit Phase
Input   **Output**
5.1.3 Phase-skill requirements   E.1 Budgeted time
E.1 Prioritized AUs
Description. Prepare time estimate by required skill level for each audit phase of each audit unit and store audit-task-skill-hour requirements in data base.

Prepare Cyclic Audit-Coverage Plan   **Process Ref: 5.1.5**
Input   **Output**
E.1 Cycled audit-task-   5.3.1 Cyclic audit-
    skill-hour requirements   coverage plan
5.2 Audit-staff requirements   5.3.1 Audit-staff requirements
Description. Given cycled audit tasks and their corresponding requirements in terms of skill levels and number of hours, prepare an ideal cyclic audit-coverage plan that lays out the audit phases to be performed on each audit unit at the specified sub-period of the audit cycle as well as the audit staff's requirements.

Budget and Allocate Resources   **Process Ref: 5.2**
Input   **Output**
5.1.5 Audit-staff requirements   4.1 Resource allotment
(MGMT) revisions   5.3.2 Resource allotment
                                     (MGMT) resource
                                     requirements; budget
Description. Submit audit staff's requirements and financial resource requirements to management for approval. Based on revisions, develop budget and summarize resource allotment.

Match Required with Available Skill Hours   Process Ref: 5.3.1

Input
5.1.5 Cyclic audit-coverage plan
5.1.5 Audit-staff requirements
D.3 Available skill hours

Output
5.3.2 Shortfalls
5.3.2 Excesses
(EXT AUD) coordination plan
(AUD CTEE) ideal vs. possible audit-coverage plan

Description. Match audit staff's requirements against personnel-time availability resulting in two possible situations: personnel-skill shortfall and personnel-skill excesses. Then develop an ideal versus a possible audit-coverage plan to submit to the audit committee. Develop a plan for purposes of coordinating internal and external audit efforts.

Balance Workload   Process Ref: 5.3.2

Input
5.2 Resource allotment
5.3.1 Shortfalls
5.3.1 Excesses

Output
6.1.2 Actual current year's audit plan

Description (Logic Summary). If shortfall and if resource allotment permits, expand the department, contract temporary services, or make adjustments guided by AU-priority scores and skill, progress, and tenure ratings of audit personnel. Adjustments may be in the form of cutback in audit coverage or a shift of work to other departments. If excesses, expand planned audit coverage, undertake special projects, and/or reduce departmental growth.

List Employees in Skill-Hour Category   Process Ref: 6.1.1

Input
D.2 Staff skill-hour inventory

Output
6.1.2 Employee-skill-hour list

Description. To facilitate assignments to audit staff, prepare a list of audit staff with corresponding skill levels and time availability.

Assign Employees to Task   Process Ref: 6.1.2

Input
6.1.1 Employee-skill-hour list
5.3.2 Current year's audit-coverage plan
4.3 Staffing factors

Output
F.1 Employee-audit assignment

Description. Match audit-work requirements with audit-personnel capabilities and time availability by taking into consideration staffing factors. Store employee-audit assignments in data base.

Work Scheduling   **Process Ref: 6.2**
Input   **Output**
Requests/suggestions (auditee) Work schedule (audit staff)
F.1 Employee's audit   F.1 Budgeted employee's time
  assignment   F.1 Start-finish dates
Description. Assign dates to employee's audit assignment by taking into consideration the auditee's requests or suggestions. Start and finish dates specifying audit-work schedule and the audit activities are included: when they will be done, the estimated time required, and the audit personnel assigned.

Work Monitoring   **Process Ref: 6.3**
Input   **Output**
Performance, experiences,   G.1 Time by employee
time report (audit staff)   and by audit task
Description. Based on time reports and performance, monitor time spent by each employee for each audit task.

Performance Evaluation   **Process Ref: 6.4**
Input   **Output**
G.1 Time by audit task   Management-control report
G.1 Time by employee
Description. Compare budgeted with time spent. Produce management-control reports and evaluation reports for purposes of staff management and to facilitate estimation of staff requirements in preparing cyclic audit-coverage plan.

Part 2: Data Flow

Current Year's Audit-Coverage Plan   **Data Flow**
Source Ref: 5.3.2   Description: Balance Workload
Destination Ref: 6.1.2 Description: Assign Employees to Task
Expanded Description. Identifies the audit tasks to carry out over a number of audit cycles. The plan outlines AUs grouped into priority categories, the audit phases for each AU, and the audit cycle in terms of audit frequency and intensity.

AU Categories   **Data Flow**
Source Ref: 3.1.1   Description: Identify AU Categories
Destination Ref: B1   Description: AU Inventory
Expanded Description. Represents general classes of areas of economic activity.

AU Category-Concern Index   **Data Flow**

Source Ref: 3.2.2   Description: Evaluate AU Categories

Destination Ref: B2   Description: AU Inventory

Expanded Description. Represents the level of audit significance attached to a category of audit units expressed in the form of a numerical score.

AU-Concern Index   **Data Flow**

Source Ref: 3.2.3   Description: Evaluate AUs

Destination Ref: B2   Description: AU Inventory

Expanded Description. Represents the level of audit significance attached to a particular audit unit in the form of a numerical score.

Audit-Cycling Policy   **Data Flow**

Source Ref: 1.0   Description: Plan, Responsibility, and Audit Approach

Destination Ref: 2.3   Description: Identify Cyclic Audit-Coverage Approach Categories

Expanded Description. It determines the length of the planning period and its component subperiods and specifies the frequency of audits.

Audit Phases   **Data Flow**

Source Ref: 2.1   Description: Define Audit Framework

Destination Ref: 5.1.2   Description: Choose Audit-Intensity Levels

Expanded Description. This represents the different stages of work involved in auditing an audit unit: planning and supervising, documentation, review and evaluation, compliance, substantiation-detailed tests of operations, and reporting.

Audit-Staff Requirements   **Data Flow**

Source Ref: 5.1.5   Description: Prepare Cyclic Audit-Coverage Plan

Destination Ref: 5.3.1   Description: Match Required with Available Skill Hours

5.2   Description: Budget and Allocate Resources

Expanded Description. Specify the number and skill level of audit personnel needed to perform the amount of audit work to do.

Audit-Work Schedule **Data Flow**
Source Ref: 6.2 Description: Work Scheduling
Destination Ref: ...
Included Data Elements: Date of Start and Finish
Included Data Structures: Auditor and Audit Tasks

Available Skill Hours **Data Flow**
Source Ref: 4.2.3 Description: Estimate Available
  Hours per Person
  D.3 Description: Personnel-Skill-Hour Inventory
Destination Ref: D.2 Description: Personnel-Skill-Hour
  Inventory

Expanded Description. Number of man-hours available per planning period for each auditor within each audit-skill level.

Categorized AUs with Priority Score **Data Flow**
Source Ref: 3.2.4 Description: Compute Priority Score
Destination Ref: AU Description: AU Inventory
Expanded Description. Audit units are grouped according to AU categories and scored to reflect the degree of audit significance.

Coordination Plan **Data Flow**
Source Ref: 5.3.2 Description: Balance Workload
Destination Ref: External Auditors
Expanded Description. This is the counterpart of the coordination requirements provided by external auditors (process 1.0). The plan serves to encourage coordination of audit techniques, methods, and terminology between internal and external auditors. It also includes the current years' audit coverage.

Categorized AUs **Data Flow**
Source Ref: 3.1.2 Description: Identify All AUs
Destination Ref: B1 Description: AU Inventory
Expanded Description. List of AUs grouped according to AU categories that were the basis for identifying individual AUs.

Available Skill Levels **Data Flow**
Source Ref: D1 Description: Personnel-Skill-Hour Inventory
Destination Ref: 4.2.3 Description: Estimate Available
  Hours per Person
Expanded Description. List of audit-skill levels possessed by audit personnel.

Coordination Requirements   **Data Flow**
Source Ref: External Auditors
Destination Ref: 1.0   Description: Plan, Responsibility,
and Audit Approach
Expanded Description. Guidelines that are set out in order
to have a well-coordinated approach that ensures proper audit
coverage with minimal duplication of effort between external
and internal auditors.

Categorized-Factor List   **Data Flow**
Alias: Categorized Factors
Source Ref: 2.2.1   Description: Identify/Maintain
Exposure Factors
Destination Ref: A1   Description: Exposure Categories
and Factors
Expanded Description. List of risk-exposure categories with
all the specific risk factors belonging to each category. This list
serves as a basis for prioritizing audits. Included data struc-
tures are factor category and risk factors.

Definition of Audit Approach   **Data Flow**
Source Ref: 1.0   Description: Plan, Responsibility,
and Audit Approach
Destination Ref: 2.1   Description: Define Audit Framework
Expanded Description. This reflects the orientation of the
audit department, its perceived goals, and its role in the organization.

Definition of Audit Unit   **Data Flow**
Source Ref: 1.0   Description: Plan, Responsibility,
and Audit Approach
Destination Ref: 3.1.1   Description: Identify AU Categories
Expanded Description. This serves as the criterion for deter-
mining whether an entity qualifies as an audit unit.

Definition of AU Categories   **Data Flow**
Source Ref: 1.0   Description: Plan, Responsibility,
and Audit Approach
Destination Ref: 3.1.1   Description: Identify AU Categories
Expanded Description. This identifies the broad areas that
serve as a basis for identifying all AUs; e.g., functions and locations.

Department Charter   **Data Flow**
Source Ref: 1.0   Description: Plan, Responsibility,
                                                   and Audit Approach
Destination Ref: . . .
Expanded Description. This establishes the department's
position within the organization and authorizes access to records, personnel, and physical properties relevant to the performance of audits. It also defines the scope of internal auditing activities.

Evaluation Reports   **Data Flow**
Source Ref: 6.3   Description: Performance Evaluation
Destination Ref: 4.1   Description: Staff Management
Included Data Elements: Budgeted Time, Actual Time, and
Variance
Included Data Structures: Auditor and Audit Tasks

Excesses   **Data Flow**
Source Ref: 5.3.1 Description: Match Required with Available
                                                   Skill Hours
Destination Ref: 5.3.2   Description: Balance Workload
Expanded Description. This is the result when available skill
hours are greater than the audit staff's requirements.

Future Goals and Requirements   **Data Flow**
Source Ref: 4.1   Description: Staff Management
Destination Ref: 4.3   Description: Training and Developing
                                                             Plan
Expanded Description. This refers to the number of staff
members needed for a certain level of audit skill at a future
point in time. It also identifies present and future needs for special skills that are not possessed by the audit staff.

Cyclic Audit-Coverage Plan   **Data Flow**
Source Ref: 5.1.5   Description: Prepare Ideal Cyclic
                                              Audit-Coverage Plan
Destination Ref: 5.3.1   Description: Match Required with
                                              Available Skill Hours

Included Data Elements: Audit Cycle, Priority Category, and
Year's Number
Included Data Structures: AU (Planned) Audit Tasks

Ideal Versus Possible Audit-Coverage Plan   Data Flow
Source Ref: 5.3.1   Description: Match Required with
                                                    Available Skill Hours
Destination Ref: Audit CTEE
Expanded Description. This compares the ideal cyclic audit-coverage plan with the actual plan constrained by human and financial resources.

Long-Range Strategic Plans   Data Flow
Source Ref: 1.0   Description: Plan, Responsibility,
                                                    and Audit Approach
Destination Ref: . . .
Expanded Description. This outlines the long-term goals for the internal auditing department and sets out the plans for reaching them. The plan must be approved by management and the board, related to specified operating plans and budget, and accompanied by measurement criteria and targeted dates of accomplishment.

Management-Control Report   Data Flow
Source Ref: 6.4   Description: Performance Evaluation
Destination Ref: . . .
Expanded Description. This reports on the progress of audits, especially deviations from plans and budgets.

Management's Expectations   Data Flow
Source Ref: Management
Destination Ref: 1.0   Description: Plan, Responsibility,
                                                    and Audit Approach
Expanded Description. This refers to management's expectations of the internal audit department: its role and its goals.

Personnel Policy   Data Flow
Source Ref: 1.0   Description: Plan, Responsiblity,
                                                    and Audit Approach
Destination Ref: 4.1   Description: Staff Management
Expanded Description. This includes policies and procedures that are provided to guide the audit staff in meeting the department's standards of performance.

Phase-Skill Requirements   Data Flow
Source Ref: 5.1.3   Description: Match Skills Needed to
                                                    Audit Task

Destination Ref: 5.1.4   Description: Estimate Time Needed
                                        per AU per Audit Phase
Expanded Description. This identifies the audit-skill level
needed for each audit phase.

Planned Audit Tasks   **Data Flow**
Source Ref: 5.1.2   Description: Choose Audit-Intensity Levels
Destination Ref: 5.1.3   Description: Match Skills Needed
                                        to Audit Task
Expanded Description. This represents an audit activity ex-
pressed in terms of an audit phase for a specific audit unit.

Prioritized AUs   **Data Flow**
Source Ref: 3.2.5   Description: Sort AUs by Score
Destination Ref: C.1   Description: Prioritized AUs
Expanded Description. This a list of all AUs ranked by prior-
ity score in descending order of audit significance.

Professional Standards   **Data Flow**
Source Ref: IIA
Destination Ref: 1.0   Description: Plan, Responsibility,
                                        and Audit Approach
Expanded Description. This includes the auditing standards
considered appropriate for discharging the responsibilities of
the internal auditing department. It also refers to the rules of
professional conduct for the internal audit staff.

Recruitment Plan   **Data Flow**
Source Ref: 4.1   Description: Staff Management
Destination Ref: . . .
Expanded Description. This is a plan for employing additional audit personnel. It considers present and future needs at
all levels in relation to the present and expected audit work-pro-
gram plus training and developing. The plan is consistent with
the personnel policy set forth by the department and approved
by management and includes considering alternatives and aspects such as:

- Sources of applicants.
- Methods of finding applicants.
- Methods of providing information to applicants.
- Methods of evaluating and selecting applicants.
- Anticipated growth.
- Personnel turnover.

- Individual advancement.
- Retirement.

The plan should include guidelines for evaluating applicants on the basis of academic background, work experience, achievements, and personal interests. It also requires periodic evaluation of the effectiveness of hiring practices, the effectiveness of personnel involved in hiring, and whether the qualifications expressed in written job descriptions are being met by newly hired personnel.

Resource Requirements   **Data Flow**
Source Ref: 5.2   Description: Budget and Allocate Resources
Destination Ref: Management
Expanded Description. This deals with the number of people and the financial resources needed to meet an ideal cyclic audit-coverage plan.

Revisions   **Data Flow**
Source Ref: Management
Destination Ref: 5.2   Description: Budget and Allocate
                                                    Resources
Expanded Description. These are revisions to the audit department's request for resources.

Risk-Type Definitions   **Data Flow**
Source Ref: 1.0   Description: Plan, Responsibility,
                                          and Audit Approach
Destination Ref: 2.2.1   Description: Identify/Maintain
                                              Exposure Factors
Expanded Description. This defines what constitutes an area of concern to management.

Skill Definitions   **Data Flow**
Source Ref: 4.1   Description: Staff Management
Destination Ref: 5.1.3   Description: Match Skills with Needed
                                                  Audit Tasks
Destination Ref: 4.2.2   Description: Evaluate Current Skill
                                                    Inventory
Included Data Elements: Audit-Skill Classifications (e.g., Assistant Auditor, Senior Auditor), Level and Type of Educational Accomplishments, Years of Work Experience, and specific abilities

Expanded Description. This is a description of skill levels for each internal audit position that provides an indication of the responsibilities for each level of personnel as well as the qualifications necessary for employment at that level.

Shortfalls   **Data Flow**
Source Ref: 5.3.1 Description: Match Required with Available
                                                    Skill Hours
Destination Ref: 5.3.2   Description: Balance Workload
Expanded Description. This is the result when available skill hours are less than the audit staff's requirements.

Weighting Schemes   **Data Flow**
Source Ref: 2.2.2   Description: Determine Weighting Schemes
Destination Ref: 2.2.3.1   Description: Evaluate Factor
                                                    Categories
              2.2.3.2 Description: Evaluate Specific Factors
Included Data Elements: Direct-Assessment and Pairwise-Comparison Methods

---

Part 3: Data Stores

Exposure Categories and Factors   **Data-Store Ref: A1**

Contents   **Source**
Categorized Factors   I = Input (User)
= (Factor Category plus Risk Factors)
  Risk-Factor Category Weights   I
Data Flow in: 2.2.1 – A1 Categorized Factors
              2.2.3.1 – A1 Risk-Factor Category Weights
Data Flow out: A1 – 2.2.2 Categorized Factor List
              A1 – 2.2.3.1 Categorized Factor List
              A1 – 2.2.3.2 Weighted Categorized Factor List

Exposure Categories and Factors   **Data-Store Ref: A2**
Contents   **Source**
Categorized Factors   A1
= (Factor Category plus Risk Factors)
Risk-Factor-Category Weights   A1
Risk-Factor Weights   I = Input (User)
Global Specific Factor Weights   C = Computed
                                            (System)
Data Flow in: 2.2.3.2 – A2 Risk-Factor Weights
Data Flow in: 2.2.3.3 – A2 Global Specific Factor Weight
Data Flow out: A2 – 2.2.3.3 Specific Categorized Factor Weight

---

Exposure Categories and Factors	Data-Store Ref: A3
Contents	**Source**
Categorized Factor	A1
= (Factor Category plus Risk	
Factors)	
Risk-Factor-Category Weights	A1
Risk-Factor Weights	A2
Global Specific Factor Weights	A2

Data Flow out: A3 – 3.2.2 Global Specific Factor Weight

Exposure Categories and Factors	Data-Store Ref: A4
Contents	**Source**
Categorized Factor	A1
= (Factor Catgory plus Risk	
Factors)	
Risk-Factor-Category Weights	A1
Risk-Factor Weights	A2
Global Specific Factor Weights	A2

Data Flow out: A4 – 3.2.3 Evaluate AUs

AU Inventory	Data-Store Ref: B1
Contents	**Source**
Categorized AUs	
= (AU Categories plus AUs)	I = Input (User)

Data Flow in: 3.1.1 – B1 AU Categories
            3.1.2 – B1 Categorized AUs
Data Flow out: B1 – 3.1.2 AU Categories
             B1 – 3.2.2 Categorized AUs

AU Inventory	Data-Store Ref: B2
Contents	**Source**
Categorized AUs	B1
= (AU Categories plus AUs)	
AU-Category-Concern Index	I = Input (User)
AU-Concern Index	I
Priority Score	C = Computed

Data Flow in: 3.2.2 – B2 AU-Category-Concern Index
            3.2.3 – B2 AU-Concern Index
            3.2.4 – B2 Categorized AUs with Priority Score
Data Flow out: B2 – 3.2.4 AU-Category-Concern Index
             B2 – 3.2.4 AU-Concern Index
             B2 – 3.2.3 Categorized AUs
             B2 – 3.2.5 Categorized AUs with Priority Score

Prioritized AUs	Data-Store Ref: C1
Contents	**Source**
Prioritized AUs	C = Computed (System)

= (AU Categories plus AUs plus Priority Scores)
Data Flow in: 3.2.5 – C1 Prioritized AUs
Data Flow out: C1 – 5.1.1 Prioritized AUs

Personnel-Skill-Hour Inventory	Data-Store Ref: D1
Contents	**Source**
Personnel Information	I = Input (User)
Skill Rating	I = Input (User)

Data Flow in: 4.2.1 – D1 Personnel Information
4.2.2 – D1 Skill Rating
Data Flow out: D1 – 4.2.2 Personnel Information
D1 – 4.2.3 Available Skill Levels

Personnel-Skill-Hour Inventory	Data-Store Ref: D2
Contents	**Source**
Personnel Information	D1
Skill Rating	D1
Available Skill Hours	I = Input (User)

Data Flow in: 4.2.3 Available Skill Hours
Data Flow out: D2 – 6.11 Staff's Skill-Hour Inventory

Personnel-Skill-Hour Inventory	Data-Store Ref: D3
Contents	**Source**
Personnel Information	D1
Skill Rating	D1
Available Skill Hours	D2

Data Flow in: . . .
Data Flow out: D3 – 5.3.1 Available Skill Hours

Audit Tasks – Skill-Hour Requirements	Data-Store Ref: E1
Contents	**Source**
Audit Work	I = Input (User)
= (AU plus Audit Phase)	
Phase-Skill Requirements	I
Budgeted Time	I

Data Flow in: 5.1.4 – E1 Budgeted Time
Data Flow out: E1 – 5.1.4 Prioritized AUs
E1 – 5.1.5 Cycled Audit Tasks – Skill-Hour Requirements

Employee's Audit-Task Assignment   **Data-Store Ref: F1**

Contents	Source
Personal Name	T = Transfer, D2
Audit Task	T = E1
= (AU plus Audit Phase)	
Start-Finish Dates	I = Input (User)
Budgeted Time	

Data Flow in: 6.1.2 – F1 Employee's Audit Assignment

                F1 Start-Finish Dates

                F1 Budgeted Employee's Time

Data Flow out: F1 – 6.2 Employee's Audit Assignment

                F2 – 6.3 Employee's Audit-Budgeted Time

Employee's Task Time   **Data-Store Ref: G1**

Contents	Source
Personal Name	I = Input (User)
Audit Task	I
= (AU plus Audit Phase)	
Time Spent	I

Data Flow in: 6.3 – G1 Employee's Time for Audit Task

Data Flow out: G1 – 6.4 Time for Employee and for Audit Task

Part 4: Data Structures

Audit Unit   **Data Structure**

Aliases: AUs, Auditable Unit

Short Description: An Area of Economic Activity

Source: I = Input (User)

Data Elements: Name, Number, Last Audit Date, Audit Time Taken, Number of Employees, Dollar Size, Dollar Throughput, Transaction Volume, Budgeted Audit Hours, Current Audit-Scheduled Completion Date, Current Audit Scheduled Start Date, Current Year-to-Date Audit Hours, Priority Score, and AU-Concern Index

---

AU Category   **Data Structure**

Short Description: General Types of Areas of Economic Activity

Source: I = Input (User)

Data Elements: Name, Number, Total Time, and AU-Category-Concern Index

Risk Factors   **Data Structure**

Alias: Specific Risk Factor
Short Description: Factors of Concern to Management Serving
as a Basis for Prioritizing Auditable Units
Source: I = Input (User)
Data Elements: Name, Risk-Factor Weight, and Global Specific
Factor Weight

Factor Category   **Data Structure**

Alias: Risk-Factor Category
Short Description: General Categories of Variables That Can
Be Used to Assess Significance of an Auditable Unit
Source: I = Input (User)
Data Elements: Name, Number, Risk-Factor-Category Weight

Auditor   **Data Structure**

Aliases: Employee, Personnel
Short Description: Refers to Staff Members of the Internal Audit
Group
Source: I = Input (User)
Data Elements: Name, Number, Total Hours Worked, and Total
Available Hours

Audit Tasks   **Data Structure**

Short Description: A Unit of Audit Work Identified by Audit
Unit and Audit Phase
Source: I = Input (User)
Data Elements: Total Budgeted Hours for Task, Total Hours for
Task, Scheduled Data, and Actual Data

Cyclic Coverage Category   **Data Structure**

Alias: Audit Cycle
Short Description: Serves as Basis for Grouping Auditable
Units in Terms of Audit Extensiveness and Audit Frequency
Source: I = Input (User)
Data Elements: Intensity and Frequency

Time Period   **Data Structure**

Short Description: Used to Specify Length of Time or Specific
Dates
Source: I = Input (User)
Data Elements: Year, Quarter, Month, Week, and Day

Part 5: Data Elements

Actual Date   **Data Element**
Short Decription: Specific Date That an Audit Task Started and
Ended
Source: I = Input (User)
Values: Year 19xx (xx = numeric), Month (1 to 12), and Day (1
to 31)

Audit Phases   **Data Element**
Short Description: Different Stages of Work Involved in Auditing an Audit Unit
Source: I = Input (User)
Values: Controlled Value Set, Planning, Documentation, Review and Evaluation, Compliance, Substantiation, and Reporting

Budgeted Audit Hours   **Data Element**
Short Description: The Amount of Time Expressed in Hours Es-
timated to Audit a Unit
Source: I = Input (User)
Values: Uncontrolled Value Set, Numeric, Greater Than Zero

Scheduled Audit-Completion Date   **Data Element**
Short Description: Specific Target Date for Completing Audit
Work on One Audit Unit
Source: I = Input (User)
Values: Year 19xx (xx = numeric), Month (1 to 12), and Day (1
to 31)

Scheduled Audit-Start Date   **Data Element**
Short Description: Specific Date When Audit of an Audit Unit
Will Start
Source: I = Input (User)
Values: Year 19xx (xx = numeric), Month (1 to 12), and Day (1
to 31)

Current Year-to-Date Audit Hours   **Data Element**
Short Description: Number of Hours Spent Auditing an Audit
Unit from the Start of the Current Year to the Present Date
Source: I = Input (User)
Values: Uncontrolled Value Set, Numeric, Greater Than Zero

Dollar Size   **Data Element**
Short Description: An Attribute Used to Characterize an Audit Unit
Source: I = Input (User)
Values: Noncontrolled Value Set, Numeric, Greater Than Zero

Frequency Data   **Element**
Short Description: Number of Audits Performed During a Specified Time Period
Source: I = Input (User)
Values: Numeric, Greater Than Zero

Intensity   **Data Element**
Short Description: Audit Extensiveness or Amount of Audit Effort Expended During an Audit
Source: I = Input (User)
Values: Expressed in Terms of Audit Phases That Will Be Carried out: Planning and Supervising, Documentation, Review and Evaluation, Compliance, Substantiation, Detailed Tests of Operations, and Reporting

Last Audit Date   **Data Element**
Short Description: Date When an Auditable Unit Was Last Audited
Source: I = Input (User)
Values: 1983 Year 1975, Month (1 to 12), and Day (1 to 31)

Name   **Data Element**
Short Description: Name Can Refer to AU, AU Category, Risk Factor, Factor Category, or Auditor
Source: I = Input (User)
Values: Uncontrolled Value Set, Alphabetic Characters

Number   **Data Element**
Short Decription: Number Can Refer to That Assigned to the AU, AU Category, Factor Category, or Auditor
Source: I = Input (User)
Values: Uncontrolled Value Set, Numerical or Alphanumeric

Number of Employees   **Data Element**
Short Description: Number of Audit Personnel Assigned to Work on a Unit for a Particular Period of Time
Source: I = Input (User)
Values: Uncontrolled Value Set, Numeric, Greater Than Zero

Priority Score   **Data Element**
Short Description: Score Computed by the System Used to Rank
the Auditable Units
Source: Computed (System)
Values: Uncontrolled Value Set, Numeric Greater Than Zero

Scheduled Date   **Data Element**
Short Description: Specific Date an Audit Task Is Scheduled to
Start and End
Source: I = Input (User)
Values: Year 19xx (xx = numeric), Month (1 to 12), and Day (1
to 31)

Total Available Hours   **Data Element**
Short Description: Number of Hours an Audit-Staff Member
Has Available to Perform Responsibilities
Source: I = Input (User)
Values: Uncontrolled Value Set, Numeric Greater Than Zero

Total Budgeted Hours for a Task   **Data Element**
Short Description: Number of Hours Estimated to Complete an
Audit Task
Source: I = Input (User)
Values: Uncontrolled Value Set, Numeric Greater Than Zero

Total Hours for Task   **Data Element**
Short Description: Total Hours Actually Spent on Each Audit
Task
Source: I = Input (User)
Values: Uncontrolled Value Set, Numeric Greater Than Zero

Total Hours Worked   **Data Element**
Short Description: Number of Hours Spent by Each Audit-Staff
Member During a Period of Time or During an Audit Cycle
Source: I = Input (User)
Values: Uncontrolled Value Set, Numeric Greater Than Zero

Transaction Volume   **Data Element**
Short Description: An Attribute Used to Characterize an Audit
Unit
Source: I = Input (User)
Values: Uncontrolled Value Set, Numeric Greater Than Zero

Summary

In this chapter, a relatively detailed analysis was provided of the elements that make up a comprehensive audit-planning approach. First, the planning system was subdivided into six main modules. Each module was successively subdivided until a set of components was obtained that was straightforward to analyze.

Second, an analysis of data flows between modules was carried out to provide insight into how modules and submodules depended on each other. This included an identification of key data stores.

Third, the data flows and data stores were broken down into their structural elements to provide an understanding of the detailed information content of the data flows and data stores.

Finally, a data dictionary was used to record in an organized way the understanding gained through the detailed analysis of the planning activities. This includes a summary of the processes (i.e., modules and submodules), data flows, data stores, data structures, and data elements.

6
Planning Tools
and Techniques

This chapter outlines the essential features of some tools and techniques that may be useful for enhancing planning and coordinating activities of internal audit departments. Some were mentioned in previous chapters. The purpose of the discussion here is to provide additional information about these techniques and, where possible, to provide appropriate illustrations of how the techniques may be applied in an internal audit-planning context.

There are many techniques which might be included in a discussion such as this. Those selected for this chapter represent techniques discussed in audit literature, techniques being used (or sometimes misused) in some organizations, and techniques which appealed to the author.

The goals of this discussion are (1) to inform internal auditors about the availability of tools for substantially improving the state of planning activities as currently practiced, including information about advantages and limitations of certain tools; (2) to illustrate particular uses of certain techniques for carrying out planning activities discussed in previous parts of this study; and (3) to provide a concise reference source in this area.

Some of the techniques may be used for a variety of purposes in addition to those described here. Others are less flexible. For our discussion, one specific application was selected for each technique to illustrate its potential usefulness in internal audit planning and coordinating activities. Other applications could easily be found.

For the sake of consistency with the other chapters, the applications of the techniques are classified into the same six main phases of planning as previously outlined:

1.0 Techniques for Enhancing Planning of the Role, Re-

sponsibility, and Approach of the Internal Audit Department

Strategy-set transformation was briefly discussed as a strategic planning tool in Chapter 2. This technique involves identifying and transforming key elements of organizational strategy sets into strategic departmental guidelines.

Delphi is a technique for eliciting an informed opinion and obtaining a consensus on a set of issues; for example, what should be the priorities of the internal audit department as viewed by external parties?

The analytical hierarchy process is a technique for hierarchically breaking down complex problems into sets of smaller, less formidable problems. It may be particularly useful for structuring audit-risk-exposure-concern evaluations.

Rating scales are used throughout auditing. Often, the theory of measurement and scaling is ignored; and the properties of measurement scales, both beneficial and restrictive, are not taken into consideration when constructing and using various types of scales. Misuse of rating scales can lead to unsupportable conclusions.

Variance analysis techniques have been proposed to aid in the discretionary allocation of audit attention to audit units. Two basic techniques introduced here will be control charts and Cusum charts.

Regression analysis is a useful statistical technique for estimating relationships. In particular, it may be used to arrive at reasonable estimates of audit-time requirements.

Management by objectives has been found to be useful for both directing attention toward desirable activities and as a basis for evaluating performance.

Zero-base budgeting is a tool for selecting subsets of desirable activities when resources are limited.

Network-scheduling techniques, including performance evaluation and review technique (PERT) and critical path method (CPM), are useful for planning an integrated set of activities so as to ensure that a work plan for a specified time period is achieved.

Gantt charts are useful graphic aids for organizing and monitoring ongoing work activities.

Mathematical programming permits the use of quantitative optimization techniques for best matching audit skills and hours available with specific audit requirements and other scheduling constraints.

Linear programming is discussed as a tool for situations in which one overriding goal is to be met; for example, minimization of all audit costs. Goal programming is a refinement which might be used to permit competing goals to be incorporated into the quantitative analysis.

These techniques will be described at a conceptual level. The intent here is not to provide a technical manual; rather, the goal of the overviews provided is to expand horizons for professionals seeking useful techniques to enhance their planning capabilities. In the outlines, there are references to useful materials which contain relatively complete discussions for purposes of implementing the techniques.

1.0 Techniques for Enhancing Planning of the Role, Responsibility, and Approach of the Internal Audit Department

1.1 Strategy-Set Transformation

Strategy-set transformation (SST) is a strategic planning

technique for management-information systems (MIS) proposed by King. Its basic aim is the design of an MIS strategy that supports the purposes, goals, and strategies of the entire organization. The approach involves identifying and transforming the elements of the organizational strategy set into strategic departmental parameters. Although the idea was originally conceived for the design of MIS, the concept can be redefined and applied to strategic planning for internal auditing.

Figure 6.1.1.A shows the concept of the transformation process from the organizational strategy set to the internal audit-strategy set. The approach requires the explicit identification of the organization's mission statements, aspirations, and character and permits, by inferences, derivation of audit objectives, constraints, and strategies.

Advantages. It makes audit planning an integral part of the organization and promotes organizational efficiency as well as organizational effectiveness. King defined efficiency as the ratio of output to input and effectiveness as the ratio of output to the goals which are being sought.

Limitations. It relies heavily on inferences. In some organizations, internal audit directors may not have access to top-management plans.

Assumption. Top-management plans can be identified either from explicit documentation or rational inferences.

General Procedures. Delineate the organization's strategy set. King described the process as consisting of the following steps:
- Identify the organizational claimants: management (M), stockholders (S), creditors (CR), customers (CU), employees (E), government (G), the general public (P), and so on.
- Identify the goals of each claimant group. King and Cleland provided an exhaustive list of claimants and their claims.
- Identify the organization's goals and strategies that directly correspond to those of the claimant groups.
- Validate the organization's apparent strategy set by submitting a formal document to management for feedback: confirmation, comments, or criticisms.
- Transform the organizational strategy set into an internal audit-strategy set by inferences guided by the broad knowledge

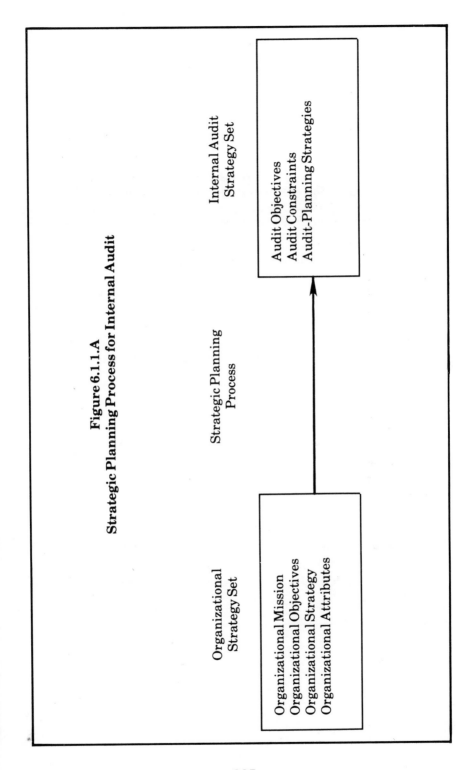

Figure 6.1.1.A
Strategic Planning Process for Internal Audit

Organizational
Strategy Set

Strategic Planning
Process

Internal Audit
Strategy Set

Organizational Mission
Organizational Objectives
Organizational Strategy
Organizational Attributes

Audit Objectives
Audit Constraints
Audit-Planning Strategies

Figure 6.1.1.B
Illustration of Strategy-Set Transformation

Organizational Strategy Set

Objectives	Strategies	Attributes
O_1: To increase earnings by 20 percent per year (S, Cr, M)	S_1: To diversify into new businesses (O_1, O_2)	A_1: Cost-conscious management
O_2: To eliminate vulnerability to the business cycle (S, Cr, M)	S_2: To set up a data-base-manage-ment system (O_3)	A_2: Recently poor performance brought about by temporary shortage of raw materials
O_3: To improve information system (S, M, Cu, Cr)		A_3: High responsiveness to regulatory agencies; e.g., SEC, IRS

Figure 6.1.1.B
(Continued)

Internal Audit-Strategy Set

Objectives	Constraints	Strategies
AO_1: Audit priority on high dollar-payoff-auditable units (A_1)	C_1: Potential audit-budget cut (A_2)	AS_1: To train audit staff for future needs of the department (e.g., EDP audit) $(S2_7C_3)$
AO_2: Cost savings from audit recommendations should at least be equal to annual budget (A_1)	C_2: Potential staff reduction (C_1)	AS_2: To coordinate financial audit activities in order to reduce external audit fees (AO_1)
AO_3: Strict compliance with taxation and reporting requirements (A_3)	C_3: Severe shortage of audit staff competent in auditing data-base systems (S_2)	AS_3: To emphasize certain operational audits to ensure compliance with established cost-effectiveness policies and procedures (AO_1)
		•
		•
		etc.

and experience of the internal audit director. See Figure 6.1.1.B for an illustration of the transformation.

Discussion. SST can provide a formal explanation for the strategies adopted at the departmental level and their relationship and contribution to overall corporate goals and objectives. It provides a clear link between the department's strategic choices and the corporation as a whole. Consequently, it can improve management's perceptions of the role of internal audit and improve the strategic choices made by internal audit through its emphasis on an explicit and rational consideration of departmental plans in light of corporate goals.

The exercise described above may seem to be a difficult and unnecessary addition to departmental paperwork. In truth, the value of the exercise can be debated. Churchman's prescription seems to apply here: Do it or don't but don't waste your time debating it.

In the case studies reported in Chapter 3, several long-term departmental plans were reviewed which had severe shortcomings. In some cases, it was difficult to understand why they were prepared or how their contents "mattered." SST, at the very least, can justify itself as a sensible communication vehicle. In some cases, it could even serve as an effective basis for making strategic choices on the basis of a defensible, explicit, and thorough analysis.

1.2 Delphi

Delphi is a group-process technique for eliciting, collating, and directing informed (expert) judgment toward a consensus on a particular topic (Delp *et alii,* 1977, p. 68). Individuals debate anonymously by mail through a set of questionnaires. The responses are then collected, collated, and analyzed by a design team. Based on the results of the analysis, another questionnaire is developed. The process continues with rounds of questionnaires until all opinions converge. This technique is useful in soliciting opinions from various groups in the organization in the process of setting audit objectives, identifying important concerns, creating a system of priorities, and designing an audit framework.

Advantages. It can assist in establishing goals and priorities which are acceptable to the entire organization, thus contributing to congruence between a department and the larger organization. It can be used to define the scope, the dimension, and the attributes of the problem and permits equal participation of groups with varying backgrounds.

The technique allows active participation of well-informed executives who are geographically scattered and also allows active participation of knowledgeable executives who cannot afford the time required for group meetings.

The anonymity provided by Delphi may reduce the impact of biased opinions of certain dominant groups and may elicit more genuine responses than might otherwise be obtained; for example, in group meetings. By having individuals think through and respond on their own, the Delphi process avoids tunnel vision and "bandwagon" thinking and encourages diverse and speculative thinking (Wedley, 1977).

Ratings from Delphi studies provide quantitative scores for evaluations even though these evaluations involve subjective and intuitive thinking. These ratings can aid in choosing a course of action (Wedley, 1977). The number of Delphi respondents can be incremented with very little extra cost.

Limitations. The desirable features of a group meeting, such as instant communication, brainstorming, and intellectual stimulation, are lost (Delp group, 1977).

Assumptions. There is ample time, approximately six weeks, to gather, assimilate, and analyze responses. The respondents have good written communication skills. There is high participant interest and commitment throughout the process to maintain the necessary quantity and quality of responses after successive rounds of questionnaires.

General Procedures. After determining the basis for a Delphi application, state the problem, identify target groups, and contact potential respondents by phone or mail. Inform them of the nature, objectives, duration, commitment, benefits, and confidentiality of the Delphi technique. The procedures continue with the following steps:

- Design the initial questions. For example, question one may ask: What are the risk factors that should influence audit planning in the manufacturing industry?
- Pretest the questionnaires on respondents from the Delphi group.

- Solicit responses from all target groups. A response rate of 85 percent is generally acceptable. If it falls below this level, carefully composed reminders should be sent to the Delphi group. The process is known as "dunning." Using the previous example, the respondents may answer by listing some items they feel are significant: quality of internal control, complexity of operations, and competence of management, etc.
- Gather, collate, and analyze responses by categories.
- Design the second round of questionnaires. The purpose is to allow respondents to understand, clarify, criticize, comment, and support specific items identified in the initial questionnaires. Respondents may also be requested to vote on or rank some items.
- Repeat steps two to four in this list. Items are ranked, and comments are summarized. Measures of central tendency and dispersion for each item are also typically calculated.
- Design a third round of questionnaires. The aim is to gather reactions and explore disagreements on the results of the responses to the second round of questionnaires. Statistical measures are provided to respondents for feedback. The items are re-ranked. Review and analysis of the statistics by the participants narrow down the dispersion, resulting in a gradual convergence of opinions.
- Repeat steps two to four.
- Design the fourth (and final) round of questionnaires. This is the last attempt toward consensus.
- Repeat steps two to four.
- Participants are informed of the results to provide a sense of closure. Additional rounds might generate greater precision; however, Wedley maintained that most Delphi exercises do not generally go beyond four rounds because the amount of convergence does not justify the effort expended after that.

Discussion. Delphi can help the internal audit department gather informed outside opinions as a basis for organizing and directing its activities. This planning exercise cannot be carried out frequently due to the effort required on the part of the participants as well as the coordination required while it is being carried out. It can be applied once every three to five years and in a very specific way help identify the key factors to be used in important planning decisions such as audit-priority determination, personnel arrangement, coordination of plans with external auditors and auditees, areas of emphasis, etc.

2.0 Techniques for Enhancing Facilities and Procedures Management

2.1 Analytic Hierarchy Process

Saaty described analytic hierarchy process (AHP) as "decomposition by hierarchies and synthesis by finding relations through informed judgment." The idea is that a system is better perceived by decomposing the complexity of the structure into its components and finding hierarchical relationships among them. The relative strength with which elements in one level influence those of the upper level is measured by a series of pairwise comparisons (i.e., evaluating components two at a time).

The concept of AHP may be useful in structuring audit-risk evaluation and personnel-development decisions among other analyses. Figure 6.2.1.A illustrates the hierarchical relationships among overall audit objectives, risk factors, and audit units. The apex shows an example of the overall objective which an organization might aim to achieve. To achieve this objective, individual risk factors have to be identified and eliminated or minimized. To minimize risk, audit resources have to be allocated among audit units depending upon their individual risk exposure and assuming that audits reduce risk.

The relative importance and extent of risks of each audit unit can be measured by pairwise comparisons based upon the professional judgment of audit planners and recorded in a table. Through the application of some mathematical techniques on the table of pairwise comparisons, the underlying scale values can be derived. The overall risk for each audit unit is determined by calculating a weighted average-risk measure.

Advantages. It provides a framework which aids in the systematic and scientific evaluation of risks affecting audit units and a logical link between the amount of risk and resource allocation. The open-group process of determining risk factors encourages intellectual stimulation. A higher level of confidence is placed on the relevant risk factors since they are agreed upon by the group, and the derived scale values represent the most consistent judgment of the group.

Limitations. The derivation of the scale values (i.e., mathematically, the eigenvector) from the pairwise-comparison

**Figure 6.2.1.A
Analytical Hierarchy**

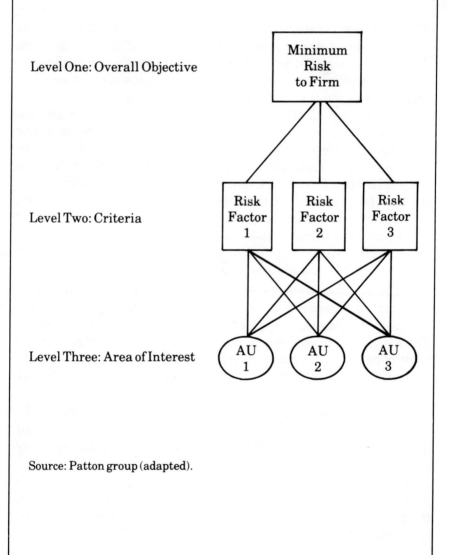

Level One: Overall Objective

Level Two: Criteria

Level Three: Area of Interest

Source: Patton group (adapted).

matrix is a complicated mathematical process and requires sophisticated computer software. The process becomes time-consuming as the number of comparisons increases.

Assumptions. People are often inconsistent, but priorities must be assigned and things done despite inconsistency. The expressed intensity of one factor over another is determinate, and all comparisons are based on informed and professional judgments.

General Procedures. The Patton group suggests several steps for risk evaluation and resource-allocation process with the AHP approach:

• Select risk factors. A reasonable number might be from five to nine selected on the basis of a Delphi approach or on the basis of the research discussed in chapters 3 and 4.

• Construct a risk-factor-importance scale. Based on the professional judgment of audit managers, enter absolute values into the comparison matrix representing the relative importance of one factor over another. Figure 6.2.1B shows that size is five times more important than liquidity but three times more important than personnel change. After the comparison matrix is completed, derive the scale values with the aid of a computer software package. Saaty and the Patton group have details of the procedure.

• Construct audit-unit-risk scales for as many risk factors as identified in procedure one. Based on the perception of audit managers, for each risk factor, enter absolute values into the comparison matrix representing the extent that risk factor impacts all audit units taken one pair at a time. To illustrate, Figure 6.2.1.C shows that size influences audit unit one three times as much as audit unit two and four times as much as audit unit three. Once again, after the comparison matrix is completed, derive the scale values for the given risk factor with the aid of a computer software package. Repeat the procedures for other risk factors. Summarize the derived scale values in a risk matrix. See Figure 6.2.1.D.

• Combine the scaled elements to arrive at the overall unit-risk evaluation. Mathematically, it is the weighted average of the unit's riskiness on each risk factor. That is, overall risk of a given audit unit is equal to the summation over "j" risk factors of:

Risk of the Audit Unit on Factor j x Importance of Factor j

Figure 6.2.1.B
Risk-Factor-Importance Scale

Risk Factor	Comparison Matrix					Scale
	1	2	3	4	5	Eigenvector*
1. Size	1	5	3	2	7	0.4475
2. Liquidity	1/5	1	1/2	1/3	2	0.0897
3. Personnel Change	1/3	2	1	1/2	3	0.1540
4. System Quality	1/2	3	2	1	4	0.2534
5. Complexity	1/7	1/2	1/3	1/4	1	0.0554
						1.0000

*The eigenvector has been normalized to sum to one.

Source: Patton group (1982).

Figure 6.2.1.C
Audit-Unit-Risk Scale

Size Factor*

	AU1	AU2	AU3	AU4	Scale
Audit Unit 1	1	3	4	8	.5735
Audit Unit 2		1	2	4	.2334
Audit Unit 3			1	2	.1287
Audit Unit 4				1	.0644
					1.0000

*The lower half of the matrix is not filled in because, under this methodology, these values are constrained to be reciprocals of the corresponding entries in the upper half; e.g., the entry for the fourth row and first column would be "forced" to be 1/8.

274

Thus, the risk measure of each audit unit is calculated by multiplying the audit-unit-risk matrix by the risk-factor-importance vector to arrive at the overall risk-measure column in Figure 6.2.1.D.

Both Delphi and AHP are useful techniques in structuring risk evaluation. Both approaches aim at reaching consensus through simple, repetitive processes. Delphi uses rounds of questionnaires, and AHP uses a series of pairwise comparisons.

With Delphi, participants respond anonymously to avoid the influence of a dominant group, whereas an important set of variables and judgments is established by an open-group process with AHP.

In Delphi, disagreements are resolved by successive review and revision of questionnaire results on an anonymous basis, whereas differences in views are resolved by open discussion among informed judges in AHP.

Delphi supports statistical and quantitative analysis of numerical responses gathered from questionnaires, whereas AHP uses absolute numbers one to nine to reflect qualitative judgments based on pairwise comparisons that are subsequently used to derive an estimate for the underlying scale. Lastly, Delphi has no built in mechanism for checking the consistency of responses, whereas AHP enters numerical values and their reciprocals into the matrix — making consistency a necessary but forced condition for valid scaling of judgments.

2.2 Rating Scales

A rating scale measures the degree to which an entity demonstrates or exhibits a specific characteristic. The rating is determined by absolute values or relative judgments. Stevens identified four rating scales:

- Ordinal scales that are useful for ranking preferences within a set of factors.
- Nominal scales that are useful for classifying or categorizing sets of factors.
- Interval scales that are useful for ordering factors and indicating the degree to which one factor exceeds another on a specified basis of comparison: time, temperature (Fahrenheit and Celsius but not Kelvin), etc.
- Ratio scales that are like interval scales but have a natural zero point: length, weight, Kelvin temperatures, etc. Rating

Figure 6.2.1.D
Audit-Unit-Risk Matrix

	Size (from Figure 6.2.1.C)	Liquidity	Personnel	System	Complexity	Overall Risk Measure *
			(figures arbitrarily selected)			
AU 1	.5735	.1167	.5609	.1602	.1096	0.4002
AU 2	.2334	.2107	.1762	.2726	.2672	0.2343
AU 3	.1287	.0770	.2006	.0999	.0560	0.1238
AU 4	.0644	.5956	.0623	.4673	.5672	0.2417
	1.0000	1.0000	1.0000	1.0000	1.0000	1.0000

*This is the normalized result of multiplying (i.e., by matrix multiplication) the eigenvector in Figure 6.2.1.B and the Audit-Unit-Risk Matrix in Figure 6.2.1.D.

scales are useful in audit-portfolio management, particularly in setting priorities for auditable units, for ranking the relative importance of audit factors, for describing the degrees of risk or complexity, and for similar uses. Illustrative examples of these rating scales are provided in Figure 6.2.2.

Advantages. Rating scales allow quantitative comparisons of qualitative factors with appropriate statistical analyses. Factors quantified on rating scales may be combined to reflect a quantitative assessment of cumulative effects: the pooled judgments of a group of raters or the repeated judgments of a single rater.

Limitations. Ranking relies heavily on subjective judgments, and discrimination along intervals is limited by human psychological and physiological limitations.

Assumptions. Raters can discriminate along the rating dimension. For example, they can make direct quantitative judgments of the amount of an attribute that is associated with the scale entries. Appropriate scale and analysis approaches are selected.

General Procedures. The Delp group suggests several steps in constructing rating scales:
- Determine the attributes or factors to rate: quality of internal control, risk level, complexity level, propriety of documentation, integrity of management, etc.
- Determine the best scale for rating factors: a nominal scale if the categories are mutually exclusive and exhaustive, an ordinal scale if the objective is to order factors according to their relative importance, and an interval scale if both order and degree of difference among the ranked factors is under consideration. In some cases, different factors must be measured on different scales. For example, when quantitative criteria such as dollar throughput, number of employees, etc., exist, interval scales might be used; however, with criteria such as quality of management, quality of internal control, etc., ordinal scales would need to be used. When very dissimilar items are to be evaluated, an ordinal scale may not be justified; and a nominal scale would be best for classifying the dissimilar items.
- Construct the rating scale: choose the origin and units (e.g., zero to nine) that are to represent degrees of factors to be evaluated.
- Rate the attributes or factors. If consistency is desired, a set

Figure 6.2.2
Examples of Rating Scales

A. Ordinal Scale

Rank (i.e., order of importance)	Audit Factors
1	Reliability of internal control system
2	Integrity of management
3	Competence of management
4	Complexity of operations
5	Volume of transactions

B. Nominal Scale

Acceptable	Not Acceptable
AU 9	AU 90
AU 1	AU 50
AU 15	

C. Interval Scale

Urgency	Audit Frequency
0	Continuous audit coverage
1	Annual audit
2	Audit every other year
3	Last audit was three years ago
4	Last audit was more than three years ago

of guidelines for the rating procedure should be developed and used by the rating personnel.

• Verify the consistency of the ratings. In scaling, it is assumed that subjects are capable of making direct quantitative judgments (given an interval). However, variability of judgments, even within a subject, is inevitable. One valid explanation is the concept of "anchoring," which states that the judge's first judgment is made at random or with reference to past experiences with the attributes or factors which he or she brings to the rating process.

Torgerson described the variability as a "shift in the position of the absolute scale": the change in judgment is brought about by the change in the origin or point of reference which influences the subject's initial perception.

In scaling, it is essential that the unit and the reference point be anchored by adequate descriptions and instructions. Otherwise, mean or median judgments given to each attribute or factor should be derived. Repeated judgment by a single subject a number of times (replication over trials) or by a number of judges (replication over raters) increases the confidence level on the scaling results. With replication, it is best to present attributes or factors in different orders for different trials or raters to ensure independence of judgments in every round.

• Analyze the scaling results. The choice of analytical techniques to apply to the evaluation of the scaling results depends on the nature and the type of scales used (Stevens, 1968). Ordinal scales can be transformed by any increasing monotonic (order-preserving) function. Such a transformation of the relative numbers assigned to the rated attributes is used in AHP, which involves only a series of pairwise comparisons.

Interval scales allow a linear transformation of the numbers (i.e., multiplication by a constant and addition of a constant) as in linear programming, goal programming, etc.

Ratio scales only permit multiplication by a constant as a means of transforming the scaled measurements. Nominal scales allow any one-to-one substitution of the assigned numbers, since all they represent are categories, not values.

The importance of adhering to only permissible transformations when analyzing scaled measurements is that only in this way can the scaled information contained in those measurements be preserved.

3.0 Techniques for Enhancing Audit-Portfolio Management

3.1 Variance Analysis Techniques

Control Charts. These were originally developed by Dr. Walter A. Shewhart and are statistical tools used primarily for study and control of repetitive, mechanical procedures. Control charts consist of a central line, upper and lower control limits, and plots of individual observations over a period of time. The main premise of this tool is that all processes exhibit two types of variation: (1) natural variation that cannot be controlled beyond certain prespecified limits, and (2) unusual variation that can be investigated (audited) and eliminated if desirable.

Control charts are developed for a unit(s) of interest from available historical data. Thereafter, observations pertaining to this unit(s) are recorded on a control chart. Action (i.e., investigation) is taken when an observation falls outside the control limits or a cluster of observations falls on one side of the central line. Although the most common application of control charts is for monitoring mechanical processes, through suitable redefinition of some variables, control charts can be used to monitor "behavior" of audit units on the basis of a performance index constructed for this purpose.

Control charts can be used for analytical review purposes by auditors and can provide a stronger basis for identifying unusual variances that would warrant audit attention. Currently, analytical reviews are performed by auditors but without the discipline inherent in the construction and the application of control charts to data at hand. Instead, subjective evaluations are made by auditors. Unfortunately, these evaluations have a tendency to be deficient for many reasons outlined in a stream of judgment literature over the past 30 years. (Refer to Libby and Ashton for reviews of this literature.)

Advantages. A control chart provides a running record of performance; allows for some variation within prescribed tolerances or limits; discloses "unusual" performance that would entail remedial action such as auditing; and saves time, effort, and money in that actions such as audits are made only when exceptions occur. It can also eliminate extensive item-by-item examination of variance reports to detect a significant variance if appropriate, composite performance indexes are established and can compensate for judgmental deficiencies by providing a decision aid for audit use in performing analyses.

Limitations. It is a detective, not a preventive tool, and highlights those areas that require more investigation but does not provide the cause of the variance. This would require actual investigation. The parameters (e.g., mean and standard deviation) may suffer from errors in estimates or construction of inadequate measures of performance. It does not take into consideration cost-benefit analysis, and an audit may cost more than the savings in eliminating a problem. It does not explicitly consider patterns over time. This can be done by using Cusum charts, discussed later.

Assumptions. Individual variation is unpredictable. Many variations when grouped form a fluctuating pattern. Statistical theory provides the basis for calculating limits of variation of a natural pattern. Ordinary sampling normally extends about six sigmas from tip to tip. Thus, the control limits are represented by ± three standard deviations (Jardine group, 1975).

General Procedures. After determining relevant factors that fairly measure the performance of each audit unit of interest – cash balance, inventory level, various ratios, etc – continue with these steps:
● Determine the acceptable range of performance based on history records of good controls. The acceptable range is that which falls on the central line or within the control limits. The central line ($\bar{x}$) is the sum of all measurements divided by the number of measurements. Control limits are set at ± three standard deviations. Details of the statistics involved in the calculation are contained in Burr's and the Jardine group's, as well as many others, books in the area of statistical quality control.
● Plot performance over a period of time on the control charts.
● Observe deviations.
● Investigate the cause of deviations which fall outside the control limits.

Enhancements. Although our discussion has focused on static and stable systems, in many audit situations, auditors may be interested in stable but not static systems such as those displaying a growth pattern or trend.

Conceptually, the points made above still apply. However, the central line must be estimated differently, most likely with

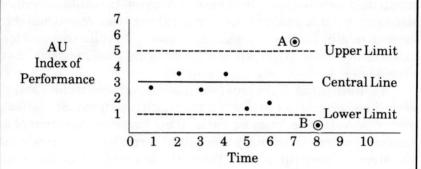

Figure 6.3.1.1.A
Control Chart

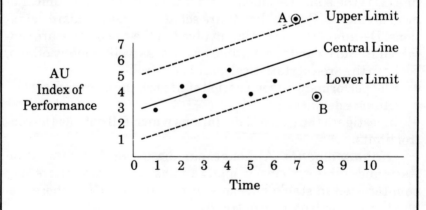

Figure 6.3.1.1.B
Control Chart

regression analysis. As a result, the control chart depicted in Figure 6.3.1.1.A will change to look like Figure 6.3.1.1.B. A slightly different evaluation of an observation that appears to be an outlier is required; for example, refer to Weisberg, especially Chapter 5. The principles behind using the techniques are similar to those outlined above.

Additional enhancements may take the form of analysis of variance and other statistical tools. Refer to Burr and the Jardine group. Also, a good review of variance-analysis techniques may be found in Kaplan. Tests of the usefulness of simple and advanced techniques are described by Magee.

Cusum Charts. Cumulative sum (i.e., Cusum) charts are commonly used when a sequential analysis is desired of a pattern of observations. The idea is to accumulate the sequence of deviations of the outcomes of performance from a prespecified standard. A graphical technique (illustrated in Figure 6.3.1.2) is typically used. A V-mask with a half-angle "θ" is placed at a distance "d" from the most recent cumulative sum. Points falling outside the limits of the V-mask are subjected to further investigation (i.e., audit).

Advantages. It indicates a departure from the standard, is more sensitive than control charts to small but persistent changes in the process mean (Jardine group, 1975, p. 145), and gives an indication of when the change took place and its magnitude. It is also a management-by-exception tool.

Limitations. It does not permit cost-benefit analysis. The decision rules are more complex than those for Shewhart (i.e., control) charts. It discloses significant deviations but does not explain the cause of variances. The two-length parameters of the V-mask (θ and d) may suffer from the subjectivity of estimates.

General Procedures. After determining relevant factors that fairly measure the performance of each audit unit of interest – cash balance, inventory level, various ratios, etc. – go on with these steps:

• Determine standard performance based on past history records of "good" control.

• Plot cumulative performance-index deviations over a period of time on Cusum charts:

$$\text{Cusum} = \text{Sum}\,(Q_i - Q_o)$$

where n is the number of observations
Q_o is the standard
Q_i is the performance during time t

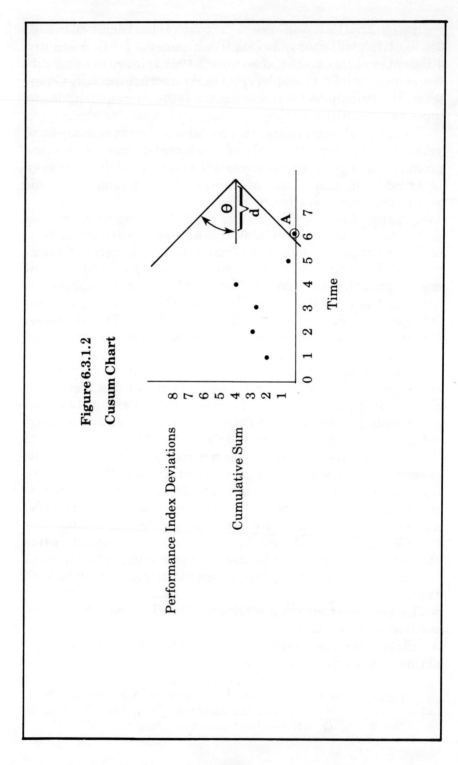

Figure 6.3.1.2
Cusum Chart

Performance Index Deviations

Cumulative Sum

θ

d

A

Time

0 1 2 3 4 5 6 7

8
7
6
5
4
3
2
1

- Determine the two design parameters of the Cusum V-mask. These are the offset distance (d) and the angle of the mask (θ). These parameters are frequently set by experimenting with different values for "d" and "θ" on charts derived from past data from the process being controlled until the right incidence of false and true signals is achieved (Kaplan, 1975, p. 317). Analogous to the Shewhart control chart, a standard set of design parameters (d and θ) has proven effective in a large number of quality-control applications. These standard parameters are:

$$\theta = \tan(\Sigma/2w)$$
$$d = 10w$$

  where "w" is a vertical to horizontal scale factor used for effective, visual display usually equal to 2 sigmas (i.e., 2 standard deviations (Jacobs, 1978, p. 201).
- Observe points outside the V-mask limit.
- Investigate (audit) the causes of the deviations.

4.0 Techniques for Enhancing Personnel-Skills Management and Development

4.1 Regression Analysis:

Regression analysis is a technique that expresses the average relationship between two or more variables. It relates a dependent variable with an independent variable(s)in the form of a mathematical equation derived by the "least-squares" method. The tool can serve various purposes; for example, it can be a forecasting tool, can be used as a control tool for identifying unusual fluctuations by observing values that substantially deviate from the regression line, or can be used for estimating audit time requirements. The following discussion is directed toward this third application.

Advantages. It is a relatively straightforward process. It establishes a norm for a given relationship (e.g. between man-hours and some other variable such as "complexity points") based on the patterns of past data (Morehead and Meyers, 1980) and can facilitate time estimation.

Limitations. The relationship between the dependent variable (e.g., man-hours) and independent variable (e.g., complexity factors) is valid only within a reasonable range. The regression model may be invalidated when factors that govern the relationships are changed and require a new model. It requires a great deal of tedious computation, so it is impractical without the aid of a computer. Programs are increasingly available for this purpose.

Assumptions. Man-hours for personnel at different levels are equivalent. Historical data required to construct the regression model are available. There is a linear relationship between the independent and dependent variables (or transformations of them).

General Procedures. After determining what variables to use for estimating a relationship (for example, assuming the audit-complexity level is associated with estimated time – as complexity increases so does audit time), construct a complexity-level chart. This chart lists the complexity elements in an audit engagement that are appropriately weighed as to their relative importance. Completing this step, continue with those below:

● Based on records of time incurred in completing audits, validate the reliability of the complexity-level chart by working on draft charts.

● Plot the validated points on an audit time-required chart where the vertical axis represents man-hours and the horizontal axis represents complexity points.

● Derive the regression line. The theory is based on summing the squares of the deviation of each data point from the corresponding value of the model and selecting coefficients of the model that minimize this sum (Delp group, 1977). The regression equation is:

$$y = a + bx$$
where y is the dependent variable (e.g., man-hours)
x is the independent variable (e.g., complexity points)
b is the slope of the line
a is the intercept (i.e., the point on the y axis crossed by the regression line).

$$b = \text{sum } (x - \bar{x})(y - \bar{y}) \text{ sum } (x - \bar{x})^2$$
$$a = \bar{y} - b\bar{x}$$
where $\bar{x}$ and $\bar{y}$ are averages of n data points for x and y

(See Figures 6.4.1 A and 6.4.1.B.)

Significant deviations between estimations and time suggest that the chart is not valid at this point, that audit time was affected by unusual circumstances, or that the model is not correct.

Figure 6.4.1.A
Example of Regression Computation

Past Data

Audit period	1	2	3	4	5
Estimated complexity points (x)	350	300	150	250	200
Audit Time (man-hours, y)	1000	950	500	750	750

Computation of Regression Coefficients

(1) x	(2) y	(3) x-x̄	(4) y-ȳ	(5) (x-x̄)(y-ȳ)	(6) $(x-\bar{x})^2$
350	1,000	100	210	21,000	10,000
300	950	50	160	8,000	2,500
150	500	-100	-290	29,000	10,000
250	750	0	- 40	0	0
200	750	- 50	- 40	20,000	2,500
Total 1,250	3,950	0	0	78,000	25,000
Aver-ages x̄ = 250	ȳ = 790	0.0	0.0		

$$b = \frac{78,000}{25,000} = 3.12$$

b = 3.12
a = 790 - (3.12)(250)
= 790-780
= 10

Regression equation is y = 10 + 3.12x

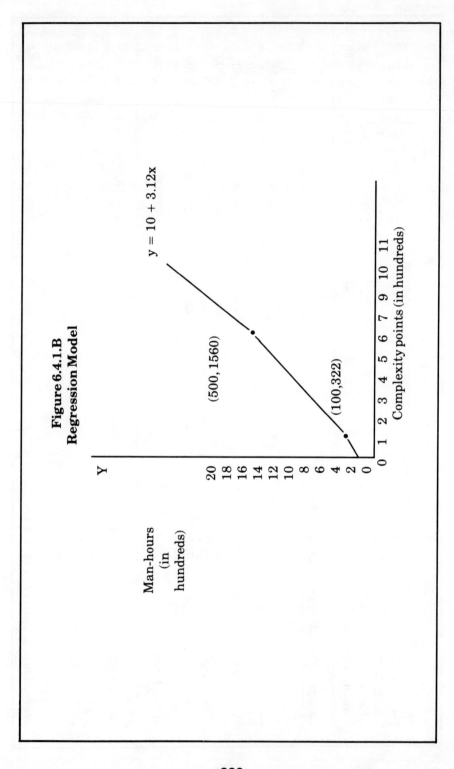

Figure 6.4.1.B
Regression Model

$y = 10 + 3.12x$

(500,1560)

(100,322)

Y

Man-hours
(in
hundreds)

20
18
16
14
12
10
8
6
4
2
0

0 1 2 3 4 5 6 7 8 9 10 11

Complexity points (in hundreds)

Once realistic charts and regression models are developed and the complexity-level of each auditable unit is determined, audit time can be readily estimated by reference to the estimated relationship, either on a graph or with the regression-derived formula. If the complexity points for an auditable unit are estimated to be at 400, the chart shows that the job will require nearly 1,260 man-hours.

Enhancements. Our discussion is based on a simple regression that necessitates preparing a variate such as complexity, which is a specified combination of eight other variables. This, however, is not necessary. Multiple regression can be used to estimate the relationship between audit-time requirements and individual variables directly without guessing at the weights to assign to the variables. For example, the following model might be used as a replacement to the simple model used above:

$$Y = A + B_1X_1 + B_2X_2 + B_3X_3 + B_4X_4 + B_5X_5 + B_6X_6 + B_7X_7 + B_8X_8$$

Where Y and A retain the same meanings as before

$X_1, X_2,...,X_8$ are individual complexity factors and

$B_1, B_2,...,B_8$ are estimated weights (automatically estimated)

4.2 Management by Objectives

Raia defined management by objectives (MBO) as a philosophy, a process and a system of management. As a philosophy, it is "results-oriented" and emphasizes accomplishments and results. As a process, it consists of four steps: (1) formulating clear, concise statements of objectives; (2) developing realistic action plans for their attainment; (3) systematically monitoring and measuring performance and achievement; and (4) taking corrective actions necessary to achieve planned results.

As a system, it enhances an organization's ability to function in a logical and systematic way. MBO may be applied to strategic planning and control, performance appraisal, managerial development, compensation, or manpower planning. In this section, the technique will be discussed from the point of performance evaluation.

Advantages. It measures performance against predetermined standards or objectives and provides an objective basis for pecuniary rewards. It also provides performers with a yardstick with which to evaluate their performance; thus, it can act as a motivating device for individual growth and development. The appraisal of individual performance and skill can provide much of the data required for manpower planning.

Limitations. It is difficult to set objectives partly because of the nature of the job, inadequacy of information, or inexperience with goal setting. Goal setting, action planning, and progress review are time-consuming. Applying MBO concepts to every function in the department can result in increased time pressures and paperwork on the part of managers.

Assumptions. Objectives can be explicitly delineated. Managers possess the skills and the abilities needed for the practice of MBO.

General Procedures. The MBO concept consists of four major steps:

- Setting performance-evaluation criteria. Initially, managers have to develop measures and standards with which to evaluate staff performance. Objective measures are most desirable. These might include objective criteria such as number of audit jobs completed, the variance between actual hours spent on the job and the budgeted time, and so on. In addition, subjective criteria are useful. These might include such characteristics as the quality of work, dependability, job knowledge, initiative, leadership, cooperation, and overall performance.

Thompson and Dalton advocated identifying specific objectives for individuals in advance and holding them responsible for outcomes during performance appraisals. This procedure avoids the negative consequences of a zero-sum situation when a staff member has to be evaluated lower because somebody has to be evaluated higher. Marked improvement in the performance of one person does not automatically require that someone else must slip.

- Development of action plans. Whereas the stated objectives reflect desired ends, action plans essentially describe specifically what, how, when, where, and how much the staff member should accomplish to reach the stated objectives.
- Controlling performance. Control involves monitoring actions in order to determine whether desired results are likely to be achieved. This includes periodic progress reviews, feedback, and corrective actions when necessary. The goal of such control is to maximize the probability of achieving prespecified goals.
- Performance appraisal. After prespecified milestones (e.g., a

deadline, an activity-end point, etc.) are completed, the individual or group performance is appraised. The appraisal should contribute to individual growth, development of compensation schemes, and future manpower planning.

5.0 Techniques for Enhancing Planning and Budgeting

5.1 Zero-Base Budgeting

Zero-based budgeting (ZBB) was designed to help management allocate scarce resources by ranking them against new and existing programs. Peter A. Pyhrr, originator of ZBB, defined it as:

> An operating, planning, and budgeting process which requires each manager to justify his entire budget request in detail from scratch (hence, zero-base) and shifts the burden of proof to each manager to justify why he should spend any money at all. This approach requires that all activities be identified in "decision packages" which will be evaluated by systematic analysis and ranked in order of importance.

All auditable units may be viewed as competitors for scarce audit resources. By applying the concepts of ZBB, the merits of each audit unit can be studied; and the resources can be systematically channeled to high-payoff audit activities.

Advantages. ZBB challenges the status quo of an audit department's activities, helps ensure the effective allocation of resources, and provides a systematic working process for evaluating competing audit units or categories of audit units. The prioritized activities show what is "first to go" or "first to add" when funding changes. It gives managers opportunities to sell their programs and challenge others and can improve the quality and acceptance of funding decisions within the department. The group process helps orient the audit director to the operations of all segments in the department.

Limitations. Organizations can absorb only a limited amount of change in a given period. Too many changes, even though valid in their own right, might drastically disrupt operations. This approach, if strictly applied and taken seriously, can create organization-wide tension and uncertainty that could result in a social cost that could quickly become a money cost

(Rubiniyi, 1980). The requirement that upper management evaluate and rank all the recommended decision packages may overburden it with details. It generates an enormous amount of paperwork.

Assumptions. Activities should compete for resources. Resources are limited. Changes do not have a rippling effect on other activities.

General Procedures. After top management provides planning and policy assumptions (e.g., general spending limits, inflation rates, salary policies, etc.), go through the following steps:

• Audit units to be subjected to ZBB are identified based on specific, prioritized objectives or classes of objectives as defined in the audit charter or policy statements.

• Audit packages for a range of feasible operating levels are developed for each audit unit. Operating levels are typically defined as minimum, intermediate, base, and expanded. The base level represents the current year's budget adjusted for the impact of inflation. The expanded level represents justifiably increased effort levels consistent with the objectives of the organization. Each decision package may be a single audit or a stand-alone set of audits. Essential information in the ranking process normally in-includes what the activity is to achieve and how, short- and long-term costs and benefits, number and skill levels of staff to be involved, and alternatives rejected and pertinent reasons.

• Audit packages are evaluated and ranked. Nelson proposed four useful ranking techniques:

1. Banding. This is useful if there is a large number of decision packages of varying scope and/or complexity. The decision packages are grouped into those that unquestionably will or will not be funded and those for which there is some question as to funding. Only the latter group of decision packages is ranked.

2. Criteria. Each decision package is subjected to established standards. Criteria could be staff-level requirements, time requirements, software availability, and others.

3. Scoring with weighted averages (i.e., rating scales). Each manager in the department assigns scores to each decision package on the basis of its specific importance to organizational goals according to a prespecified rating system. The packages are then ranked according to a composite score.

4. Delphi. See section 1.2 of this chapter. Figure 6.5.1 pro-

Figure 6.5.1
ZBB Working Paper*

Levels of audit intensity	Major Objectives of the Department											
	First Objective				Second Objective				Third Objective			
	ZBB$_1$				ZBB$_2$				ZBB$_3$			
	Audit Packages				Audit Packages				Audit Packages			
	1	2	3	...	1	2	3	...	1	2	3	...
Minimal level	✓	✓	✓	✓	✓	✓	✓	✓	✓	✓	✓	✓
Intermediate level	✓	✓	✓	✓	✓	✓						
Base level	✓	✓	✓	✓	✓							
Expanded level	✓	✓										

*Notes:

1. For the first departmental objective, all audit packages are assigned at least a base level of audit intensity. In addition, packages one and two are assigned the expanded level.

2. For the second departmental objective, all audit packages are assigned at least a minimal level of audit intensity. In addition, package two is assigned the intermediate level; and package one is assigned the base level.

3. For the third departmental objective, all audit packages are assigned the minimal level of audit intensity.

vides a conceptual framework of the foregoing discussion.

● A final budget is produced in contingency form. ZBB establishes budgets that can cope with changing funding environments. It provides a mechanism for reducing budgets systematically and rationally rather than imposing across-the-board cuts that impact high and low priority areas equally. Using Figure 6.5.1 as an example, an internal audit director can develop an audit plan that is intended to be extensive in that it covers a wide range of objectives and decision units; but the degree of audit does not go beyond the base level. On the other hand, the plan may be intensive in that it stresses audits on high-priority-decision units at the maximal level.

5.2 Simulation

As defined by Mize and Cox, simulation is a process of conducting experiments on a model of a dynamic system in lieu of either direct experimentation with the system itself or direct analytical solution of some problems associated with the system. It is a symbolic or numerical abstraction of the process under study and not the process itself.

Audit plans are vulnerable to changes in business operations such as acquisitions of new subsidiaries, automation, budget cuts, manpower shortages, changes in key audit personnel, changes in risk factors, and similar events. By changing relevant parameters to correspond with expected changes in relevant factors, possible effects of changes on audit plans can be observed and studied.

Advantages. It is the most effective means of analyzing complex systems when analytic and numeric solution methods are deficient for unravelling a problem or are impractical to apply. The approach shows the effects on system components of varying conditions, assists in forecasting system behavior, and permits study of a wide range of alternative policies without actually working on the physical system.

Limitations. It does not by itself provide a solution to any problem but provides an understanding of the relationship among the components of a system. Simulation experiments may require volumes of data. The unavailability of adequate data is often a major obstacle in developing simulation models. Strict application of this technique requires familiarity with simulation statistics, computers, and interactive terminals. A payoff may come only after auditors gain necessary experience. This potential learning curve may be costly and is time-consuming. The usefulness and reliability of conclusions derived depend on how closely the model represents reality.

Assumptions. Necessary data are available. Relevant components, variables, parameters, and relationships can be identified and quantified.

Key Definitions. Some common terms used with this approach are:

- System – a collection of components joined by some form of interaction or interdependence.
- Model – an abstraction or representation of the real system.
- Experiment – the process of observing the performance of the simulation model under certain conditions.
- Components – the objects making up the system.
- Variables – the attributes of a system that change values as a function of time.
- Parameters – the attributes of a system that do not change values over the entire range of the system behavior being simulated.
- Verification – the process of testing a computer-simulation program to ensure that it functions as intended.
- Validation – the process of building an acceptable level of confidence that an inference about a simulated process is a correct or valid inference for the process (Van Horn, 1971).

General Procedures. After identifying parameters of the proposed audit plan to be studied – acquisition of a new subsidiary, budget and staff levels, audit frequency-intensity combinations, etc. – do the following:

- Identify the important variables and the cause-effect relationships in the plan. Delphi or AHP might be useful techniques.
- Develop a descriptive model.
- Computerize and verify the model.
- Validate the model. Naylor and Finger suggested a three-stage approach: (1) construct hypotheses and postulates for the process with all available information, observations, general knowledge, relevant theory, and intuition; (2) attempt to verify the assumptions of the model by subjecting them to empirical testing; and (3) compare the input-output transformations gener-

ated by the model to those generated by the real world.

- Express policies or decisions as changes in parameter values or in some structural relationships. Simulate and infer.

6.0 Techniques for Enhancing Work Scheduling and Performance Monitoring

6.1 Network-Scheduling Techniques

Critical Path Method (CPM). CPM is a network-scheduling technique. A network is a flow plan of all the interdependencies and interrelationships of activities and events that must be accomplished to reach specified objectives. Events and activities are the two basic components of the network.

An event (depicted by a circle or node) is a specific instant of time. It can be the start or the end of a mental or physical task, a point in time which can be clearly delineated. An activity (depicted by an arrow) is the work which is required to accomplish an event. A dummy activity (depicted by a broken arrow) represents no work or expenditure of time but is inserted to maintain the logic of the network.

In CPM, the sequence of activities is defined and arranged so that a predecessor-successor relationship exists for all tasks with the exception of project start and project finish. Subsequently, the estimated completion time for each activity is derived by taking into consideration the available resources and the desired performance standards. A critical path or a bottleneck route is then determined. This path consists of the sequence of activities with zero slack. Slack is the amount of leeway allowed in starting or completing an activity. It determines the duration of the project. The project may be shortened or lengthened depending upon the time it takes to complete critical activities.

Although CPM is commonly used for managing construction projects, it can be applied to audit planning by a redefinition of the project concept. In this study, the project may be considered to be a quarter's or a year's work plan. CPM may be used to ensure that the planned series of work activities can be fulfilled.

Advantages. It is a "management-by-exception" tool that helps planners identify critical activities requiring special attention from management, assists in estimating minimal project duration, and assists in job scheduling in order to meet target dates at minimal cost. It also enables planners to determine the effects of shortening jobs in projects and enables planners to evaluate the cost of a "crash" program. A crash program assumes that no cost is spared to reduce the time consumed to a minimum for the activity. The simplicity of the graphical representation effectively communicates complex plans. It is a control tool that helps monitor the progress of a plan and facilitates the construction of Gantt charts (Delp group, 1977).

Limitations. The exact nature and timing of each activity included in the plan must be estimated in advance. It does not provide alternative actions contingent upon information subsequently gathered (e.g., shortage of manpower) and does not support the flexibility of resource shifting or resource allocation. Time estimates do not consider the relative skills and experience of audit personnel. It cannot graphically represent iterative activities. As the CPM network grows complex, project analysis becomes cumbersome.

Assumptions. All activities are known and well defined during the planning phase. There are unconstrained resources. Time estimates are determinate. Future events are anticipated with a reasonable amount of certainty.

Key Definitions. Some common terms used with this approach are:
● Activity – an operation with a well-defined beginning and end and a specific purpose (Delp group, 1977).
● Critical path – a path through a network on which activities on this path have zero slack.
● Duration – the period within which an activity will be completed.
● Earliest start (ES) – the estimated time of an activity measured from the start of the project, if all preceding activities are started as early as possible.
● Earliest finish (EF) – the sum of its (an activity) earliest start time and duration.
● Latest finish (LF) – the estimated time when an activity must be completed without delaying the completion of the project.
● Latest start (LS) – an activity's latest finish time minus its duration.
● Slack – the difference between the earliest expected occurrence time for an event and its latest allowable occurrence time.

The difference, expressed in time units, indicates how much the occurrence of that event can be delayed without delaying the end event in the network.

General Procedures. After identifying and listing all activities necessary to complete the project, carry out these steps:
- Estimate the duration of each activity in the manner described below:

Audit Activities	Duration in Weeks
Audit Unit A	3
Audit Unit B	5
Audit Unit C	10
Audit Unit D	4
Audit Unit E	13
Audit Unit F	3
Audit Unit G	5
Audit Unit H	7

- Draw a project network. Arrange activities in a logical sequence and show predecessor-successor relationships (see Figure 6.6.1.1.A).
- Determine each activity's ES and EF.
- Determine each activity's LS and LF.
- Compute slack time for each activity.
- Identify the critical path for the project.
- Determine the duration of the project (see Figure 6.6.1.1.B).

Program Evaluation and Review Technique (PERT). PERT is similar to CPM in concept and methodology. The primary difference lies in the way time estimates are made. Whereas with CPM, activity times are fixed and are varied only by changing resource (e.g., total man-hours) levels; the activity time is deemed a random variable described by a probability distribution with PERT. Thus, PERT takes into account possible slippage in time due to factors beyond a planner's control. Three time estimates are typically made for each activity:
- Most probable time (m) – the realistic time required to complete an activity under normal conditions. Statistically, it is the mode (the highest point) of the probability distribution for the activity time.
- Most optimistic time (o) – the time required if no complications or unforeseen difficulties arise in performing an activity. Statistically, it is the lower bound of the probability distribution.
- Pessimistic time (p) – the time required if unusual complica-

298

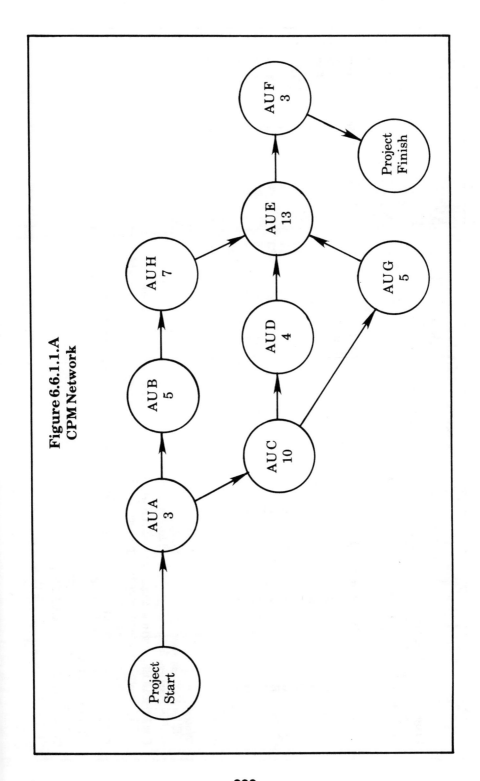

Figure 6.6.1.1.A
CPM Network

299

Figure 6.6.1.1.B
Computation of ES, EF, LS, LF, Slack, and Critical Path*

Project: Audit-Work Plan
Network Planner: J. Smith
Start Date: January 1, 198X
Time Units: Week(s)

Activity	Duration	Immediate Predecessor	Immediate Successor	ES	LS	EF	LF	Slack	Status
Project start	—	—	—	0	0	0	0	0	—
AU A	3	—	B,C	0	0	3	3	0	Critical
AU B	5	A	H	3	8	8	13	5	
AU C	10	A	D,G,H	3	3	13	13	0	Critical
AU D	4	C	E	13	16	17	20	3	
AU E	13	D,G,H	F	20	20	33	33	0	Critical
AU F	3	E	—	33	33	36	36	0	Critical
AU G	5	C	E	13	15	18	20	2	
AU H	7	B,C	E	13	13	20	20	0	Critical
finish	—	—	—	20	20	20	20	0	—

*Notes

ES = Earliest start   LS = Latest start
EF = Earliest finish   LF = Latest finish

For ES and EF, begin with project start and work forward through the network.
ES: If there is only one immediate predecessor, ES = predecessor's EF, (else ES = largest EF among predecessors
EF: EF = ES + duration

For LS and LF, begin at the project stop and go backward through the network.
LF: If there is only one immediate successor LF = successor's LS, else LF = successor's smallest LS
LS: LF – duration

Slack = EF – ES or LF – LS

Thus, the critical path is ACEFH; project duration is 36 weeks.

300

tions or unforeseen difficulties arise in carrying out an activity. Statistically, it is the upper bound of the probability distribution.

PERT-time distribution of an activity is illustrated in Figure 6.6.1.2.A.

Advantages. PERT shares the aforementioned advantages of CPM. Moreover, its time-estimate feature provides additional advantages: it allows prediction of time under the uncertainties of task duration and permits simulation of alternative plans and schedules.

Limitations. PERT suffers from the last four aforementioned limitations of CPM.

Assumptions. The tails of many probability distributions are considered to lie at about three standard deviations from the mean so that there would be a spread of about six standard deviations between the upper and lower tails. Activity times are statistically independent. The project time has a normal distribution.

General Procedures. The procedures involved in PERT-network construction are similar to those relating to CPM except that, in the former, three time values are estimated for each activity. This allows greater flexibility. For example, with the probability distribution of the three estimates defined, concepts in statistics can be applied to calculate the mean or the estimated expected value of elapsed time for an activity (Te) and standard deviation (s) by using the following formulae:

$$Te = \frac{o + 4m + p}{6}$$

$$s = \frac{p - o}{6}$$

"Te" and "s" are calculated as follows:

Activities		o	m	p	Te	s
A		3	3	4	3	0.17
B	(not critical)					
C		9	10	16	11	1.17
D	(not critical)					
E		11	13	14	13	0.5
F		2	3	5	3	0.5
G	(not critical)					
H		7	7	7	7	0.0
					37	2.34

"Te" is the estimated time to complete the project with critical activities A, C, E, F, and H. The probability that the project

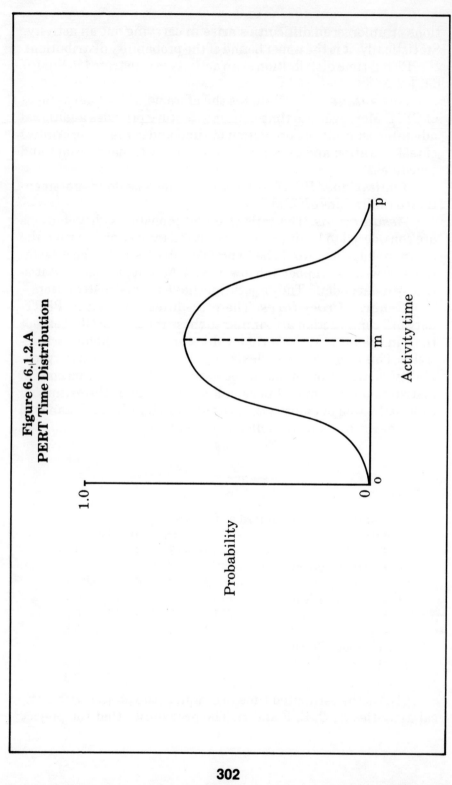

Figure 6.6.1.2.A
PERT Time Distribution

will be finished in 40 weeks or less is 89 percent:

$$P(z < \frac{(40-37))}{2.34} = P(z < 1.28) = 0.8925$$

Where, z is an entry in a standard probability table, and P is the corresponding probability.

Choosing Between PERT and CPM. The choice between the two techniques depends upon the type of project and managerial objectives. PERT is more appropriate if there is a high degree of uncertainty in estimating activity times. This is useful for new audit projects when there are no historical records to rely on in the process of estimating activity times. Likewise, it is particularly applicable to those audit projects when time records show marked fluctuations due to the impact of frequent unforeseen events. On the other hand, CPM is appropriate if activity times are well predicted on the basis of experience or when arbitrary cutoffs to audit-time expenditures can be made.

6.2 Gantt Charts

Gantt charts are premised on network scheduling and resource allocation. They are time-scaled CPM networks: each activity is represented by a bar, the length of which represents the duration of an activity. Gantt charts are an enhancement over CPM. Required resources and available resources may be assessed for each unit of time. Activities can be shifted so that the project stays within the resource constraint.

Advantages. This approach schedules activities, resources, and staff assignments and marks milestones. It determines the minimal project duration within the resource constraint, is simple and intuitive, and identifies critical activities that require special attention from management. Using these charts also permits allocating limited resources by rescheduling activities.

Limitations. It does not emphasize the logical sequence of activities as clearly as CPM. Its resource-allocation feature does not consider differences in skill levels. It does not necessarily lead to optimum allocation of scarce resources.

Assumptions. All activities are known and well defined during the planning phase and are determinate.

General Procedures. After constructing a CPM network for the project, follow these steps:
- Construct a Gantt Chart for unlimited resources (see Figure 6.6.2).

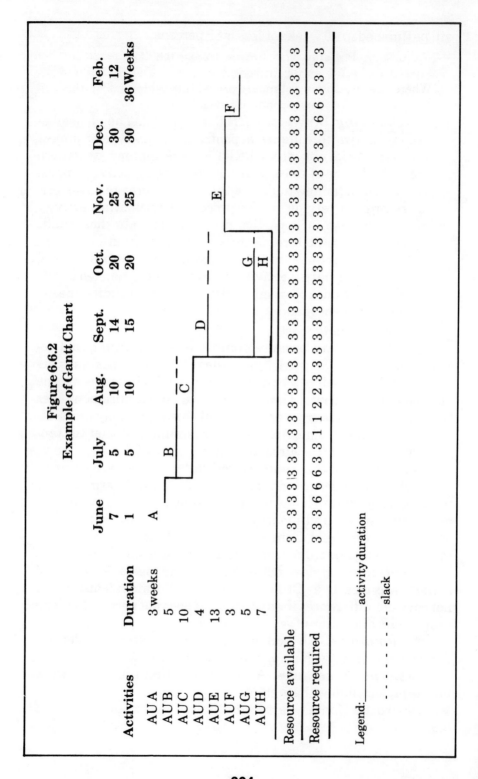

Figure 6.6.2
Example of Gantt Chart

Activities	Duration	June 7 1	July 5 5	Aug. 10 10	Sept. 14 15	Oct. 20 20	Nov. 25 25	Dec. 30 30	Feb. 12 36 Weeks
AU A	3 weeks	A							
AU B	5		B						
AU C	10			C					
AU D	4				D				
AU E	13						E		
AU F	3								F
AU G	5					G			
AU H	7					H			

Resource available   3 3 3 3 3 3 3 3 3 3 3 3 3 3 3 3 3 3 3 3 3 3 3 3 3 3 3 3 3 3 3 3 3 3 3 3

Resource required   3 3 3 6 6 6 3 1 1 2 2 3 3 3 3 3 3 3 3 3 3 3 3 3 3 3 3 3 3 3 6 6 3 3 3 3

Legend: _____ activity duration

 - - - - - slack

304

- Determine resource requirements (see Figure 6.6.2).
- Adjust the schedule for limited resources. By tabulating the resources available and required, they can be clearly and readily shifted and allocated so as to stay within the limit. This may be done by utilizing the slack time if the activities are not critical. If critical, the project duration has to be lengthened to match resource requirements by resource availability. In the foregoing example, the manpower problem during the fourth and fifth weeks can be solved by extending audit-unit B by four weeks. This does not lengthen the project duration because the extension only consumes the slack time. On the other hand, the manpower problem during the 32nd and 33rd weeks is resolved by extending audit-unit E by two more weeks, thereby causing the project to be completed after the 38th week.

6.3 Mathematical Programming

Staff Assignment (Linear Programming). Linear programming is a mathematical method of determining an optimal solution that satisfies multiple objectives and numerous interrelated restrictions and constraints. A linear programming problem has three essential elements:
- Alternative courses of action. There must be two or more controllable variables that must be handled simultaneously.
- Constraints. The alternative courses of action or the variables of the model are interrelated through some type of restriction. Restrictions define the feasibility of a proposed course of action.
- Objectives. There must exist a clear-cut criterion by which the relative merits of each of the alternative courses of action may be evaluated.

Advantages. It assists the planner of staff assignments so that the professional and economic objectives of the department are met subject to specified resource limitations. It allows flexibility by permitting numerous "what-if" kinds of operations through post-optimality analysis and does not require the planner to explicitly assign weights to objectives.

Limitations. Each objective plus qualitative criteria must be expressed in quantitative terms. The variables must be linearly related in terms of resource usage and objective contribution to the specialized objectives. The process is difficult, and the estimated values are subjective.

Assumptions. Trueman (1974, p. 231) stated three basic assumptions in a linear programming model:

● Proportionality (i.e., the amount of each resource used or requirement supplied) and the associated contribution to profit or cost must be exactly proportional to the value of each decision variable.

● Additivity (i.e., the total amount of each resource utilized or requirement supplied) and the total profit or cost are equal to the sum of the respective amounts. The two foregoing assumptions mean that all constraints and objective functions are characterized by linear relationships.

● Certainty (i.e., the linear programming model is completely deterministic, having no stochastic elements) is present.

General Procedures. After setting up a job-auditor matrix and associated job-auditor parameters (see Figure 6.6.3.1.A), carry out the following:

● Identify constraints such as: (a) the maximum and minimum hours of work each auditor may perform, (b) the maximum and minimum standard hours of work to do on each audit activity, (c) time-off periods alloted to auditors, (d) training periods for auditors, (e) specific audit tasks requiring specific auditors assigned to them because of experience or other reasons, (f) budget constraints, and (g) allowable overtime and idle time.

● State audit objectives such as: (a) maximize profit, (b) minimize staff increases and reductions, (c) minimize excessive overtime, and (d) minimize idle times.

● Convert the constraints and objectives into algebraic functions: (a) constraints describing most available number of hours of "jth" auditor.

$$\text{Sum}(X_{ij}) < 160$$

where X_{ij} is summed over the number of audit activities during a scheduled period including audit engagements, professional education, vacation, idle time.

$$X_{ij} = \text{hours by jth auditor on ith activity}$$

(b) constraints describing the maximum number of hours to spend on "ith" activity.

$$\text{Sum}(X_{ij}) < 400$$

where X_{ij} is summed over the number of audit staff

Figure 6.6.3.1.A
Job-Auditor Matrix and Associated Job-Auditor Parameters

			Type of Position (j)					
	Billing Rate/hour b_i	Projected Annual Bookings W_i	1	2	3	4	5	6
Type of job (i) 1	$40	3,500	x_{11}					
2	35	5,800	x_{21}	x_{22}				
3	30	25,000	x_{31}	x_{32}	x_{33}			
4	25	45,000		x_{42}	x_{43}	x_{44}		
5	15	85,000			x_{53}	x_{54}		
6						x_{64}	x_{65}	x_{66}

Auditor Parameters	1	2	3	4	5	6
Annual base salary/ employee/year (C_j)	52,000	41,000	31,200	20,800	16,640	12,480
Number of base salary hours/ employee/year (y_j)	1,760	1,760	1,840	1,880	1,920	1,920
Variable overhead/ hour (V_j)	18	16	14	9	8	7
Overtime rate/ hour (r_j)	0	0	0	15	12	9
Maximum reasonable overtime hours/employee/year (s_j)	200	200	300	500	500	500
Professional development hours/employee/year (h_i)	160	160	120	80	40	120
Staff addition cost/position (h_j)	—	—	20,000	10,000	8,000	6,000
Staff-reduction cost/ position (t_j)	—	—	6,000	5,000	4,000	3,000
Number of present employees (n_{1j})	2	3	10	15	20	35
Number of contemplated employees (n_{2j})	2	3	*	*	*	*
Organization-design ratios (g_j)	—	—	10	6	5	4

Fixed fair overhead = $200,000/hour

*To be determined.

Source: Balachandran and Steuer.

(c) constraints describing the limitations on the flexibility of staff assignments:

1. The staff as a whole should take at least 200 hours of vacation during the slack period.

$$\text{Sum} = (X_{ij}) \geq 200$$

2. Auditor j should work exactly 50 hours on activity i.

$$x_{ij} = 50$$

3. Only seniors should have time off. This can be done by specifying $X_{ij} = 0$.

where j is nonsenior, and i is time off

(d) objective describing the maximization of profit.

$$\text{Max Sum} = (X_{ij} a_{ij})$$
$$a_{ij} = b_{ij} + s_{ij} + t_{ij}$$

where a_{ij} = aggregate dollar equivalents of the jth auditor working on ith activity

b_{ij} = billing rate in dollars of the jth auditor working on ith activity.

s_{ij} = the dollar equivalent of the benefit of assigning the jth auditor on ith activity as a result of past training and experience

t_{ij} = the dollar equivalent of the benefit of assigning the ith auditor to jth activity in terms of the experience this activity will provide him/her.

● Derive the optimal solution by (a) graphical analysis (impractical on complex models), (b) algebraic analysis (simplex method), and/or (c) computer-aided linear programming tools. Figure 6.6.3.1.B is an illustrative example of an optimal solution.

As is evident from the solution, all auditors are assigned 160 hours of activity. The maximum time spent on any one activity is for audit unit D, which is limited to 400 hours. Several other constraints have been satisfied, and auditors have been assigned to audits accordingly.

Goal Programming. This is a decision aid for solving problems with multiconflicting objectives through the use of a system of priorities. Low-order objectives are considered only when high-order objectives are satisfied or have reached a point beyond which no further improvements are desired. Instead of trying to maximize or minimize the objective function directly, deviations from goals given a set of constraints are minimized. Goal-programming problems are always minimization problems. Deviations from the highest priority goal are minimized to the fullest possible extent, followed by the minimization of deviations from

Figure 6.6.3.1.B
Summary of Optimal Assignment Problem

Auditor

	Activity	One	Two	Three	Four	Five	Six	Total
AU A	1	0	0	0	0	40	40	80
AU B	2	0	0	10	30	30	40	110
AU C	3	0	10	25	25	30	40	130
AU D	4	110	100	85	75	20	10	400
Time off	5	0	0	0	0	20	20	40
Vacation	6	50	50	40	30	20	10	200
	Total	160	160	160	160	160	160	960

the next goal, and so on.

Goal programming, like linear programming, can be used to assign audit personnel to engagements. Its primary advantage is that it increases the dimensions of the objective function by accommodating multiconflicting objectives; for example, Welling applied the technique to the analysis and reconciliation of conflicting objectives of job productivity, human-resource development, and individual satisfaction.

Advantages. It is a flexible technique for decision problems that involve conflicting objectives, allows for an ordinal solution (Lee, 1972, p. 22), and satisfies goals in their order of importance. It also does not require that all goals be expressed in monetary terms and reduced to a composite function.

Limitations. The variables must be linearly related in terms of resource usage and objective contribution to the specified objectives. The process of deriving the optimal solution is complicated and time-consuming and requires computer aids.

Assumptions. Goal programming shares the same assumptions as linear programming: proportionality, additivity, and certainty.

General Procedures. After setting up a job-auditor matrix and associated job-auditor parameters, go on with the following steps:
- Identify constraints.
- State audit goals in order of importance: (a) completion of all audit jobs, (b) investment in human resources for professional development, and (c) satisfaction of individual needs such as low overtime, sufficient leisure time, but minimal idle time.
- Convert the constraints and objectives into algebraic functions. Deviational variables are assigned to functions depending on whether over- or underachievement of the goal is satisfactory or not. If overachievement is satisfactory, the positive deviation from the goal can be eliminated from the stated functions. On the other hand, if underachievement is acceptable, the negative deviation should not be included in the stated functions. If exact achievement is desired, both positive and negative deviations must be represented in the functions (Lee, 1972) in these manners: (a) to express the audit productivity goal, the equation is:

$$\text{Sum} (a_i \times_{1i} + b_{1 \times 3i} + d_{-1i} - d_{+1i} = R$$

a_i = billing rate of regular auditor i

b_i = billing rate of auditor i in on-the-job training program

x_{1i} = total number of hours charged by regular auditor i on audit engagements

x_{3i} = total number of hours charged by auditor i under on-the-job training programs

R = fixed audit personnel and overhead cost plus target profit

d_{-1i} = underachievement of the productivity goal

d_{+1i} = overachievement of the productivity goal

(b) to express the professional development goal:

$$\text{Sum}(X_{2i} + d_{-2i} - d_{+2i} = T$$

where x_{2i} = total number of hours charged by auditor i on formal training programs

d_{-2i} = insufficient formal training for auditor i

d_{+2i} = excess formal training for auditor i

T = maximum hours allotted to formal trianing

(c) to express the individual satisfaction goal:

$$\text{Sum}(X_{1i} + X_{2i} + X_{3i} + d_{-4i} - d_{+4i}) = M$$

where d_{-4i} = underutilization of regular auditor hours

d_{+4i} = overtime hours

M = maximum regular working hours of all auditors

● Assign priority to the deviation variables. Consider the following deviations:

d_{-1i} = underachievement of productivity goals by auditor i

d_{+4i} = overtime hours for auditor i

If the policy states that overtime hours be incurred to complete all audit jobs, the objective is to minimize

$$(P_{1d-1i} + P_{2d+4i})$$

where P_1 is the first priority, and P_2 is the second

● Derive the optimal solution by (a) graphical analysis, (b) algebraic analysis-simplex method, and/or (c) computer-aided goal programming tools.

The structure of the optimal solution with goal programming looks similar to that of linear programming as shown in Figure 6.3.4.1.B. The values change with changes in parameters, preemptive priority factors, and/or weights on goal deviations at the discretion of audit managers. For additional information, refer to chapters four to six of Lee's work.

Linear programming optimizes one objective function, whereas goal programming optimizes several conflicting objectives in the order of their importance. In linear programming, goals and subgoals have to be quantified and reduced to one composite function, whereas in goal programming, this unidimensionality of the objective function is eliminated by treating goals and subgoals separately.

In the linear-programming-solution approach, the values of choice variables are dictated by the objective-function criterion and tend to "drive" the value of the slack variables, whereas in goal programming, deviational variations "drive" the values of the choice variables. In linear programming, the relationships of the variables should be expressed in cardinal numbers. In goal programming, subgoals may be stated in upper or lower limits. The value of good programming is, therefore, the solution of problems involving multiconflicting goals according to a manager's priority structure (Lee, 1972, p. 22).

There are other approaches for handling conflicting goals. The interested reader should refer to Balachandran and Steuer.

Summary

In this chapter, a number of tools and techniques for enhancing various aspects of planning have been described. Several of the techniques require additional support in the form of programmed aids to be useful. These techniques, unfortunately, are not widely available at this time.

The material presented here was intended to be illustrative of the techniques rather than definitive. Readers interested in pursuing a particular technique further should refer to the cited references found in the bibliography for additional information.

Appendix A
Management of the
Internal Auditing
Department*

500 MANAGEMENT OF THE INTERNAL AUDITING DEPARTMENT

The director of internal auditing should properly manage the internal auditing department.

.01 The director of internal auditing is responsible for properly managing the department so that:

.1 Audit work fulfills the general purposes and responsibilities approved by management and accepted by the board.

.2 Resources of the internal auditing department are efficiently and effectively employed.

.3 Audit work conforms to the *Standards for the Professional Practice of Internal Auditing.*

510 Purpose, Authority, and Responsibility

The director of internal auditing should have a statement of purpose, authority, and responsibility for the internal auditing department.

.01 The director of internal auditing is responsible for seeking the approval of management and the acceptance by the board of a formal written document (charter) for the internal auditing department.

520 Planning

The director of internal auditing should establish plans to carry out responsibilities of the internal auditing department.

.01 These plans should be consistent with the internal auditing department's charter and with the goals of the organization.

.02 The planning process involves establishing:

.1 Goals

.2 Audit work schedules

.3   Staffing plans and financial budgets

.4   Activity reports

.03   The *goals* of the internal auditing department should be capable of being accomplished within specified operating plans and budgets and,to the extent possible, should be measurable. They should be accompanied by measurement criteria and targeted dates of accomplishment.

.04   *Audit work schedules* should include (a) what activities are to be audited; (b) when they will be audited; and (c) the estimated time required taking into account the scope of the audit work planned and the nature and extent of audit work performed by others. Matters to be considered in establishing audit work schedule priorities should include (a) the date and results of the last audit; (b) financial exposure; (c) potential loss and risk; (d) requests by management; (e) major changes in operations, programs, systems, and controls; (f) opportunities to achieve operating benefits; and (g) changes to and capabilities of the audit staff. The work schedules should be sufficiently flexible to cover unanticipated demands on the internal auditing department.

.05   *Staffing plans and financial budgets,* including the number of auditors and the knowledge, skills, and disciplines required to perform their work, should be determined from audit work schedules, administrative activities, education and training requirements, and audit research and development efforts.

.06   *Activity reports* should be submitted periodically to management and to the board. These reports should compare (a) performance with the department's goals and audit work schedules and (b) expenditures with financial budgets. They should explain the reasons for major variances and indicate any action taken or needed.

530   Policies and Procedures

The director of internal auditing should provide written policies and procedures to guide the audit staff.

.01   The form and content of written policies and procedures should be appropriate to the size and structure of the internal auditing department and the complexity of its work. Formal administrative and technical audit manuals may not be needed by all internal auditing departments. A small internal auditing department may be managed informally. Its audit staff may be directed and controlled through daily, close supervision and written memoranda. In a large internal auditing department, more formal and comprehensive policies and procedures are essential to guide the audit staff in the consistent compliance with the department's standards of performance.

540   Personnel Management and Development
The director of internal auditing should establish a program for selecting and developing the human resources of the internal auditing department.

.01   The program should provide for:

.1   Developing written job descriptions for each level of the audit staff.

.2   Selecting qualified and competent individuals.

.3   Training and providing continuing educational opportunities for each internal auditor.

.4   Appraising each internal auditor's performance at least annually.

.5   Providing counsel to internal auditors on their performance and professional development.

550   External Auditors
The director of internal auditing should coordinate internal and external audit efforts.

.01   The internal and external audit work should be coordinated to ensure adequate audit coverage and to minimize duplicate efforts.

.02   Coordination of audit effort involves:

.1   Periodic meetings to discuss matters of mutual interest.

.2   Access to each other's audit programs and working papers.

.3   Exchange of audit reports and management letters.

.4   Common understanding of audit techniques, methods, and terminology.

560   Quality Assurance
The director of internal auditing should establish and maintain a quality assurance program to evaluate the operations of the internal auditing department.

.01   The purpose of this program is to provide reasonable assurance that audit work conforms with these *Standards,* the internal auditing department's charter, and other applicable standards. A quality assurance program should include the following elements:

.1   Supervision

.2   Internal reviews

.3   External reviews

.02 *Supervision* of the work of the internal auditors should be carried out continually to assure conformance with internal auditing standards, departmental policies, and audit programs.

.03 *Internal reviews* should be performed periodically by members of the internal auditing staff to appraise the quality of the audit work performed. These reviews should be performed in the same manner as any other internal audit.

.04 *External reviews* of the internal auditing department should be performed to appraise the quality of the department's operations. These reviews should be performed by qualified persons who are independent of the organization and who do not have either a real or an apparent conflict of interest. Such reviews should be conducted at least once every three years. On completion of the review, a formal, written report should be issued. The report should express an opinion as to the department's compliance with the *Standards for the Professional Practice of Internal Auditing* and, as appropriate, should include recommendations for improvement.

*Excerpted from the *Standards for the Professional Practice of Internal Auditing,* published by The Institute of Internal Auditors, Inc., in 1978), pp. 500-1 to 500-3.

Appendix B
Company E: Guidelines for Completing Risk-Calculation Worksheet

I. NATURE OF TRANSACTIONS

1. Value per transation – a measure of the exposure to loss or embarassment arising from one average transaction, loan, or deposit.

Risk Level	Average Transaction Dollar Amount
0	None
1	0 - 10,000
2	10,000 - 100,000
3	100,000 - 1,000,000
4	over 1,000,000

2. Total value of transactions (daily) – a measure of exposure to loss or embarassment arising from the total dollar amount of all transactions on an average day.

Risk Level	Average Daily Dollar Amount
0	None
1	0 - 1,000,000
2	1,000,000 - 10,000,000
3	10,000,000 - 100,000,000
4	over 100,000,000

3. General ledger balance – a measure of the exposure to loss or embarassment due to the size of the general ledger balances associated with the area.

Risk Level	Average Total Assets and Liabilities
0	None
1	0 - 10,000,000
2	10,000,000 - 100,000,000
3	100,000,000 - 1,000,000,000
4	over 1,000,000,000

4. Liquidity/negotiability – a measure of the exposure to loss or embarassment due to the ease or difficulty of assets controlled by the department being converted to cash.

Risk Level	Asset Type
0	None
1	difficult to transport or convert to cash
2	moderately easy to transport or convert to cash
3	very easily transported and converted to cash
4	cash

5. Income/expense – a measure of the exposure to loss or embarassement due to the size of the income-expense balances associated with the area.

Risk Level	Year-End Total Income and Expense
0	None
1	0 - 1,000,000
2	1,000,000 - 10,000,000
3	10,000,000 - 100,000,000
4	over 100,000,000

II. NATURE OF OPERATIONS

1. Pressure (meeting deadlines) – a measure of exposure to loss or embarassment due to accuracy being sacrificed in favor of speed in executing transactions, usually because of meeting deadlines.

Risk Level	Department Deadlines
0	None.
1	Quality is high priority, and existing deadlines have limited influence on the work.
2	The department tries to meet certain deadlines but is frequently late if errors exist.
3	Department must meet certain deadlines but will delay if there are material problems.
4	Department must meet certain deadlines, and anything late is not acceptable.

2. Volume (of transactions) – a measure of the exposure to loss or embarrassment due to accuracy being sacrificed because of the volume of transactions which must be handled.

Risk Level   **Volume**

0	None.
1	Department has low volume and enough time to re-check work.
2	Volume is moderate, but time is available to re-search most problems.
3	Volume is high, and only serious problems are handled immediately.
4	Volume is very high. Almost all error research is put off, and only material problems are looked into.

3. Complexity of transactions – a measure of exposure to loss or embarrassment due to difficulty or level of skill involved in the task performed.

Risk Level   **Level of Complexity**

0	None.
1	Task is simple and routine.
2	Task is moderately simple and requires limited judgment.
3	Task is fairly complex and requires personal judgment.
4	Task is complex and requires an involved thought process.

4. Compliance with regulations – a measure of exposure to loss, embarrassment, or regulatory sanction due to complexity and volume of regulations or penalties for noncompliance.

Risk Level   **Regulations**

0	None.
1	Few regulations and little risk for noncompliance.
2	Either substantial regulations or substantial penalties.
3	Substantial volume of regulations with substantial penalties.
4	Heavily regulated with serious ramifications for noncompliance.

III. DEPARTMENT-CONTROL ENVIRONMENT

1. Audit trail – a measure of how the exposure to loss or embarrassment has been mitigated by transaction documentation and audit trail.

Risk Level	Quality of Audit Trail
0	No activity.
1	All activity is well documented and can be easily researched.
2	Activity is documented but is difficult to reconstruct.
3	Activity is poorly documented and hinders research efforts.
4	Documentation of activity is so poor that time needed to research items is seldom justified.

2. Separation of duties – a measure of how exposure to loss or embarrassment has been mitigated by separating duties within critical operations.

Risk Level	Separation of Duties
0	Separation of duties is not warranted.
1	Separation of duties provides good error detection and requires collusion to defraud.
2	Responsibilities for certain functions is divided; however, individuals have control over certain transactions.
3	Individuals have control over transactions, but their work is subject to periodic review.
4	Individuals have full authority and responsibility for transactions, no separation of duties.

3. Management review and accountability – a measure of how exposure to loss or embarrassment has been mitigated by department review of the activities.

Risk Level	Quality of Review
0	Department management is fully aware of all department activity.
1	Department management adequately monitors department activity.
2	Department management monitors problem areas in the department.
3	Department management only becomes involved if there are no major problems.

4	No communication between staff and department management.

4. Compliance to internal accounting controls – a measure of how exposure to loss or embarrassment has been mitigated by good accounting practices.

Risk Level	Accounting Practice
0	No entries.
1	Entries are properly approved and always in compliance with bank-accounting guidelines.
2	Entry approval is discretionary, but entries are usually made in accordance with bank guidelines.
3	Accounting policies in the department are discretionary.
4	Past reviews have revealed unorthodox accounting practices.

5. Accuracy of information – a measure of exposure to loss or embarrassment which has been mitigated by the accuracy of department information.

Risk Level	Accuracy
0	Information processed or retained by the department has an excellent record of complete accuracy.
1	Inaccuracy existing in information is not material.
2	Department has experienced or is periencing information-accuracy problems, but the effect is only slightly material.
3	The accuracy of information is often suspect.
4	Department has or is experiencing serious information-accuracy problems.

IV. SENIOR MANAGEMENT/ MANAGEMENT-COMMITTEE CONTROLS

1. Senior management's concern and awareness of an area – a measure of the degree of control exercised by the management committee over an area and the inversely related need for in-depth audit coverage.

Risk Level	Level of Involvement
0	There is full awareness by bank's senior management of the activity.

1	Senior management has periodic appraisal of the activity and sees little need for increased involvement.
2	Senior management has limited awareness of the activity but perceives exposures which could cause potential problems.
3	Past, current, or potential problems and limited awareness by senior management.
4	Serious exposures or actual problems have not been communicated to senior management.

2. Internal audit coverage – a measure of control provided by frequent internal audit coverage.

Risk Level	Frequency
0	Continuous audit coverage (more than annual.
1	Generally reviewed once a year by internal audit.
2	Generally reviewed every other year.
3	Last internal audit was three years ago.
4	Last internal audit was more than three years ago.

3. External audit coverage – a measure of control provided by external audit coverage.

Risk Level	External Audit
0	Reviews the area annually.
1	Has an intense interest in internal audit coverage and does additional testing.
2	Critically reviews internal audit coverage.
3	Does passive review of internal audit work.
4	Does not review the area.

4. Resolution of previous findings – a measure of control provided by the department's acceptance and correction of previous control problems.

Risk Level	Findings and Resolution
0	No previous findings.
1	Department quickly resolves reasonable findings.
2	Department accepts findings but is slow in implementing changes.
3	Department considers control findings a low priority.
4	Department usually can not justify the need to implement audit findings.

V. EXPERIENCE AND TRAINING

1. Experience of management – a measure of the experience of department's management and its effect on limiting exposures.

Risk Level	Experience
0	Department management has exceptional experience, enabling performance of its job at an optimun level.
1	Department management's experience is good. There are no perceived problems worthy of concern.
2	Department management's experience is satisfactory. There are no major problems, but there are some areas of minor concern.
3	There is evidence of a lack of experience recognized by department management; otherwise, substantiated that is cause for concern.
4	Department management's lack of experience has clearly and repeatedly proven to be a serious problem.

2. Training – a measure of training provided the staff and its effect on limiting exposures.

Risk Level	Level of Training
0	Staff is well trained and can handle any situation.
1	Departmental training is good.
2	Training is provided but not consistently.
3	Training is provided only as problems arise.
4	Little or no training.

3. Delegation of duties – a measure of how well jobs are delegated so that success of the department does not depend on one individual.

Risk Level	Delegation
0	Responsibility is spread evenly within the area
1	Responsibility is delegated well with the manager retaining more important duties.
2	Limited delegation with manager handling a significant portion of work.
3	Staff has authority to perform routine work; manager handles all others.
4	No delegation of duties.

4. Staff experience – a measure of how exposure is mitigated by the experience of the staff.

Risk Level	Experience
0	Staff is well experienced and is familiar with all departmental procedures.
1	Staff experience is good. This causes few operating problems.
2	There is a mix of experienced and new staff.
3	The staff is mostly inexperienced.
4	Staff inexperience is responsible for frequent errors.

Appendix C
Company H: Operating Information Worksheet

Store No. _____

	Store	Region	High 0	1	Avg. 2	3	Low 4	5	Weighted Average	Total
			Priorities for Audit							
Volume (total)	$ ____	____							× .5 =	
Percentage of change	____	____							× .5 =	
Complexity (No. of key subsystems)	____	____							× 1 =	
Shrinkage/overage	____	____								
Percentage ____ prior year	____	____							× 1 =	
Sales/square feet	____	____							× .5 =	
Gross profit (merchandise)	____	____							× .5 =	
Operating profit ____ % prior year	____	____							× .1 =	
Store profit ____ % prior year	____	____							× .5 =	
Catalog sales	$ ____	____								
Controllable profit	____	____							× .5 =	
Shrinkage/overage	____	____							× .5 =	
Inventory control:	____	____							× .5 =	
Inventory turnover	____	____								
Average annual stock position	____	____							× .5 =	

Appendix D
Company H:
Audit-Evaluation
Worksheet

Store
No. _____ Location _____ Auditor _____ Date audit Completed _____

Store Rating _____

Revisit Code	Weighted Value	Audit Rating	Weighted Rating (Cols. 1 x 2)	Potential Rating (4 x Col. 1)	Percentage (Col. 3 ÷ Col. 4)
GENERAL					
Till verification	4			16	
Cash security	3			12	
Building security	4			16	
Store-security activity	2			8	
Bank reconciliation	1			4	
Disbursements	5			20	
Sales audit	5			20	
Sales adjustment media	4			16	
Layaways	3			12	
House sales	2			8	
SUBTOTAL: GENERAL				132	
Procedures/accuracy	5			20	
Affirmative action	2			8	
Corp. Loss/acc. prev.	2			8	
SUBTOTAL: PAYROLL/PERSONNEL				36	
MERCHANDISE					
Merchandise sample/invoice	5			20	
Stockroom	3			12	
Chargebacks	3			12	
Claims	3			12	
Period-end cutoffs	3			12	
Price adjustments	5			20	
Year-end cutoff	4			16	
Inventory review	2			8	
SUBTOTAL MERCHANDISE				112	

KEY SUBSYSTEMS					
Catalog	5			20	
Automotive centers	5			20	
Customer pickup	4			16	
Custom decorating	2			8	
Deliverable merch. system	5			20	
Restaurant	2			8	
Firearms and ammunition	3			12	
Fine jewelry	5			20	
In-store production services	4			16	
In-store carpet	4			16	
Beauty salon	2			8	
SUBTOTAL:					
KEY SYSTEMS				164	
TOTAL STORE RATING				444	

LEGEND:

No audit exceptions	100%	REVISIT CODE:
Major control weakness	50%	A = Below 60%, return early (unsatisfactory)
Extensive control weakness	25%	B = 60%-84%, regular audit schedule
Unacceptable	0%	C = 85%-100%, can be delayed
		D = Return earlier than normal

Appendix E
Company H:
Management-Evaluation
Worksheet

Please rate the following categories for each of your listed store/units from zero to four – four is the best rating and zero is the worst for operating results and associate-experience level. If you feel an audit is not necessary, a four is assigned under audit priority. A zero is assigned if you feel an audit is urgent.

						1.5						1.5						2.0	Total
	Operating Results						Associate Experience Level						Audit Priority						
	Good	Avg.	Poor				Good	Avg.	Poor				Low	Avg.	High				
Stores/units	4	3	2	1	0		4	3	2	1	0		4	3	2	1	0		

Appendix F

An Internal Audit Charter

1.1 Statement of Responsibilities of the Internal Auditor

Internal auditing is an independent appraisal activity for the review of the corporation's business activities as a service to management at all levels. It is a managerial control which functions by measuring and evaluating the effectiveness of other controls.

The objective of internal auditing is to assist all members of management in the conduct of the corporation's affairs by providing analyses, appraisals, recommendations, and pertinent comments concerning the business operations reviewed. The attainment of this objective involves such activities as:

- Reviewing and appraising the soundness, adequacy, and application of accounting, financial, and other controls and promoting effective control at reasonable cost.
- Ascertaining the extent of compliance with established policies, procedures, and statutory requirements.
- Ascertaining the extent to which corporate assets are accounted for and safeguarded from losses of all kinds.
- Appraising the reliability and usefulness of information developed within the corporation for management.
- Recommending improvements.
- Carrying out audit work in conjunction with the work of external auditors.

1.2 Authority and Reporting Responsibilities

The related authority for carrying out this mandate empowers internal auditors to:
- Conduct audits of corporate activities as they consider desirable, decide the nature and scope of such audits, and formulate programs and methods of investigation to ensure complete and effective audit coverage and reporting.
- Have access at all reasonable times to all corporate properties, records, and personnel relevant to the fulfillment of their re-

sponsibilities.
- Review and appraise policies, plans, procedures, and records.
- Inform and advise management.
- Coordinate their activities with others so as to best achieve their audit objectives and the objectives of the corporation.

The organizational status of the internal auditing function and the support accorded to it by management are major determinants of its range and value. It is essential, therefore, that internal auditors report to an officer whose status and level of independence of the functions subject to audit are sufficient to ensure the broadest range of audit coverage and the adequate consideration of and effective action on the audit findings and recommendations. In this regard, internal auditors report directly to the audit committee. Because the audit committee is independent of normal line operations, this reporting structure allows the internal audit function to operate with a high degree of independence and considerable latitude.

1.3 Coordination with External Auditors

In carrying out their responsibilities, it is essential that internal auditors coordinate their work with external auditors in areas such as review of accounting controls. Although their primary objectives differ, there are areas where both need to perform similar tests to meet their objectives such as in the review of internal controls and the substantiation of assets, liabililities, income, and expenditures. A well-coordinated approach helps ensure proper audit coverage with minimum duplication of effort. In this regard, internal auditors undertake work in conjunction with external auditors in three ways by:
- Coordinating their approach to certain aspects of the internal control review and financial verification program where work can be shared.
- Working under the direction of and assisting external auditors in their financial verification program.
- Undertaking certain phases of the internal controls of the audit and financial verification program on behalf of external auditors.

1.4 Rules of Professional Conduct

The following rules of professional conduct (IIA, 1968), which are consistent with those of the accounting and auditing professions, are deemed an appropriate code of ethics for all members of the internal audit staff. On this basis, all members are obligated to:

- Exercise honesty, objectivity, and diligence in the performance of their duties and responsibilities.
- Exhibit loyalty in all matters pertaining to the affairs of the corporation and not knowingly be a party to any illegal or improper activity.
- Refrain from entering into any activity which may be in conflict with the interest of the corporation or which would prejudice their ability to objectively carry out their duties and responsibilities.
- Refrain from accepting fees or gifts from customers or business associates of the corporation or from internal sources without the knowledge and written approval of senior management.
- Be prudent in the use of information acquired in the course of their duties and not use confidential information for any personal gain or in a manner which knowingly would be detrimental to the welfare of the corporation.
- Use reasonable care to obtain sufficient, factual evidence to support the conclusions drawn and, in reporting, reveal such material facts known to them which, if not revealed, could distort the report of the results of operations under review or conceal an unlawful practice.
- Continually strive for improvement in the proficiency and effectiveness of their serivce.
- Be mindful of their responsibility to the corporation to maintain a high standard of competence, morality, and dignity.

In recognizing that individual judgment is required in the application of one's professional principles, members of the internal audit staff have a responsibility to conduct themselves so that their good faith and integrity shall not be open to question. While having due regard for the limit of their skills, they shall promote the highest possible internal auditing standards within the corporation.

1.5 Auditing Standards

In keeping with the *Standards for the Professional Practice of Internal Auditing* adopted by The Institute of Internal Auditors in 1978, the following are considered to be appropriate auditing standards for the corporation's internal auditing department.

Professional Proficiency. Audit tasks should be carried out with professional proficiency and due professional care:

- The technical proficiency and educational background of candidates for internal auditing positions should be appropriate for the tasks they will perform.
- The internal audit department should possess collectively the disciplines and technical skills needed to carry out its responsibilities.
- Auditors should be skilled in dealing with people and in communicating effectively.
- Auditors should maintain technical competence through a program of continuing education.
- Auditors should receive adequate guidance and direction.

Scope of Work. The scope of internal auditing should include evaluating the reliability and the integrity of information systems; compliance with policies, plans, procedures, laws, and regulations; safeguarding assets; economical and efficient use of resources; and the accomplishment of established objectives and goals for operations or programs.

- Audits should be carried out to assess the soundness, adequacy, and application of accounting, financial, and other controls and assuring integrity of the management-information systems.
- Audits should be carried out to determine the degree of compliance with relevant laws and regulations and with corporate policies, plans, and procedures.
- Audits should be carried out to determine the extent to which corporate assets are safeguarded.

Performance of Audit Work. Audit work should include planning, examining and evaluating information, communicating results, and following up.

- Audit work should be adequately planned.
- Adequate information should be properly collected, analyzed, interpreted, and documented to support audit results.
- Audit results should be adequately reported.
- Audit reports should be followed up to ensure that they have been appropriately acknowledged.

Bibliography

AICPA. *Statement on Auditing Standards No. 9.* New York: AICPA, 1976.

Albrecht, L. *Organization and Management of Information Processing Systems.* New York: MacMillan, 1973.

Anderson, J.R. *Cognitive Psychology.* San Francisco: Freeman, 1980.

Anderson, U. *Quality Assurance for Internal Auditing.* Altamonte Springs, Florida: The Institute of Internal Auditors, 1983.

Ansoff, H.I., and R.C. Brandenburg. "A Program of Research in Business Planning." *Management Science.* February 1967, pp. 219-239; reprinted in A. Rappaport (editor). *Information for Decision Making.* Englewood Cliffs, New Jersey: Prentice-Hall, 1970, pp. 199-237.

Anthony, R.N. "Framework for Analysis." *Management Services.* March-April 1964, pp. 18-24; reprinted in A. Rappaport (editor). *Information for Decision Making.* Englewood Cliffs, New Jersey: Prentice-Hall, 1970, pp. 99-108.

Argenti, J. *Corporate Planning: A Practical Guide.* Homewood, Illinois: Dow Jones – Irwin, 1969.

Ashton, R. *Human Information Processing in Accounting.* Studies in Accounting Research No. 17, Sarasota, Florida: American Accounting Association, 1982.

Bailey, Jr., A.D.; W.J. Boe; and T. Schnack. "The Audit Staff Assignment Problem: A Comment." *The Accounting Review.* July 1974, pp. 572-574.

Balachandran, K.R. and R.E. Steuer. "An Interactive Model for the CPA Firm Audit Staff Planning Problems with Multiple Objectives." *The Accounting Review.* January 1982, pp. 125-139.

Barefield, R.M. *The Impact of Audit Frequency on the Quality of Internal Control.* Studies in Accounting Research No. 11, Sarasota, Florida: American Accounting Association, 1975.

Barrett, M.J., and V.Z. Brink. *Evaluating Internal/External Audit Services and Relations.* Altamonte Springs, Florida: The Institute of Internal Auditors, 1980.

Benveniste, G. *The Politics of Expertise.* Berkeley, California: The Glendessary Press, 1972.

Blumenthal, S. *Management Information Systems: A Framework for Planning and Development.* Englewood Cliffs,

New Jersey: Prentice-Hall, 1969.

Bostrum, R.P. and J.S. Heinen. "MIS Problems and Failures: A Sociotechnical Perspective, Part I: The Causes," and "Part II: The Application of Sociotechnical Theory." *MIS Quarterly.* September 1977, pp. 17-32, and December 1977, pp. 11-28.

Bowman, B.; G.B. Davis; and J. Wtherbe. "Modeling for MIS." *Datamation.* July 1981, pp. 155-164.

Brehm, J.W. *A Theory of Psychological Reactance.* New York: Academic Press, 1966.

Brubaker, P., Jr. "Managing the Audit – Planning for Resource Usage." *The Internal Auditor.* January-February 1976, pp. 73-75.

Burr, I.W. *Statistical Quality Control Methods.* New York: Marcel Dekker, Inc., 1976.

Carlis, J.V., and S.T. March. "A Computer-Aided Physical Database Design Methodology." *MIS Research Center Working Paper Series.* University of Minnesota, October 1981.

Chambers, A.D. *Internal Auditing.* Chicago: Commerce Clearing House, 1981.

Churchill, N.C. *Behavioral Effects of an Audit: An Experimental Study.* Unpublished Thesis, University of Michigan, 1962.

Churchman, C.W. *The Systems Approach.* New York: Dell, 1968.

Churchman, C.W. *The Systems Approach and Its Enemies.* New York: Basic Books, 1979.

Crouse, D.W. "Risk Analysis in an EDP Audit Environment." *The Internal Auditor.* December 1979, pp. 69-77.

Darou, G.B., and J.G. Miller. "An Audit Management System." *The Internal Auditor.* January-February 1975, pp. 68-72.

Davidson, A.R. "A Criteria-Matrix Approach to Project Selection in Operational Auditing." *The Internal Auditor.* August 1976, pp. 62-64.

Davis, G.B. "Strategies for Information Requirements Determination." *IBM Systems Journal.* 1982, pp. 1-30.

DeMarco, T. *Structured Analysis and System Specification.* Englewood Cliffs, New Jersey: Prentice-Hall, 1979.

Delp, P.; A, Thesen; J. Motiwalla; and J. Beshadri. *System Tools for Product Planning; Program of Advanced Studies in Institution Building and Technical Assistance Methodology,* Bloomington, Indiana: International Development Institute, Indiana University, 1977.

334

DeSilva, M.G. *Some Aspects of Quality Control in Industry.* Bloomington, Indiana: International Development Institute, Indiana University, Ranjana Printers, 1967.

Drucker, P.F. "Long-Range Planning: Challenge to Management Science." *Management Science.* April 1959, pp. 238-249; reprinted in A. Rappaport (editor). *Information for Decision Making.* Englewood Cliffs, New Jersey: Prentice-Hall, 1970, pp. 109-118.

Franklin, W.H., Jr. "Why Training Fails." *Administrative Management.* July 1981. pp. 42-74.

Freedman, D.P., and G.M. Weinberg. *Handbook of Walkthroughs, Inspection, and Technical Reviews.* Boston: Little Brown & Co., 1982.

Gane, C., and T. Sarson. *Structured Systems Analysis: Tools and Techniques.* Englewood Cliffs, New Jersey: Prentice-Hall, 1979.

Hillier, F.S., and G.J. Lieberman. *Introduction to Operations Research. 3rd ed., San Francisco: Holden Day, Inc., 1980, pp. 246-259.*

Hofer, C.W., and D. Schendel. *Stategy Formulation: Analytical Concepts. St. Paul, Minnesota: West, 1978.*

Hughes, J.S. "Optimal Audit Planning, Part I." Paper No. 437, Krannert Graduate School of Industrial Administration, Purdue University, January 1974.

Hughes, J.S. "Optimal Internal Audit Timming." The Accounting Review. Vol. LII, No. 1, January 1977, pp. 56-68.

Institute of Internal Auditors. Standards for the Professional Practice of Internal Auditing. Altamonte Springs, Florida: The Institute of Internal Auditors, 1978.

Institute of Internal Auditors. *Survey of Internal Auditing – 1979.* Altamonte Springs, Florida: The Institute of Internal Auditors, 1979.

Jacobs, F.H. "An Evaluation of the Effectiveness of Some Cost-Variance Investigation Models." *Journal of Accounting Research.* Vol. 16, No.1, Spring, 1978, pp. 190-203.

Jardine, A.K.S.; J.D. MacFarlane; and C.S. Greensted. *Statistical Methods for Quality Control.* London: Heinemann, 1975.

Kaplan, R.S. "The Significance and Investigation of Cost Variances: Survey and Extensions." *Journal of Accounting Research.* Autumn, 1975, pp. 311-337.

Keen, P.G.W., and M.S. Scott-Morton. *Decision Support Sys-*

tems: An Organizational Perspective. Reading, Maine: Addison-Wesley, 1978.

King, W.R., and D.I. Cleland. "A New Method for Strategic Systems Planning." *MIS Quarterly.* March 1978, pp. 10-17.

Kling, R. "Social Analysis of Computing: Theoretical Perspectives in Recent Empirical Research." *Computing Surveys.* Vol. 12, No.1, March 1980.

Lee, S.M. *Goal Programming for Decision Analysis.* Philadelphia: Auerbach Publishers, Inc., 1972.

Levingston, A.C. "How Well Are You Controlling Your Audit Assignments?" *The Internal Auditor.* December 1977, pp. 36-41.

Levy, F.K.; G.L. Thompson; and J.D. Wiest. "The ABC's of the Critical Path Method." *Harvard Business Review.* September-October 1963, pp. 98-108.

Libby, R. *Accounting and Human Information Processing.* Englewood Cliffs, New Jersey: Prentice Hall, 1981.

Macchiaverna, P. *Internal Auditing.* New York: The Conference Board, 1978.

Mautz, R.K., and R.D.Neavy. "Corporate Audit Committees – Quo Vadis?" *Journal of Accountancy.* Ocober 1979, pp. 83-88.

Mautz, R.K. *et al. Internal Control in U.S. Corporations.* New York: Financial Executives Research Foundation, 1980.

McLean, E.R., and J.V. Soden. *Strategic Planning for MIS.* New York: John Wiley & Sons, 1977.

Mize, J.H., and J.G. Cox. *Essentials of Simulation.* Englewood Cliffs, New Jersey: Prentice-Hall, Inc., 1968.

Moskow, M.H. *Strategic Planning in Business and Government.* New York: Committee for Ecomomic Development, 1978.

Moskowitz, H., and G. Wright. *Operation Research Techniques for Management.* Englewood Cliffs, New Jersey: Prentice-Hall, Inc., 1979.

Morehead, R.D., and D.W. Myers. "Audit Management and Control." *The Internal Auditor.* February, 1980, pp. 58-68.

Naylor, T.H., and J.M. Finger. "Verification of Computer Simulation Model." *Management Science.* Vol. 14, No., 2, October 1967, pp., B-92 to B-101.

Nelson, R.E., Jr. "A Practical Guide to Zero-Base Budgeting." *Interpreter.* July, 1979.

Neumann, F. "How DCAA Uses Risk Analysis in Planning and Programming Audits." *The Internal Auditor.* June 1979, pp. 32-39.

Neumann, F.L. "Corporate Audit Committees and the Foreign Corrupt Practices Act." *Journal of Accountancy.* March 1981, pp. 78-80.

Palmer, R.E. "Audit Committees – Are They Effective? An Auditor's View." *Journal of Accountancy.* September 1977, pp. 76-79.

Patton, J.M.; J.H. Evans; and B.L. Lewis. *A Framework for Evaluating Internal Audit Risk.* Altamonte Springs, Florida: The Institute of Internal Auditors, 1982.

Perry, W.E. *Planning EDP Audits.* Altamonte Springs, Florida: EDP Auditors Foundation, 1981.

Perry, W.E. *Selecting EDP Audit Areas.* Altamonte Springs, Florida: EDP Auditors Foundation, 1981.

Porter, W.W. "The Fully Functioning Internal Audit Organization." *The Internal Auditor.* January-February 1973, pp. 39-41.

Pyhrr, P.A. "Zero-Base Budgeting." Speech delivered at the International Conference of the Planning Executives Instituted, New York, May 15, 1972. Quoted by L.M. Cheek in *Zero-Base Budgeting Comes of Age.* New York: AMACOM, 1977, p. 12.

Raia, A.P. *Managing by Objectives.* Glenview, Illinois: Scott, Foresman and Co., 1974.

Rainey, R.C., Jr., and M.T. Lynch. "Setting up Management Training and Development for the Audit Department." *The Internal Auditor.* August 1978. pp. 65-71.

Rappaport, A. (editor). *Information for Decision Making.* Englewood Cliffs, New Jersey: Prentice-Hall, Inc., 1970.

Rittenberg, L.E., and G.B. Davis. "The Roles of Internal and External Auditors in Auditing EDP Systems." *Journal of Accountancy.* December 1977, pp. 51-58.

Rubinyi, P. "ZBR Instead of ZBB?" *CA Magazine.* April 1980, pp. 46-51.

Saaty, T. *The Analytic Hierarchy Process.* New York: McGraw-Hill, Inc., 1980.

Sawyer, L.B. *The Practice of Modern Internal Auditing.* exp. ed. Altamonte Springs, Florida: The Institute of Internal Auditors, 1981.

Shewhart, W.A. *Economic Control of Quality of Manufactured Product.* New York: Van Nostrand, 1931.

Shornack, J.J. "The Audit Committee – A Public Accountant's View." *Journal of Accountancy.* April 1979, pp. 73-77.

Simon, H.A. *Administrative Behavior.* 3rd ed. New York: Free Press, 1976.

Simon, H.A. *The Sciences of the Artificial.* 2nd ed. Cambridge, Massachusetts: MIT Press, 1981.

Steiner, G. *Comprehensive Managerial Planning.* The Planning Executives Institute, 1972; reprinted in E.R. McLean and J.V. Soden's (editors) *Strategic Planning for MIS.* New York: John Wiley & Sons, 1977, pp. 31-63.

Stevens, S.S. "On the Theory of Scales of Measurement." *Science.* Vol. 684, June 1946, pp. 677-680.

Summers, E. "The Audit Staff Assignment Problem: A Linear Programming Analysis." *The Accounting Review.* July 1972, pp. 443-453.

Sutton, C.J. *Economics and Corporate Strategy.* Cambridge, Massachusetts: Cambridge University Press, 1980.

Thompson, P.H., and G. Dalton. "Performance Appraisal: Beware." *Harvard Business Review.* January-February 1970, pp. 149-157.

Torgerson, W.S. *Theory and Methods of Scaling.* New York: John Wiley & Sons, 1958.

Trueman, R.E. *An Introduction to Quantitative Methods for Decision Making.* New York: Holt, Rinehart and Winston, Inc., 1974.

Van Horn, R.L. "Validation of Simulation Results." *Management Science.* Vol. 17, No. 5., January 1971, pp. 247-258.

Ward, D.D., and J.C. Robertson. "Reliance on Internal Auditors." *Journal of Accountancy.* October 1980, pp. 62-73.

Wedley, N.C. "New Uses of Delphi in Strategy Formulation." *Long-Range Planning.* Vol. 10, December 1977, pp. 70-78.

Welling, P. "A Goal Programming Model for Human Resource Accounting in a CPA Firm." *Accounting, Organization, and Society.* Vol. 2, No. 4, 1977, pp. 307-316.

Wesberry, J.P. "Preparing for Managing Reporting on Internal Control." (2 parts) *The Internal Auditor.* October 1980, pp. 62-71, December 1980, pp. 59-66.

Williams, H.M. "The Internal Auditor's Role in Internal Controls." *Journal of Accountancy.* April 1979, pp. 77-78.

Williams, H.M. "Audit Committees – The Public Sector's View." *Journal of Accountancy.* September 1977, pp. 71-74.

Wilson, D.E., and R.D. Ranson. "Internal Audit Scheduling – A Mathematical Model." *The Internal Auditor.* July-August 1971, pp. 42-50.

The Institute of Internal Auditors Research Foundation: 1983-84

The Institute
of Internal Auditors
International Research
Committee:
1983-84

O. Jack McGill – Gulf Oil Corporation
 – Committee Chairman

Kathryn L. Auten – California First Bank
Michael J. Barrett, DBA, CIA – University of Illinois at Chicago
Kenneth D. Carner, CIA – Security Pacific
John H. Cary, CPA – Price Waterhouse
James F. Deen, CPA – Gifford Hill & Co., Inc.
Michael F. Foran, Ph.D., CIA, CPA – Wichita State University
Jennifer M. Fox, CIA – Southern Company Services, Inc.
Arthur R. Gates, CIA, CPA – Norton Company
Michael Guenard, CPA – Peugeot Citroen
Keith R. Howe, DBA, CIA – Brigham Young University
James G. Johnson, CPA
Danny R. Kelly, CPA – Koch Industries, Inc.
Betty J. Kercher – Dalgety, Ltd.
Barbara O. Kvernes, CIA – Penn Mutual Life Insurance Company
Jean-Pierre Larrivee, CA – Metro-Richelieu, Inc.
Richard N. Lemieux, CPA – Ernst & Whinney
C. Richard MacWilliams, CISA – Union Mutual Life Insurance Company
Robert J. Mitchell – McIlwraith-Davey Industries, Ltd.
Lindsey S.W. Montgomery
Paul E. Nelson, CIA – 3M Company
Claire B. Nilson – Wilmington Savings Fund Society
Frederick L. Page – Pikes Peak Audit Associates, Inc.
James W. Pattillo, CPA, CMA – Indiana University
Walter D. Pugh, CPA, CDP, CISA – Price Waterhouse

Donald R. Ricketts, DBA – University of Cincinnati
David H. Rosenstein, CISA – Deloitte Haskins & Sells
Bradley J. Schwieger, DBA, CPA – St. Cloud State University
Melvin F. Skindzier, CIA – JCPenney Co., Inc.
Oscar Suarez, CIA, CMA – Great West Life Assurance Co.
William W. Warrick III, CPA – Coopers & Lybrand
Theodore R. Wenrich, CPA – Scott Paper Company
Timothy M. Wise – Veterans Administration
Lawrence J. Zigmont, CIA, CDP, CISA – Southeast Bank, N.A.